Photographer's Guide to the Nikon Coolpix P510

Photographer's Guide to the Nikon Coolpix P510

Getting the Most from Nikon's Superzoom Digital Camera

Alexander S. White

White Knight Press
Henrico, Virginia

Copyright © 2012 by Alexander S. White. All rights reserved. No part of this publication may be reproduced, stored in a retrieval system or transmitted in any form or by any means, electronic, mechanical, photocopying, recording or otherwise, without the prior written permission of the copyright holder, except for brief quotations used in a review.

Published by
White Knight Press
9704 Old Club Trace
Henrico, Virginia 23238

ISBN: 978-1-937986-05-6

Printed in the United States of America

This book is dedicated to my wife, Clenise.

Contents

Acknowledgments	**12**
Introduction	**13**
Chapter 1: Preliminary Setup	**17**
Setting Up the Camera	17
Charging and Inserting the Battery	17
Inserting the Memory Card	20
Introduction to Main Controls	25
Top of Camera	26
Back of Camera	26
Front and Sides of Camera	27
Setting the Language, Date, and Time	28
Chapter 2: Basic Operations	**31**
Taking Pictures	31
Fully Automatic—Auto Mode	31
Basic Variations from Fully Automatic	34
Focus	35
Manual Focus	38
Exposure	39
Exposure Compensation	39
Flash	42
Motion Picture Recording	44
Viewing Pictures	46
Review While in Shooting Mode	47
Reviewing Images in Playback Mode	47
Playing Movies	48
Chapter 3: The Shooting Modes	**50**
Auto Mode	50
Program Mode	51
Shutter Priority Mode	53
Aperture Priority Mode	59
Manual Exposure Mode	64
Scene Modes	66
Night Landscape	69
Landscape	71
Backlighting/HDR	72
The SCENE Setting on the Mode Dial	77
Portrait	79
Sports	79
Night Portrait	80
Party/Indoor	80
Beach	81
Snow	82
Sunset	83
Dusk/Dawn	83
Close-up	84
Food	86

Museum	87
Fireworks Show	88
Black and White Copy	88
Panorama	89
Easy Panorama	89
Panorama Assist	91
Pet Portrait	93
3D Photography	94
Special Effects Mode	97
Soft	99
Nostalgic Sepia	99
High-contrast Monochrome	100
High Key	100
Low Key	101
Painting	103
High ISO Monochrome	104
Silhouette	105
User Setting Mode	106
Chapter 4: The Shooting Menu	**109**
Image Quality	114
Image Size	115
Picture Control	119
Standard	119
Neutral	119
Vivid	120
Monochrome	121
Adjustments to Picture Control Settings	122
Custom Picture Control	125
White Balance	126
Metering	132
Continuous shooting	134
ISO Sensitivity	142
Minimum Shutter Speed	144
Exposure Bracketing	146
AF Area Mode	147
Face Priority	147
Auto	148
Manual	149
Center	150
Subject Tracking	151
Target Finding AF	152
Autofocus Mode	152
Flash Exposure Compensation	153
Noise Reduction Filter	154
Active D-Lighting	155
Save User Settings	157
Reset User Settings	157
Zoom Memory and Startup Zoom Position	157
Chapter 5: Other Controls	**161**
Power Switch	162
Shutter Release Button	162

CONTENTS

Mode Dial	162
Zoom Lever	163
Function Button	164
Flash Pop-up Button	166
Side Zoom Control	167
AF Assist/Self-timer Lamp	168
Playback Button	169
Monitor Button	170
Diopter Adjustment Wheel	171
Display Button	171
Movie Button	173
Flash/Charging Lamp	173
Command Dial	173
Menu Button	175
Trash Button	175
Multi Selector and its Buttons and Dial	177
Multi Selector Dial	177
OK Button	178
Direction Buttons	178
USB and HDMI Ports	183
Tilting LCD Screen	184
Chapter 6: Playback	**186**
Normal Playback	186
Index View and Enlarging Images	187
Calendar View	189
Different Playback Screens	190
Viewing Shots Taken in a Sequence	193
The Playback Menu	196
Quick Retouch	196
D-Lighting	198
Skin Softening	198
Filter Effects	199
Print Order	202
Slide Show	203
Protect	205
Rotate Image	206
Small Picture	207
Voice Memo	208
Copy	209
Black Border	210
Sequence Display Options	211
Choose Key Picture	212
Printing Images	213
Printing Directly from the Camera	214
Chapter 7: Setup and GPS Menus	**216**
The Setup Menu	216
Welcome Screen	217
Time Zone and Date	218
Monitor Settings	219
Print Date	222
Vibration Reduction	223

9

Motion Detection	224
AF Assist	225
Assign Side Zoom Control	229
Sound Settings	230
Auto Off	231
Format Card/Format Memory	232
Language	233
TV Settings	233
Fn Button	234
Charge by Computert	235
Toggle Av/Tv Selection	235
Reset File Numbering	236
Blink Warning	237
Filmstrip	237
Eye-Fi Upload	238
Reverse Indicators	239
Reset All	239
Firmware Version	240
GPS Options Menu	241
GPS Options	242
Record GPS Data	242
Synchronize	243
Update A-GPS File	244
Create Log	244
View Log	244
Viewing GPS Location Screen	245
Chapter 8: Motion Pictures	**246**
Movie-making Overview	246
Quick Guide to Recording a Movie Clip	247
Other Settings for Movies	249
Still Photo Settings Available for Movies	249
Focus Mode	249
Exposure Compensation and Exposure Lock	250
Self-timer	251
Picture Control	252
White Balance	252
Metering	253
Vibration Reduction	253
Zoom	253
Shutter Release Button: Does Not Operate	254
Fn Button: Does Not Operate	254
Settings That Are Not Adjustable for Video Recording	255
The Movie Menu	255
Movie Options	255
HS Movie Options	258
Autofocus Mode	261
Movie Playback and Editing	263
Playback	263
Editing	265
Chapter 9: Other Topics	**269**
Using the Superzoom Lens	269

Macro (Close-up) Shooting	279
Using Flash	283
Infrared Photography	290
Street Photography	292
Connecting to a Television Set	297
APPENDIX A: Accessories	**299**
Cases	299
Batteries	301
AC Adapter	302
Add-on Filters and Lenses	304
External Flash	306
APPENDIX B: Quick Tips	**309**
APPENDIX C: Resources for Further Information	**314**
Photography Books	314
Web Sites	314
Digital Photography Review	315
Reviews of the Coolpix P510	315
Flickr Discussion Group	316
Infrared Photography	316
Index	**317**

Acknowledgments

In August 2011, I published *Photographer's Guide to the Nikon Coolpix P500*, which covers the operation and features of the predecessor to the Coolpix P510. When Nikon announced in February 2012 that it would be producing an updated version of the P500 camera, I had no hesitation in deciding to write another book to cover the new model. Although these Coolpix models are not as compact as the other cameras I have written about, they have proved to be excellent choices for general photography, with their superior image quality and impressive array of advanced features.

As with earlier books, I turned to participants in the photography forums at dpreview.com for assistance in reviewing a draft to catch errors and to improve the discussion of the features and use of the P510. I am particularly indebted to John Brodie, Jeri Corbitt, Kerry Crutcher, Brian Gilbert, and Marvin Reinhart, whom I contacted through the "Nikon Talk" forum, and who provided invaluable comments that greatly improved the quality of the final book. Any remaining errors or problems, of course, are solely my own responsibility.

As has always been the case, the greatest support in every possible way, from joining me on trips to take photographs for this book to editing and proofreading the final text, has come from my wife, Clenise.

Introduction

This book is a guide to using the features and controls of the Nikon Coolpix P510 camera to get excellent results with still photography and videos. The P510 is equipped with most of the major capabilities shared by other cameras in its class, but, at this writing at least, it outshines just about all of them in the extent of its zoom range. If you are one of the many photographers who prefer not to get involved with the added effort and expense associated with DSLR (digital single-lens reflex) cameras, the P510 is one of the best choices available today. DSLRs give you great quality, but at considerable expense, and with the bulk and complications that come with changing lenses on a camera body that is quite heavy even with no lens. Or, if you already have a DSLR, you might want to have a second camera such as the P510 for occasions when you need to travel light.

You could opt for a truly "compact" camera, like the Panasonic Lumix LX5, the Fujifilm X10, the Canon PowerShot S100, or the Nikon Coolpix P310, among others. Such cameras can more readily fit in a pocket and offer a great variety of features, but, because of the need to keep their size to a minimum, their built-in lenses cannot offer the powerful image-magnifying performance of a DSLR's zoom (or non-zoom telephoto) lens.

The Coolpix P510 fits into a niche between the powerful DSLR and the pocketable compact. A camera in this class is often labeled a "bridge" camera—that is, a camera that has several of the attributes of a more robust DSLR model, but, because it is smaller and has a non-interchangeable lens, is considered a "bridge" between the bulky but highly capable DSLR and the more compact "point-and-shoot" type of camera.

When you choose a model like the P510 you are, of course, giving up the ability to slip it into a pocket or purse and forget about it until a photo opportunity arises, as you can with a true compact. On the other hand, you gain some attributes not shared by smaller models. For example, you get a camera with a solid construction that lets you get a good, firm grip, almost like holding a DSLR. You also get a strong array of features, such as continuous shooting, various scene modes, and options for things like setting ISO and white balance, and dealing with difficult lighting situations. Perhaps most importantly, especially with the P510, you get a virtually unmatched range of focal lengths with the camera's "superzoom" lens, which offers an array of focal lengths all the way from the very wide 24mm to the amazing telephoto extent of 1000mm (measured in "35mm-equivalent" terms, as discussed in Chapter 9).

Besides its superiority in zoom range, the P510 brings with it a full order of sophisticated features. The camera offers complete manual control of focus and exposure, several advanced modes of rapid continuous shooting, exposure bracketing, excellent low-light performance, and numerous special features, including a variety of ways to manipulate colors, a built-in HDR (High Dynamic Range) shooting mode, high-speed video shooting, GPS capability to track the locations of your shots, and time-lapse photography. And, as would be expected of a modern camera in this class, the P510 provides HD (high-definition) video shooting. In addition, it has an electronic viewfinder, which provides a clear view of your image even in bright sunlight, when the LCD screen would be washed out by the glare. And the LCD display has very high resolution, with 921,000 dots, providing fine detail when viewing your images. Moreover, the screen swivels to positions that allow you to take low-level shots near ground level and to hold the camera over your head to overcome crowds of people or other obstacles.

The P510 is not the perfect camera, of course; no camera can serve as the ideal tool for all situations. In this case, one drawback often cited is that the camera lacks an accessory shoe, which could be used to attach items such as an optical viewfinder or an external flash unit. (There are other ways to use external flash units with the P510, as discussed in Appendix A.) In addition, the camera does not offer the very useful RAW format for its images, although it does provide a wide array of high-quality JPEG formats. Also, the camera has a limited range of aperture settings available: from f/3.0 to f/8.3 at the widest focal length, and only from f/5.9 to f/8.3 when the lens is zoomed in fully. This narrow range can limit your ability to make certain kinds of shots, such as those requiring slow shutter speeds, although you can compensate to some extent by using other techniques for such shots.

This discussion of the camera's features is not complete, but it serves to illustrate that the Coolpix P510 has a solid set of capabilities that should be attractive to serious amateur photographers—those who want a camera that gives them numerous options for creative control of their images and that is light enough to be carried around at all times, so they will have a substantial photographic apparatus with them when a good picture-taking opportunity pops up. The P510 should be especially attractive to those photographers who have an interest in capturing images of birds and other wildlife, in situations that call for the use of a powerful telephoto lens for long-distance shots.

My goal with this guide is to provide a thorough introduction to the camera's features, explaining how they work and when you might want to use them. The book is aimed largely at beginning and intermediate photographers who are not satisfied with the technical documentation that comes with the camera and who need a more user-friendly explanation of the camera's many controls and menus. For those who are seeking more advanced information, I provide some discussion of topics that go beyond the basics, and I include in the appendices information to help you uncover additional resources. This book is not a replacement for the official Nikon Coolpix P510 Reference Manual, which contains a great deal of useful information; my book should be viewed as a supplementary resource to explain the use of the camera's features.

One note on the scope of this guide: I live in the United States, and I bought my camera in the U.S. market. I am not familiar with any variations for cameras sold in Europe, the United Kingdom, or elsewhere, such as different batteries or chargers. The photographic functions are not different, though, so this guide should be useful to photographers in all locations, apart from that narrow range of issues. I have stated measurements in both the Imperial and metric systems for the benefit of readers in various countries around the world.

All photographs in this book that illustrate the capabilities of the Coolpix P510 are ones that I took with that camera. The menu illustrations are screen captures taken from the P510 using the EyeTV 250 Plus video receiver and capture device by Elgato Systems. The photographs of the P510 and accessories used with it are ones that I took using a Sony DSLR-A850 camera with a Sony f/2.8 SAM 28-75mm zoom lens and a Sony f/2.8 50mm macro lens.

One final note: If you find any problems in this book, including typographical errors or information that appears to be confusing or incorrect, please let me know through the contact form at whiteknightpress.com or by e-mail to contact@whiteknightpress.com. Also, if the images do not look good on a particular device, such as an iPad or Kindle, let me know that as well so I can take steps to remedy the situation. Feedback from readers is the best source of information for improving books such as this one. If you have general comments or feedback to provide, you also may want to post a review of the book at Amazon.com or one of the other sites that sells the book.

Chapter 1: Preliminary Setup

Setting Up the Camera

I will assume your Nikon Coolpix P510 has just arrived at your home or office, perhaps purchased from an internet site or a retail store. The box should contain the camera itself, battery, battery terminal cover, battery charging adapter, neck strap, USB cable, audio-video cable, lens cap with cord for attaching it to the camera, software and user's manual on two CDs, and the brief "Quick Start Guide" instruction pamphlet. There also should be a warranty card and one or two other items, such as an advertising sheet or safety notice.

It is a good idea to attach the neck strap to the camera right away, and in the same procedure to attach the lens cap to its cord. In this process, you loop the other end of the lens cap cord over the neck strap before it is attached to the camera. When you're finished, the lens cap should be tethered by its cord to the strap. The lens cap cord should be attached to the neck strap where it joins the camera, on the left side as you hold the camera.

Charging and Inserting the Battery

The Nikon battery for the Coolpix P510 is the EN-EL5. With this camera, the standard procedure is to charge the battery while it's inside the camera, by connecting the supplied AC charger to the Nikon USB adapter or to the USB port on a computer or other device. There are pluses and minuses to this approach to battery-charging. On the positive side, you don't need an external charger and the camera can charge automatically when it's connected to your computer. The main drawbacks are that you cannot use the camera while the battery is charging, and you cannot charge another battery outside the camera. The solution to this situation is to purchase extra batteries and a device that will charge those batteries outside the camera. I'll discuss batteries and other accessories in Appendix A.

For now, let's get the battery charged by inserting it into the camera and connecting the charger. You first need to open the battery compartment door on the bottom of the camera and put in the battery. You can only insert it fully into the camera one way; the way I prefer to do this is to look for the small raised lip at one edge of the battery, and insert the battery so that lip is next to the outside edge of the camera, just under the trash-can icon on the camera's back, as it goes into the compartment. Figure 1-1 shows the battery going into the camera.

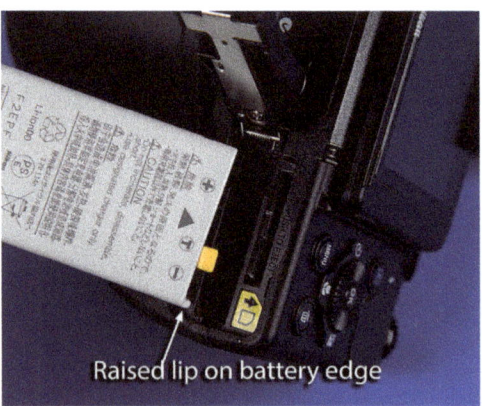

Figure 1-1: Inserting the Battery

If the battery will not go all the way down into the compartment, don't force it; check its orientation and make sure it is being inserted the correct way. You may have to push the small orange plastic retaining latch to one side to allow the battery to slip all the way into its slot; the latch will then anchor the battery in place, as shown in Figure 1-2.

CHAPTER 1: PRELIMINARY SETUP

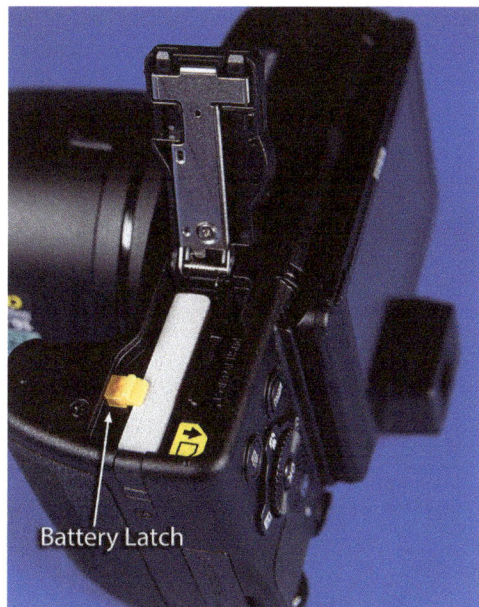

Figure 1-2: Battery held in place by latch

With the battery inserted into the camera, plug the small end of the USB cable into the USB port under the door marked HDMI on the right side of the camera, as shown in Figure 1-3, and plug the other end of the USB cable into the AC adapter that ships with the camera.

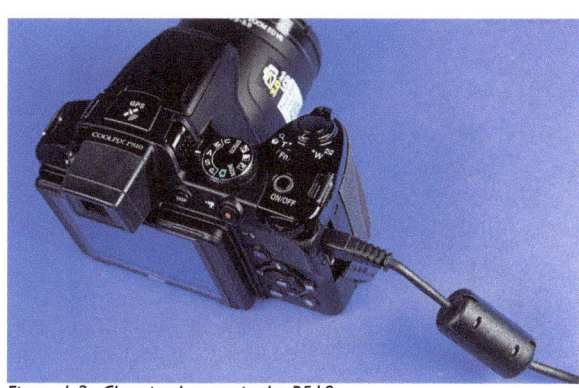

Figure 1-3: Charging battery in the P510

19

Then plug that AC adapter into a standard electrical outlet or surge protector. The green light on the back of the camera, next to the lightning bolt icon, will blink slowly to indicate that the battery is charging. When the light goes off, the battery is fully charged and ready to use. It can take almost five hours to charge a fully depleted battery using this system. (This length of time is another factor that makes it practically a necessity to obtain other batteries and an external charger, as discussed in Appendix A.)

You also can charge the battery in the camera by connecting the USB cable to a compatible USB port on a computer, if that option is selected in the camera's menu system. I'll discuss that process in Chapter 7.

Inserting the Memory Card

The Coolpix P510, like most cameras these days, does not ship with a memory card included. With this camera, unlike some others, this is not a fatal omission, because the P510 has some built-in memory that will let you take a few pictures even with no memory card inserted. The amount of built-in memory is only about 90 megabytes (MB), which is pretty minuscule compared to the capacity of modern storage cards that can hold up to 128 gigabytes (GB), more than a thousand times more. But if you're in a situation where you need to take a picture and don't have an available card, 90 MB might be enough.

The internal memory can hold about 11 still photos at the largest size of 4608 X 3456 pixels at Fine quality, or 1137 photos at the lowest quality of 640 X 480 pixels, with proportional figures for intermediate levels of image size and quality. This memory can hold only a few seconds of the highest-quality movie footage, or slightly more than 4 minutes of the lowest-quality movie footage.

If you have no card inserted in the camera, the letters IN will display in the lower right corner of the display, indicating that internal memory is being used, next to the number of remain-

CHAPTER 1: PRELIMINARY SETUP

ing images, as shown in Figure 1-4.

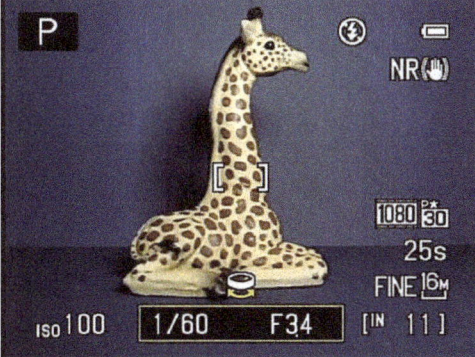

Figure 1-4: Letters "IN" mean internal memory in use

If a card is inserted, the letters IN are not displayed; only the number of remaining images is shown inside the brackets. If you fill up the internal memory, you will be greeted with the message Out of Memory on the camera's display, and your shooting will come to a halt unless you delete some images from the internal memory or insert an SD card that has some free space on it.

Because of its limited capacity, you don't want to rely on the built-in memory if you don't have to, so you need to insert a separate memory card. The P510 uses SD cards, which are quite small, about the size of a large postage stamp. They come in several varieties, as shown in Figure 1-5.

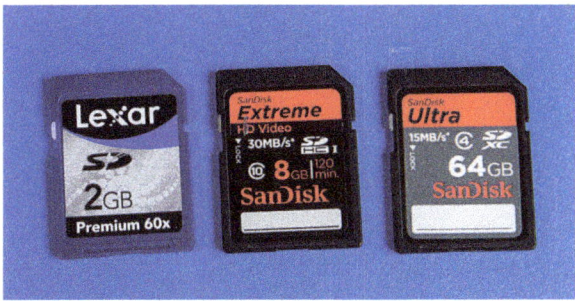

Figure 1-5: From left: SD, SDHC, SDXC

The standard card, called simply SD, comes in capacities from

21

8 MB to 2 GB. The next higher-capacity card, SDHC, comes in sizes from 4 GB to 32 GB. The newest, and highest-capacity card, SDXC (for extended capacity), comes in sizes of 48 GB, 64 GB, and up to 128GB at this writing; this version of the card can have a capacity up to 2 terabytes (TB), theoretically, and SDXC cards have faster transfer speeds than the smaller-capacity cards. Note that the P510 cannot use another type of memory card called a MultiMediaCard (MMC), even though those cards are the same size as SD cards.

What card and size should you use? It depends on your needs and intentions. If you're planning to record a good deal of high-definition (HD) video or large numbers of high-resolution still photos, you should get the biggest card you can afford. There are several variables to take into account in computing how many images or videos you can store on a particular size of card, such as which aspect ratio you're using (16:9, 4:3, 3:2, or 1:1), picture size, and quality. To cut through the complications, here are a few samples of what can be stored on a 4 GB SDHC card: At the largest size of 4608 X 3456 pixels and with Fine quality, a 4 GB card can hold 470 still photos; at the next-lower size of 3264 X 2448 pixels and with Normal quality, the same card can hold 1,650 images.

If you're interested in video, here are some guidelines. You can fit about 25 minutes of the highest-quality 1080p HD video on a 4 GB card. The same size card will hold about 40 minutes of lesser-quality HD 1080p video, 60 minutes of HD video at a still lower quality of 720p, or about 2 hours and 50 minutes of video at the lowest quality, VGA, or 640 X 480 pixels. In any of these formats, though, you can record no more than about 29 minutes of video in any one scene.

One other consideration is the speed of the card. If you plan to record high-quality video, you should get a card that is rated as Class 6 or higher for its speed.

Finally, you need to realize if you have an older computer with a built-in card reader, or just an older external card reader, there is a chance it will not read the newer SDHC cards. In that case, you would have to either get a new reader that is compatible with SDHC cards, or download images from the camera to your computer using the USB cable.

Using the newest variety of card, SDXC, used to be somewhat problematic because of compatibility issues with cameras, computers, and card readers, but at this writing in mid-2012 those issues appear to have faded away. For example, I installed a Patriot 64 GB SDXC card in my Coolpix P510, and the camera immediately recognized it and recorded images to it with no problems, even though the same card could not be used in my Coolpix P500. When I tried a SanDisk Ultra 64 GB SDXC card (shown in Figure 1-5), it also worked as expected. If you want to be safe when purchasing a memory card, check the list of approved cards at page 23 of the Coolpix P510 Reference Manual; those on the approved list are cards by SanDisk, Toshiba, Lexar, and Panasonic.

Finally, if you will have access to a wireless (Wi-Fi) network where you use your camera, you may want to consider getting an Eye-Fi card. This special type of storage device, shown in Figure 1-6, looks very much like an ordinary SDHC card, but it includes a tiny transmitter that lets it connect to a wireless network and send your images to your computer over that network as soon as the images have been recorded by the camera.

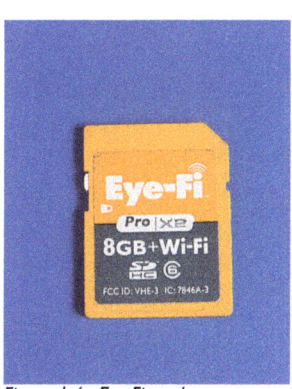

I have tested the 8 GB Eye-Fi card, the Pro X2 model shown here, with the P510, and it works well. Within a few seconds after I snap a picture with this card installed in the camera, a little thumbnail image appears in the upper right corner of my computer's screen showing the progress of the upload. When all images are uploaded, they are available in the Pictures/Eye-Fi folder on my

Figure 1-6: Eye-Fi card

computer. Also, I have installed a free Eye-Fi app for my iPad, which automatically uploads the P510's images to the iPad as they are taken. (You can also use this feature with the iPhone and with Android phones and tablets.)

The Pro X2 Eye-Fi card handles RAW files as well as smaller JPEG and video files. At this writing, the Pro X2 is the only variety of Eye-Fi card that can handle RAW files. Of course, this capability does not matter with the P510, which does not use the RAW format, but you may want to use your Eye-Fi card with other cameras that do shoot in RAW, and the Pro X2 card will serve you well in both cases. An Eye-Fi card is not a necessity, but it is nice to have your images go straight to your computer without having to use a card reader or a USB cable.

In summary, you have quite a few options for choosing a memory card. Personally, I like to use a high-speed 16 GB or 32 GB SDHC card, just to have extra capacity and speed in case they are needed. I like the convenience of the Eye-Fi card also, but, unless you do a lot of photography within range of a wireless network so the images can be uploaded quickly, it may not be worth your while to get that type of card, which costs considerably more than a regular card that provides only storage capacity.

Once you have selected your memory card, open the same little door on the bottom of the camera that covers the battery compartment, and slide the card into the card slot until it catches, with the label facing the back of the camera. To remove the card, push down on it until it releases and springs up so you can grab it. Once the card has been pushed down until it catches, close the compartment door and push the latch back to the locking position. Figure 1-7 shows a card being inserted into the P510.

CHAPTER 1: PRELIMINARY SETUP

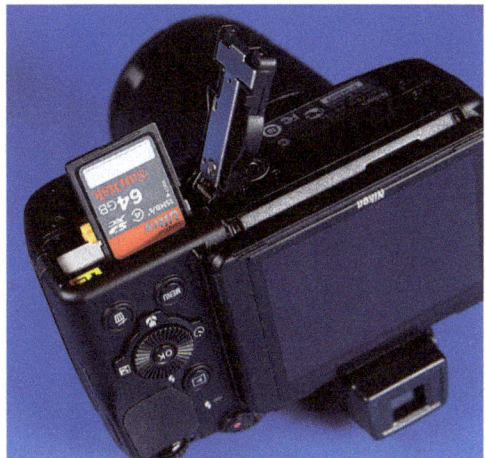

Figure 1-7: Card inserted in camera

One note for when you're shooting continuous pictures with the P510: When the camera is writing its image data to the memory card, the indicator showing the number of remaining images, in the lower right of the display, blinks. When that indicator is blinking, it's important not to turn off the camera or otherwise interrupt its functioning, such as by taking out the battery or disconnecting an AC power adapter. You need to let the card complete its recording process in peace.

Introduction to Main Controls

Now it's time to discuss some of the basic options for setting up the camera using the menu system and controls. Before I start that discussion, I will introduce the main controls, so you'll have a better idea of which button or dial is which as I discuss them later in this and other chapters. I won't discuss the functions of the controls here; they will all be covered in some detail in Chapter 5. For now, here is a series of images that show the major controls. As I discuss each one for the first time, I will describe its position and function; you may want to refer to these images for a reminder about each control.

25

Top of Camera

On top of the camera are several important controls and dials, shown in Figure 1-8.

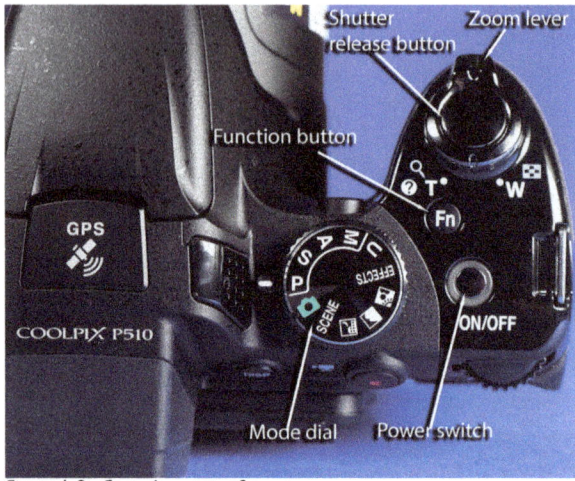

Figure 1-8: Controls on top of camera

Back of Camera

There are numerous major controls on the camera's back, as seen in Figure 1-9.

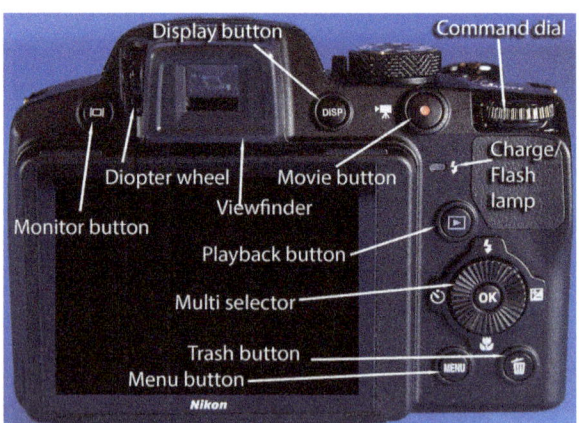

Figure 1-9: Controls on back of camera

Front and Sides of Camera

On the front and sides of the camera, there are several controls and other functional items, as shown in Figures 1-10 through 1-12.

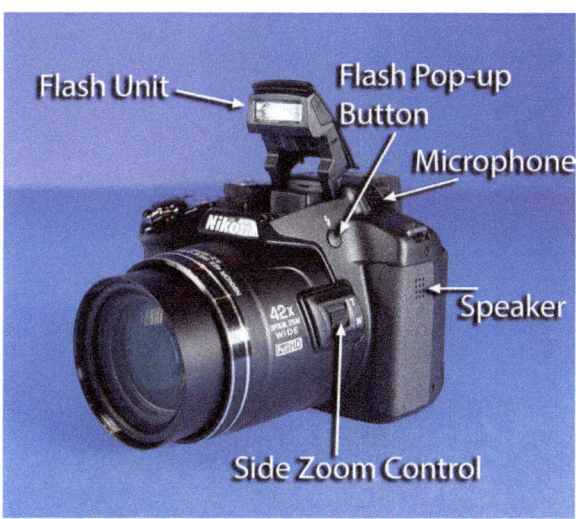

Figure 1-10: Controls on front left of camera

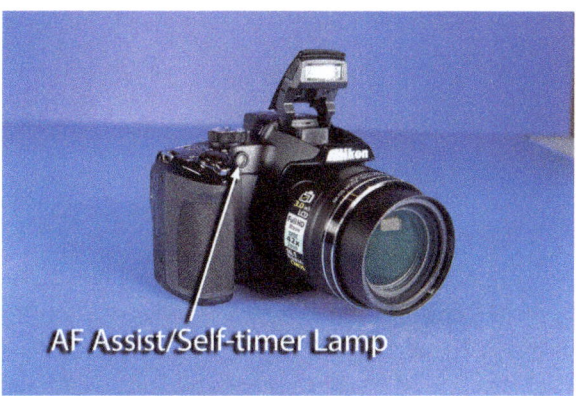

Figure 1-11: AF Assist/Self-timer lamp

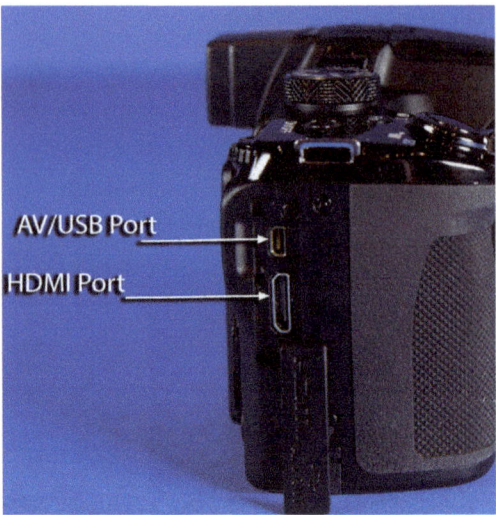

Figure 1-12: Ports on side of camera

Setting the Language, Date, and Time

You need to make sure the date and time are set correctly before you start taking pictures, because the camera records that information (sometimes known as "metadata," meaning data beyond the information in the picture itself) invisibly with each image, and displays it later if you want. Someday you may be very glad to have the date (and even the time of day) correctly recorded with your archives of digital images. If you purchase the camera brand new, it will prompt you to set the date and time when you first power it on.

If you later need to set the time and date, here is how to do so. Remove the lens cap and press down on the camera's power switch, marked On/Off, on top of the camera, to turn the camera on. Then press the Menu button at the lower right of the camera's back. Press the left side of the large round control pad on the back of the camera, known as the multi selector. That spot is marked with a clock (timer) icon. When you press on that spot, the yellow selection block will move to the far left of the screen, to the list of icons, with an icon or letter representing the current shooting mode, such as P for Program or an

CHAPTER 1: PRELIMINARY SETUP

icon for Effects or Backlighting, at the top of the list.

Then use the bottom of the multi selector, marked with a flower icon, to move the selection block down to highlight the wrench icon that represents the Setup menu. Press the right side of the multi selector, marked with a plus and minus sign, to move the highlight back to the right, where it becomes a yellow rectangle highlighting a menu item. Then use the up and down parts of the multi selector to move the yellow selection bar to the Time Zone and Date line on the menu, and press the center button in the multi selector, marked OK, to move to the screen with a selection of settings, shown in Figure 1-13.

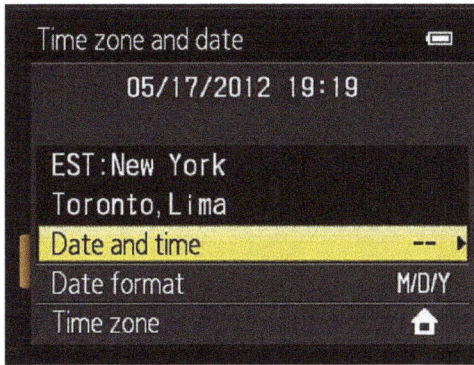

Figure 1-13: Time Zone and Date menu option

On that screen, move the selection block to the Date and Time item, and press OK to activate the date and time settings.

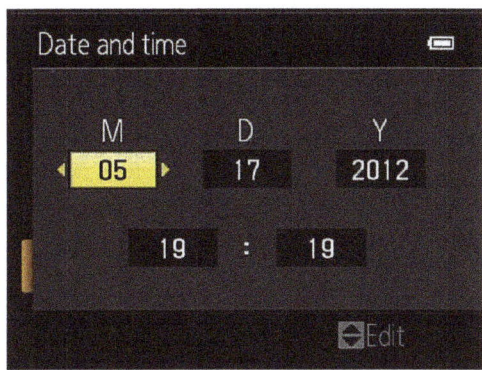

Figure 1-14: Date and time settings screen

29

Move left and right through the date, year, and time settings, as shown in Figure 1-14, and change the settings with up and down movements of the cursor. When everything is set correctly, press the center OK button to confirm and press the Menu button to exit the menu system.

If you need to change the language that the camera uses for the menus and other messages, navigate on the Setup menu to the line that says Language, and press the OK button or the right direction button (right edge of multi selector) to select the Language menu item. Then navigate with the up and down direction buttons (the top and bottom edges of the multi selector) to the language of your choice, as shown in Figure 1-15, and press the OK button to select it. Then press the Menu button to exit from the menu system.

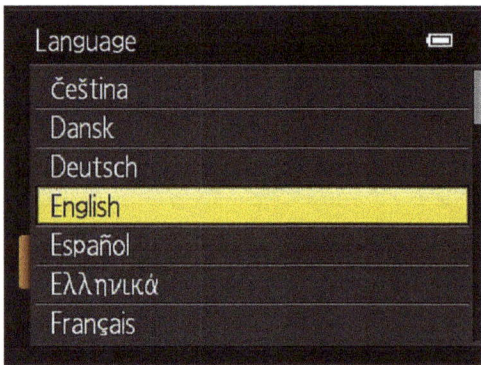

Figure 1-15: Language menu option

Chapter 2: Basic Operations

Taking Pictures

Now that the Coolpix P510 has the correct time and date set and has a fully charged battery inserted along with a memory card, let's explore some scenarios for basic picture-taking. For now, I won't get into discussions of what the various options are and why you might choose one over another. I'll just discuss a reasonable set of steps that will get you and your camera into action and will deposit a decent image on your memory card.

Fully Automatic—Auto Mode

Here's the procedure to use if you want to set the camera to its most automatic mode and let it make (almost) all of the decisions for you. This is a good way to go if you're in a hurry and need to grab a quick shot without fiddling with settings, or if you're new at this and would rather let the camera do its magic without having to provide much input.

1. Remove the lens cap from the lens and let it dangle by its cord. (If you forget to remove the cap before turning on the camera, that's okay; Nikon has engineered the P510 to have the lens cap attached to the moving part of the lens, so the cap will not block the motion of the lens in extending out from the camera. But you will notice that the camera's display is black, because the lens cap will be blocking the view.)

2. Press the On/Off button. The LCD screen will illumi-

nate to show that the camera has turned on. (Or, if you have previously selected the viewfinder using the Monitor button to the left of the viewfinder, the view inside the viewfinder will be illuminated, rather than the LCD screen.)

3. Find the mode dial on top of the camera, and turn the dial until the green camera icon is next to the white indicator line. This selects Auto shooting mode, as shown in Figure 2-1.

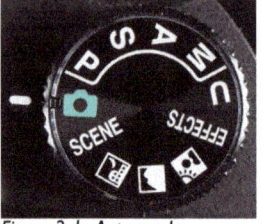

Figure 2-1: Auto mode

4. Press the Menu button at the bottom of the control area on the back of the camera. Use the direction buttons (four edges of the ridged multi selector dial) to navigate to the entry for Image Quality, select that line with the OK button or the right direction button, highlight the Fine setting, and press OK. Then navigate down to the Image Size setting, select it, and choose 4608 X 3456 pixels, the top option, as shown in Figure 2-2. (Of course, you can choose other settings for both of these options if you wish, but the ones I have mentioned provide the highest quality.)

Image size	
16M	4608×3456
8M	3264×2448
4M	2272×1704
2M	1600×1200
VGA	640×480
16:9 12M	4608×2592
16:9 2M	1920×1080

Figure 2-2: Image Size menu option

5. If you want to compose your image on the LCD screen on the back of the camera, no action is needed. If you want to use the electronic viewfinder instead, find the Monitor button to the left of the viewfinder, with an icon that looks like a TV

screen between two vertical lines. Press that button, and the display will switch to the viewfinder, turning off the LCD. You can then look inside the viewfinder to compose the shot and view the camera's settings. You can adjust the view for your eyesight by turning the diopter adjustment dial on the left side of the viewfinder's housing. Toggle between the LCD and the viewfinder whenever you want, using the Monitor button.

    6. If you are indoors or otherwise in conditions that might call for the use of flash, press the button on the left side of the camera's built-in flash unit, marked with a lightning bolt, to pop up the flash.

    7. If you have popped up the flash, press the up direction button on the large round control pad, marked with another lightning bolt, to bring up the Flash menu. Make sure the Auto setting, at the top of this menu, is highlighted. (Later, in Chapter 9, I'll discuss the other flash options.)

    8. Aim the camera toward the subject and look at the LCD screen (or into the viewfinder window, depending on your choice in Step 5) to compose the image as you want it. Locate the zoom lever on the ring that surrounds the shutter button on the top right at the front of the camera. Push that lever to the left, moving its indicator toward the letter W, to get a wider-angle shot (including more of the scene in the picture), or to the right, moving the indicator toward the letter T, to get a telephoto, zoomed-in shot. Or, if you prefer, use the equivalent zoom switch on the left side of the lens, moving it up for telephoto or down for wide-angle.

    9. Once the picture is composed as you want it, push the shutter release button halfway down. You should hear a little beep and see one or more green rectangles on the display, indicating that the picture will be in focus. If you see a red rectangle, that means the camera is having difficulty achieving focus. In that case, try moving the camera to a different angle before pressing the shutter button halfway down again.

10. Push the shutter button all the way down to take the picture.

Basic Variations from Fully Automatic

I won't discuss all of the various shooting modes now, except to name them. Besides Auto, which I just discussed, there are Program, Shutter Priority, Aperture Priority, Manual, User Setting, Scene, Night Landscape, Landscape, Backlighting, and Special Effects. I'll discuss all of those modes in Chapter 3, and movie shooting in Chapter 8. For now, I'm going to discuss some of the functions and features of the Coolpix P510 that you can adjust to suit whatever picture-taking situation you may be faced with. Not all of the settings can be adjusted in Auto mode, so we'll set the camera down to a lower level of automation, to Program mode. In that mode, you'll be able to control most of the camera's functions for taking still pictures.

I'm not going to repeat the preliminary steps for taking a picture, because those are pretty basic. If you need a refresher on those items, see the list in the above discussion of Auto mode.

Start by setting the mode dial on top of the camera to P, for Program, as shown in Figure 2-3.

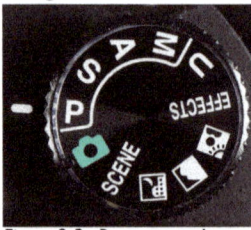
Figure 2-3: Program mode

You will immediately see some different indications on the LCD screen, to show that some of the Auto mode settings have changed. More dramatically, if you press the Menu button you will see that a great many more options are now available for you to set on the Shooting menu—instead of the two menu lines available in Auto mode, you are presented with three menu screens containing 18 settings that you can adjust, including white balance, ISO, metering mode, exposure bracketing, and others. In the Program shooting mode, the camera will determine the proper exposure, both the aperture (size of opening to let in light) and the shutter speed (how long the shutter is open to let in light). In this mode you won't be making any decisions about those two settings; you can have more control over your settings in other modes, which we'll discuss later. That still leaves lots of decisions you can make, though, so let's talk about the various settings you can adjust in Program mode.

Focus

Now that the camera is no longer set to Auto mode, you have more control over focus. More specifically, you now have the option of setting the camera to the MF setting, for manual focus, which is not available in Auto mode. You also have the ability to select which of several types of autofocus operations you want the camera to use, if you opt for autofocus.

I'll discuss focus modes in Chapter 4 in some detail. For now, let's just make sure a standard autofocus mode is selected. First, press the down direction button on the multi selector (marked by a flower icon). This action puts a small menu with four options on the display, as shown in Figure 2-4. Starting at the top, they are the letters AF, for normal autofocus; the flower icon, for macro (close-up) focus; the mountain icon, for focus on infinity; and the letters MF, for manual focus.

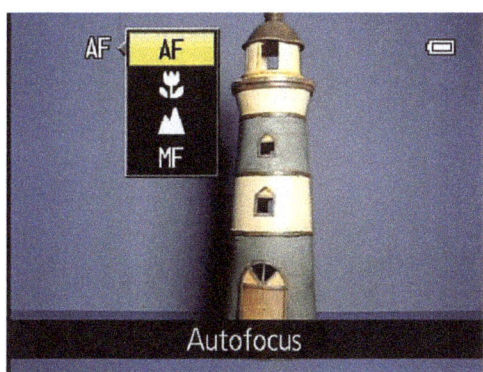

Figure 2-4: Focus mode selection

For the present, use the direction buttons to select the top icon, for normal autofocus. (You have to be quick; the four choices disappear within a few seconds.) Press the OK button to select and confirm your choice. The letters or icon for your choice will appear at the upper left of the display, unless the choice is AF; if you select AF, those letters will appear for a few seconds and then disappear, because that is the default setting.

There are several other focus-related options you can set, but for present purposes let's just use one of them. Press the Menu button at the lower right of the camera's back to enter the shooting menu. With the selection block in the list of menu items, scroll with the up and down direction buttons until the yellow selection rectangle highlights the line for AF Area Mode, at the top of the second screen of the menu.

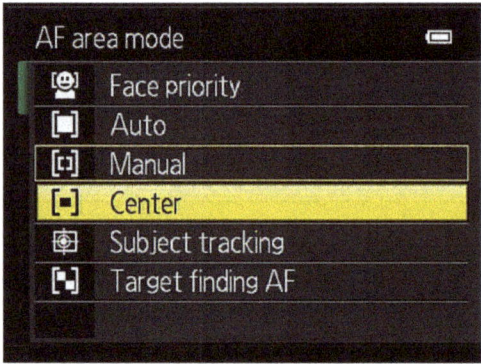

Figure 2-5: AF Area Mode set to Center

Press OK to select that item, then use the up and down direction buttons to change the value for this item to Center, as shown in Figure 2-5. With this setting, the autofocus system will place a focus frame in the center of the screen and will focus on that area. Press OK to confirm, and press the Menu button again to exit the menu system.

Now, when you aim the camera at a scene, center the most important subject between the white focus brackets, as shown in Figure 2-6.

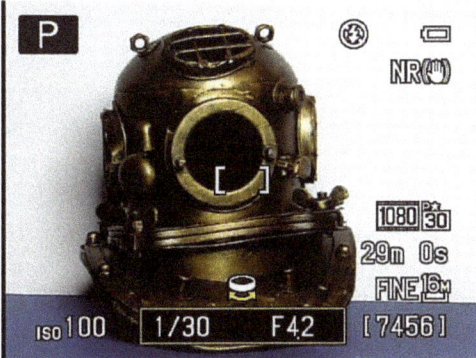
Figure 2-6: Brackets in AF Area Mode Center

Press the shutter button halfway down so the camera will evaluate the exposure and the focus. You should hear a beep and the focus brackets should turn green to confirm the focus. If everything looks okay to you, go ahead and press the shutter button all the way down to take the picture.

Suppose you want to take a picture in which your main subject is not in the center of the screen. Maybe your shot is set up so that a person is standing off to the right of center, and there is some attractive scenery to the left in the scene. Place the focus frame over the part of the picture that needs to be in focus—in our example, the person to the right. Then press the shutter button halfway down until the camera focuses and beeps. Keep the button pressed halfway to lock in the focus (and exposure) while you move the camera back to create your desired composition, with the person off to the right. Then take the picture, and the area you originally focused on will be in focus.

There is another way to handle this sort of situation, by setting AF Area Mode to Manual, a feature that lets you move the focus area around the display so it covers an off-center subject; I'll discuss that option, as well as several other options for autofocus, in Chapter 4.

Manual Focus

Now I will discuss manual focus, the other major option for focusing. Why would you want to use manual focus when the camera will focus for you automatically? Many photographers like the amount of control that comes from being able to set the focus exactly how they want it. And, in some situations, such as focusing in dark areas or areas behind glass, taking extreme close-ups, or cases where there are objects at various distances from the camera, it may be useful for you to control exactly where the point of sharpest focus lies.

For example, when I first got my Coolpix, I went into the back yard to experiment with using the superzoom lens to capture images of birds in our small fountain. It was a cloudy day, and the autofocus mechanism was having problems settling on a sharp focus. I finally decided to switch to manual focus, and the results improved. Of course, manual focus was useful on that occasion partly because I was sitting in one place, the birds tended to stay in one place to take a bath, and the fountain wasn't going anywhere; with a moving subject, manual focus is not going to be as useful.

To activate manual focus, with the camera in Program mode, press the down direction button, with the flower icon; on the menu that pops up on the display, navigate to the MF icon and select it by pressing the OK button.

Now the camera is set for manual focusing. All you need to do at this point to adjust the focus is to press the up and down direction buttons. Press the up button to focus farther from the camera, and press the down button to bring the focus closer. As you move the focus point, you will see a white bar go up and down inside a scale on the right side of the display, indicating the approximate focusing distance, as shown in Figure 2-7. In addition, the view on the screen will be enlarged, to help you focus on details in the subject. Continue adjusting until the focus is as sharp as you can get it, and then take the picture.

CHAPTER 2: BASIC OPERATIONS

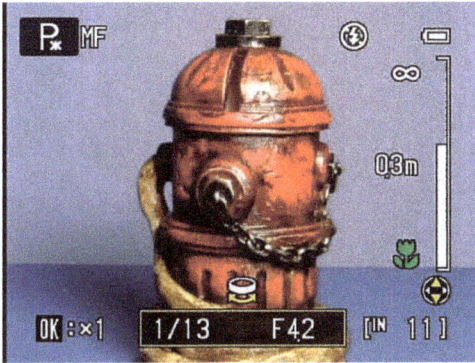

Figure 2-7: Manual focus

If you want to lock the manual focus at a particular distance, press the OK button, and the focus will be locked. At that point, you can use the up and down buttons on the multi selector for their normal functions, flash control (up button) and focus mode selection (down button). To return to adjusting manual focus, press the OK button again.

Exposure

Next, I'll discuss some possibilities for controlling exposure, beyond just letting the camera make the decisions. The Coolpix P510's Auto mode is very good at choosing the right exposure, and so is the Program mode. But there are going to be some situations in which you want to override the camera's automation.

Exposure Compensation

First, let's take a look at the control for adjusting exposure to account for an unusual, or non-optimal, lighting situation. For example, consider Figure 2-8, which shows the P510's view of a decorative cowboy boot. Because the boot is in front of a white background, the camera's autoexposure system makes the exposure too dark, to account for the large expanse of white.

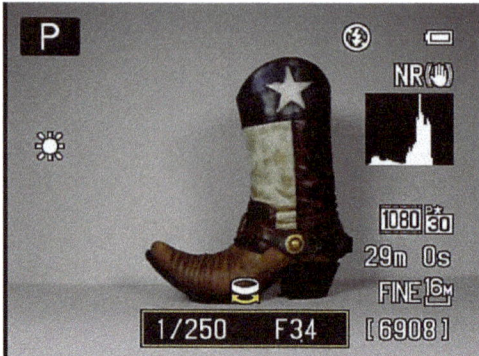

Figure 2-8: Before using exposure compensation

One solution to this problem, which the Coolpix P510 makes very easy to carry out, is to use the exposure compensation control. Look closely at the right direction button on the multi selector. That button is labeled with little plus and minus signs, with the plus on a black background and the minus on white. This control activates the exposure compensation system, which will override the automatic exposure as much as you tell it to, within limits.

Select Program mode and aim at your subject. Press the right button, and a vertical scale will appear on the left side of the display, with a plus sign at the top and a minus sign at the bottom, as shown in Figure 2-9.

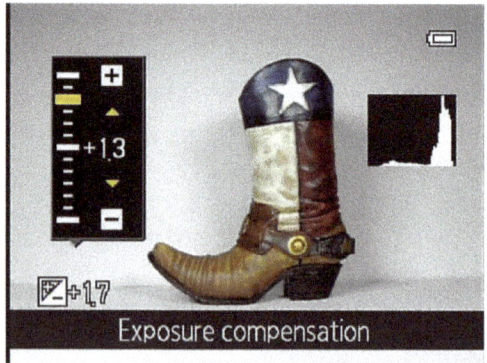

Figure 2-9: Using exposure compensation

(If the camera is in manual focus mode with focus not locked, you have to press the OK button first, before you can use the right direction button; otherwise, that button will adjust the focus position.)

Once the exposure compensation scale has appeared, press the up and down direction buttons on the multi selector to move the values higher and lower, as indicated by a yellow tick mark that appears on the scale to show the value that is being set. If you use the buttons to move the yellow mark all the way to the bottom of the scale, the picture will be considerably darker than the automatic exposure would produce. If you move the yellow tick mark to the top, the picture will be noticeably brighter.

The camera's screen brightens and darkens to show you how the exposure is changing, before you take the picture. The camera also displays a histogram—a chart showing peaks and valleys of brightness values—on the right side of the screen. In this case, you would adjust the exposure to be brighter, so the camera will expose for the boot properly, and let the background show up as a brighter white than in the first image.

I'll discuss the meaning of the histogram in more detail in Chapter 6. For now, you should know that brighter values in your image skew the peaks in the chart to the right, and darker ones skew them to the left. As you adjust exposure compensation, you should generally try to keep the white peaks of the chart in the center of the histogram. In this case, I adjusted the exposure upward by 1.3 EV (exposure value), resulting in a more normally exposed image. The peaks of the histogram are skewed somewhat to the right, because this image required adjusting the exposure to be brighter than normal.

After taking the picture, you should reset the exposure compensation back to zero, in the middle of the scale, so you don't unintentionally affect the pictures you take later. You need to be careful about this, because the camera will retain any exposure compensation value you set, even when it's turned off and then on again.

Flash

Later on, I'll discuss several other topics dealing with exposure, such as the Manual exposure, Aperture Priority and Shutter Priority modes, exposure bracketing, Active D-Lighting, and others. For now I'm going to discuss the basics of using the Coolpix P510's built-in flash unit, because that is something you may need to use on a regular basis. In Chapter 9 I'll discuss other options for using the flash, such as controlling its output and correcting "red-eye," and, in Appendix A, I'll discuss using other flash units.

The built-in flash on the P510 is not especially powerful, but it can provide enough illumination to let you take pictures in dark areas and to brighten up areas that would otherwise be lost in shadows, even outdoors on a sunny day. Here is one fundamental point that you need to be aware of: The built-in flash will not pop up by itself. If you are in a situation in which you think flash may be needed or desirable, you need to take the first step of popping up the flash unit. To do so, find the small, round button on the left side of the flash unit, marked by a lightning bolt. Press in on this button, and the flash springs up into place. (Later, when you're done with the flash, just push down on the unit until it catches again.)

Even though you have popped up the flash unit, in some shooting situations it will never fire. In the situations in which you're likely to want it to, though, it will be ready and willing to illuminate your subject as well as it can.

Let's explore a common scenario to see how the flash works. Make sure the camera is turned on and the flash unit has been released by pressing the flash pop-up button. Now turn the mode dial on top of the camera to select the Night Landscape shooting mode, represented by the white icon just below the Scene mode icon, as shown in Figure 2-10.

Go ahead and press the up direction (Flash mode) button, with

CHAPTER 2: BASIC OPERATIONS

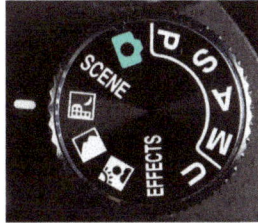
Figure 2-10: Night Landscape

the lightning bolt icon on it. Nothing will happen. You will see the universal negative symbol—a circle with a line through it—over a lightning bolt, indicating that the flash is turned off. (If you don't see this symbol, press the Display button, just to the right of the viewfinder, to switch to the more detailed shooting screen.) In this situation, because you have chosen a shooting mode (Night Landscape) that will not use flash under any circumstances, you cannot turn the flash on.

Next, with the flash still popped up, set the mode dial to P, for Program mode, and then press the Flash button on the multi selector. You will see a menu on the screen with six options available: Auto, Auto with Red-eye Reduction, Off, Fill Flash, Slow Sync, and Rear-curtain Sync, as shown in Figure 2-11.

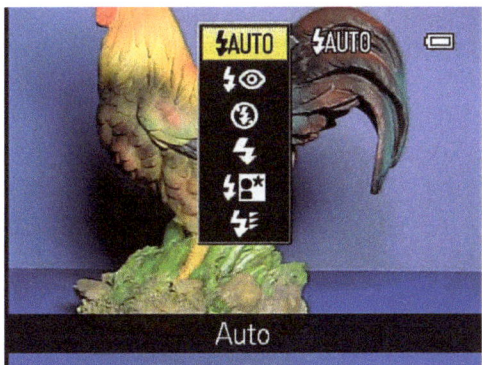
Figure 2-11: Flash mode menu

You can move through this list by pressing the up and down buttons or by turning the command dial or the multi selector dial. Once you have selected a flash mode, you can find out if the flash is going to fire or not by looking at the small lamp that sits to the left of a lightning bolt icon just below the red Movie button on the back of the camera. Set up your shot in the current lighting conditions and press the shutter button halfway. If that lamp lights up in solid red, that means that the

43

flash will fire, either because you have selected Fill Flash, or because you have selected Auto Flash and the camera senses that the flash will be needed. If the lamp does not light up, that means the flash will not fire, either because it is not available in this mode (such as Off) or because the lighting conditions do not require it. If the lamp is blinking red, that means the flash unit is not available because it is charging.

Later on, in Chapter 9, I'll talk more about the various flash options, such as Slow Sync, and how they work. For now, you know how to choose them, and you know that they will not all be available at all times.

Motion Picture Recording

Let's take a look at recording a short video sequence with the Coolpix P510. In Chapter 8, I'll discuss other options for video recording, but for now, let's stick to the basics. First, make sure the flash unit is pressed down in the off position, because it will not be needed. Then, once the camera is turned on, press the Menu button and then press the left direction button to place the yellow selection block in the line of icons at the far left of the screen. Navigate down to the second icon, which looks like a movie camera, then press the right direction button to move the selection rectangle back into the list of menu items. You will see only two items on this menu screen, which provides the options for Movie mode.

Navigate to the top option on the menu screen, which is Movie Options, and then select the top item in the list of those options, called HD 1080p, followed by a star, as shown in Figure 2-12. This is the highest-quality mode for shooting movies with the P510.

CHAPTER 2: BASIC OPERATIONS

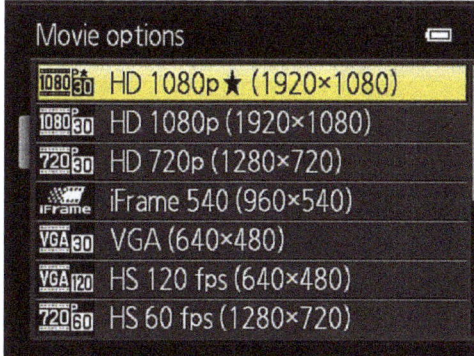

Figure 2-12: Movie Options menu item

Then press the left direction button to move back one screen, and navigate down to the second option on the screen, for Autofocus Mode. Move to the next screen by pressing the OK button or the right direction button, and then select the second option, called Full-time AF, as shown in Figure 2-13.

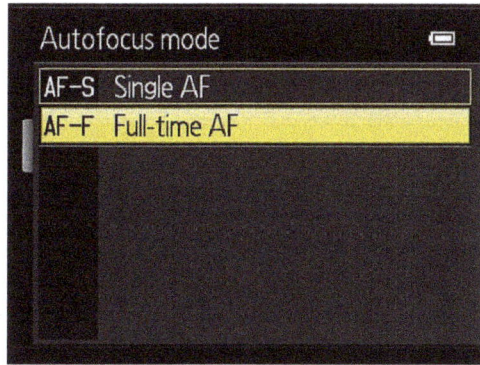

Figure 2-13: Autofocus mode for movies

Press the OK button to confirm this selection. This option will cause the camera to adjust its focus continuously as you shoot your movie. Exit from the menu system by pressing the Menu button.

That is all the preparation you need at this point. Now compose the shot the way you want it, and when you're ready, press the red Movie button once. (That button is at the top of the camera's back, just below the mode dial.) You don't need

45

to hold the button down; just press and release. The camera's display will blank out briefly, then it will show a flashing red REC indicator at the upper left and the minutes and seconds remaining for your recording at the lower right, as shown in Figure 2-14.

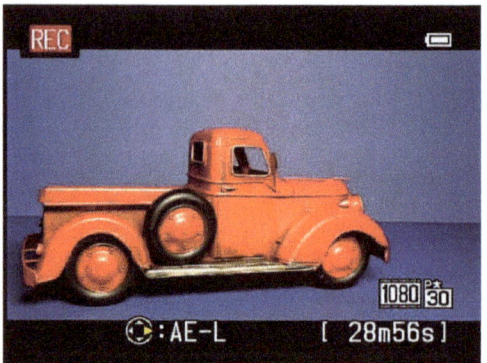
Figure 2-14: Movie recording screen

The camera will keep recording until it reaches a recording limit, or until you press the red button again to stop the recording. Don't be concerned about the level of the sound that is being recorded, because you have no control over the audio volume while recording.

The camera will automatically adjust the exposure and focus as lighting conditions and the distance from the subject change.

One other point that's not specific to the Coolpix P510: Unless you have a good reason to do otherwise, try to hold the camera as steady as possible (use a tripod or monopod if possible), and don't zoom unnecessarily or move the camera except in very smooth, slow motions, such as a pan (side-to-side motion) to take in a wide scene gradually. Video from a jerkily moving camera can be very disconcerting to the viewer.

Viewing Pictures

Before I delve into more advanced settings for taking still pictures and movies, as well as other matters of interest, I need to discuss the basics of viewing your images in the camera.

CHAPTER 2: BASIC OPERATIONS

Review While in Shooting Mode

First, every time you take a still picture, the recorded image will show up on the screen (or in the viewfinder) for a brief amount of time, if you have the Setup menu's Monitor Settings option set to turn on the Image Review function. I'll discuss the details of that setting in Chapter 7. By default, your image will stay on the screen for about two seconds after you take a new picture.

Reviewing Images in Playback Mode

To review images that were taken previously, enter playback mode by pressing the Playback button, marked with a small triangle, to the right side of the upper edge of the LCD screen. You can then scroll through the recorded images using the left and right or up and down direction buttons on the multi selector or by turning the multi selector dial (the dial that surrounds the OK button). You can enlarge any image using the zoom lever on top of the camera, and you can scroll around in the enlarged image using the direction buttons. If you have used the continuous-shooting features of the camera, you may see some images labeled with an OK followed by a colon and a triangle at the bottom center, as shown in Figure 2-15.

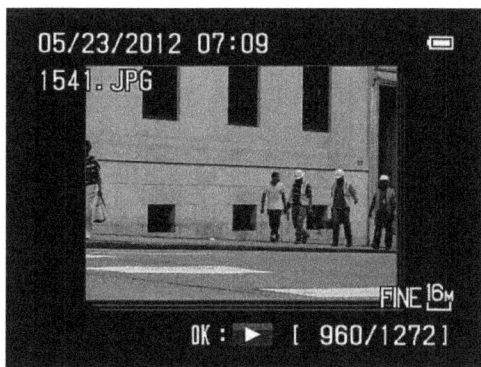

Figure 2-15: Playback of continuous shots

In those cases, you can press the center OK button to "open" a series of continuous shots, and then use the direction buttons

47

to move among the various individual shots in that series. To exit back to the main viewing screen so you can see other images and series of images, press the up direction button. (I'll discuss playback options in more detail in Chapter 6.)

Playing Movies

To play back motion pictures, move through the recorded images by the methods described above until you find an image for which there is a movie options icon at the right of the screen, showing a movie format such as 1080p, as shown in Figure 2-16.

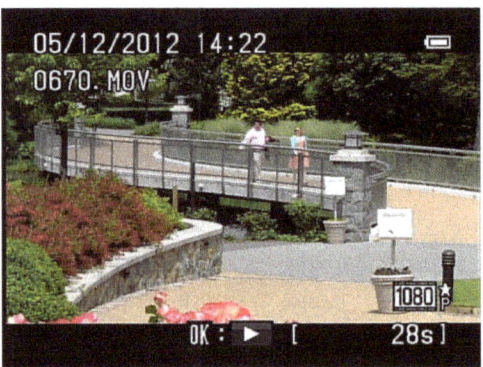

Figure 2-16: Movie ready for playback

While the still frame from the motion picture is displayed on the screen, press the OK button (the button in the center of the multi selector) and the movie will start playing on the LCD, or in the electronic viewfinder if that display option is active instead of the LCD.

At the top of the display there will be a menu of VCR-like controls, as seen in Figure 2-17. Scroll through the line of controls using the direction buttons on the multi selector, and press the OK button to activate one. You also can turn the multi selector dial to the right to fast-forward or to the left to rewind. You can raise or lower the volume of the audio by turning the zoom lever (surrounding the shutter button) towards the T position (louder) or the W position (softer). You will see a little set of volume "waves" increase or decrease next to a speaker icon at the lower left of the screen when you adjust the sound in this way. Note, though, that you cannot adjust the sound with this control if the camera is connected to a TV set; in that case, you must use the TV's volume control to change the sound level.

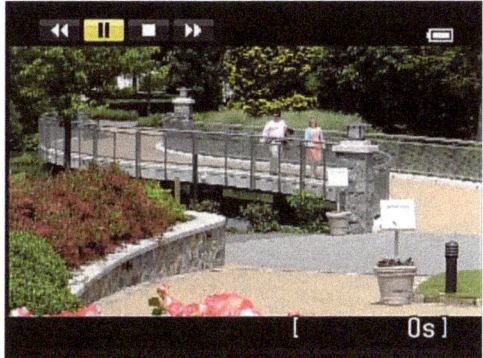

Figure 2-17: Movie playback controls

If you want to play the movies on a computer or edit them with video-editing software, they will import nicely into software such as iMovie for the Macintosh or any other program for Mac or Windows that can deal with video files with the extension .mov. This is the extension for Apple Computer's QuickTime video playback software; QuickTime itself can be downloaded from Apple's web site. For some Windows-based video editing software, you may need to convert the P510's movie files to the .avi format before importing them into the software. You can do so with a program such as mp4cam2avi, which is easily found through an internet search.

I will discuss more of your options for playing movies and editing them in the camera in Chapter 8.

Chapter 3: The Shooting Modes

Up to now I have discussed the basics of how to set up the camera for quick shots, relying heavily on features such as Auto mode for taking pictures whose settings are controlled mostly by the camera's automation. As with others of the more sophisticated digital cameras, though, with the Coolpix P510 there is a wide range of options available for setting the camera, particularly for shooting still images. One of the main goals of this book is to provide clear guidance about this broad range of features. To get started, I will first turn my attention now to the P510's several shooting modes, which provide you with many options for your photography.

Whenever you set out to record still images, you need to select one of the available shooting modes: Auto, Program, Shutter Priority, Aperture Priority, Manual, User Setting, Scene, Backlighting, Night Landscape, Landscape, or Special Effects. So far, we have worked with the Auto and Program modes. Now we will look at the others, after some review of the first two.

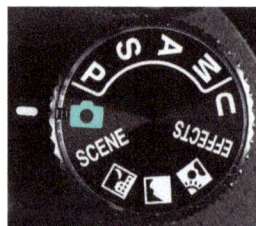
Figure 3-1: Auto mode

Auto Mode

I've already talked about the Auto shooting mode. This is the one you'll want if you just need to have the camera ready for a quick shot, maybe in an environment with fast-paced events when you won't have much time to fuss with settings.

To set this mode, turn the mode dial, on top of the camera to the right of the viewfinder, to the green camera icon, as shown in Figure 3-1. When you select this mode, the camera makes quite a few decisions for you and limits your options in several ways. For example, you can't set ISO or white balance to any value other than Auto, and you can't choose the metering method, use exposure bracketing, or use the Picture Control settings to alter the appearance of your images. In addition, you cannot select continuous shooting.

There are still a few settings you can make, however. For instance, you can choose any of the options for Image Size and Image Quality, you can use exposure compensation, and you can select any of the six available modes for the built-in flash (if you have raised the flash unit). You also can select macro (close-up) focus or infinity focus (but not manual focus), and you can use the self-timer, including its Smile Timer option.

Program Mode

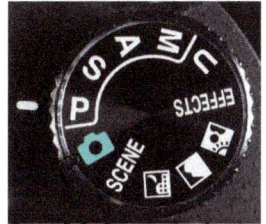
Figure 3-2: Program mode

Choose this option by turning the mode dial to the P slot. The Program shooting mode lets you control many of the settings available with the camera, apart from shutter speed and aperture. However, even though you can't directly set those two values, you still can override the camera's automatic exposure to a fair extent by using exposure compensation, the Flexible Program feature, and exposure bracketing.

I discussed exposure compensation in Chapter 2, and I'll explain exposure bracketing in Chapter 4. Flexible Program is the name Nikon uses for what is often called "Program Shift" for some other cameras. This option lets you adjust the values the camera selects in Program mode for shutter speed and aperture. For example, if the camera selects, say, 1/80 second at f/3.4, the Flexible Program feature will find equivalent combinations that result in the same exposure, such as 1/60 second at f/3.5, 1/50 second at f/4.0, or 1/40 second at 4.5. To use this feature, when the camera is in Program mode, aim at your

51

subject and just turn the command dial (the wheel at the very top right corner of the camera's back) to find an equivalent pair of shutter speed and aperture, as shown in Figure 3-3.

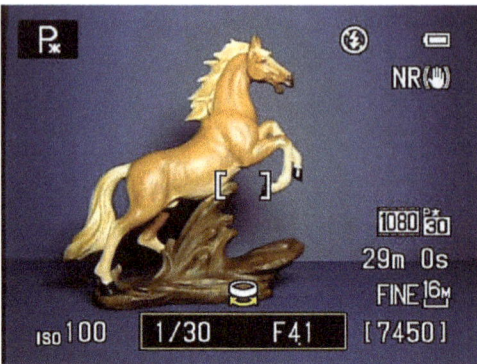

Figure 3-3: Flexible Program

When the camera is using one of these equivalent match-ups of settings rather than the originally chosen setting, it displays an icon to the lower right of the letter P that signifies Program mode in the upper left of the display. That icon, which represents Flexible Program, looks like an X with a vertical line down through its center, as seen in Figure 3-3.

Why would you use the Flexible Program option? Does it make sense to let the camera make its best calculation of the proper exposure and then override it? Well, yes, it may, in some cases. For example, you may want to see what the "proper" exposure is, and then see if you can use a wider aperture to achieve a blurred background, or a faster shutter speed to stop the action or prevent blur from camera motion. And, when you're experimenting with the camera to see what it is capable of, it can be very helpful to try various combinations of aperture and shutter speed to find out which combination gives you the best results in different situations. With a digital camera, there's no added cost for trying these different approaches, and Flexible Program is a useful way to experiment.

One way to look at Program mode is that it greatly expands the choices available through the Shooting menu. You will be able to make choices involving image size and quality, white balance, ISO sensitivity, metering method, autofocus mode, and others. I won't discuss all of those choices here; if you want to explore that topic, go to the discussion of the Shooting menu in Chapter 4 and check out all of the different selections that are available to you.

Shutter Priority Mode

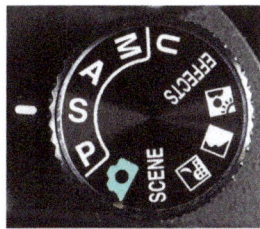

Figure 3-4: Shutter Priority

In Shutter Priority mode, you set the shutter speed, and the camera will set the corresponding aperture in order to achieve a proper exposure of the image. In this mode, you can set the shutter to be open for intervals ranging from 4 full seconds at the lowest ISO settings to 1/4000 of a second at the highest ISO settings. (For example, if the ISO is set to 800, the slowest shutter speed available is 2 seconds.) If you are photographing fast action, such as a baseball swing or a hurdles event at a track meet, and you want to stop the action with a minimum of blur, you will need a fast shutter speed, such as 1/1000 of a second. In other cases, for creative purposes, you may want to use a slow shutter speed to achieve a certain effect, such as leaving the shutter open to capture a trail of automobiles' taillights at night.

Controlling shutter speed is a powerful tool for creative photography. Here are some examples. First, take a look at Figures 3-5 through 3-7, which were taken with the Coolpix P510 of a small waterfall in a shaded area.

For the first image, Figure 3-5, I used a shutter speed of 1/400 second. As you can see, this fast shutter speed stopped the action of the flowing water quite well, "freezing" it so you can just about see some individual drops or streams of water.

For the second image, Figure 3-6, I used a considerably slower shutter speed of 1/80 second. In this image, you can see that the longer shutter speed captured a steady stream of water, making it look more like a continuous flow, although this shutter speed was still fast enough to stop the action of the water effectively.

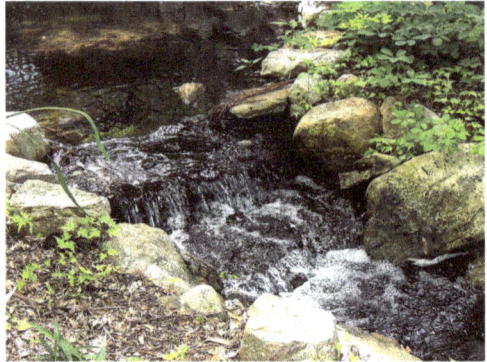
Figure 3-5: Shutter speed 1/400 second

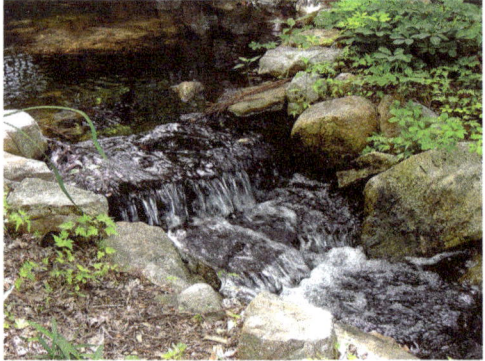
Figure 3-6: Shutter speed 1/80 second

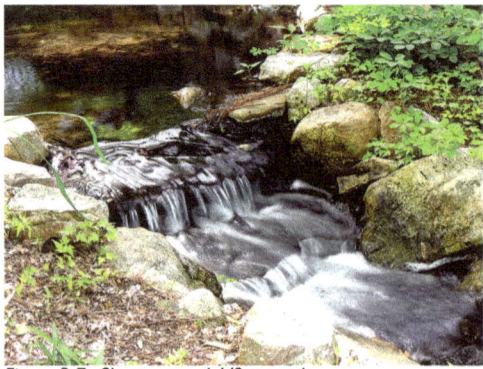
Figure 3-7: Shutter speed 1/2 second

For the final image in the series, Figure 3-7, I used a much slower shutter speed of one-half second. Keeping the shutter open for this length of time caused the flowing water to blend together into a smooth and continuous stream with a somewhat blurry and milky appearance. I was fortunate that the location was shady enough to allow the use of this slow shutter speed without resulting in overexposure. Often, to take shots such as this one it is necessary to place a neutral density filter over the lens to block some of the light, allowing the use of a slow shutter speed without making the image too bright.

Because shutter speed can be used for great creative purposes, I'm going to include one more set of photos as a second example. In this case, I used a working model of a Ferris wheel, with small white lights on the edge of the wheel. All three shots were taken indoors under artificial light at f/3.6, which was the widest aperture available at the camera's focal length of 50mm.

For the first exposure, Figure 3-8, I used a fast shutter speed of 1/800 second, in order to be sure to stop the motion of the wheel. In this image, the wheel is basically frozen in place; you can see the wheel and its seats standing still. This speed turned out to be overkill, because the wheel was not turning all that fast. For the second exposure, Figure 3-9, I used a much slower shutter speed of 1/8 second, which was still fast enough to make the wheel look as if it's basically stopped, though blurred.

For the next photo, Figure 3-10, I used an even slower shutter speed of 1/4 second. This turned out to be the first speed at which the wheel is blurred to the point of changing its appearance as its parts overlap each other. Finally, for the last shot, Figure 3-11, I turned out the lights in the room to allow the lights on the edge of the wheel to show up during an exposure of one full second. This approach resulted in the solid, circular trails of light traced by the wheel as it rotated in the dark room. Using the slowest shutter speed essentially transformed the subject of the picture into a different object.

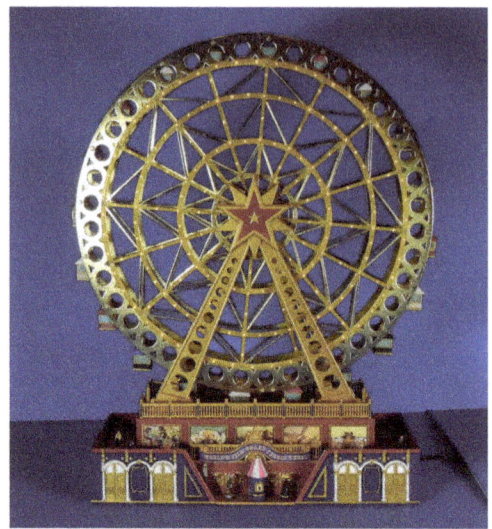

Figure 3-8: Shutter speed 1/800 second

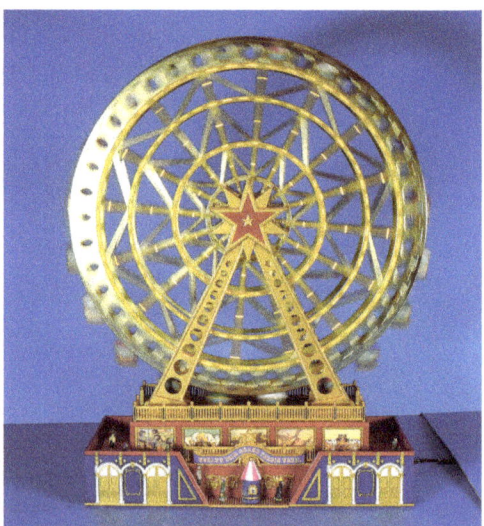

Figure 3-9: Shutter speed 1/8 second

CHAPTER 3: THE SHOOTING MODES

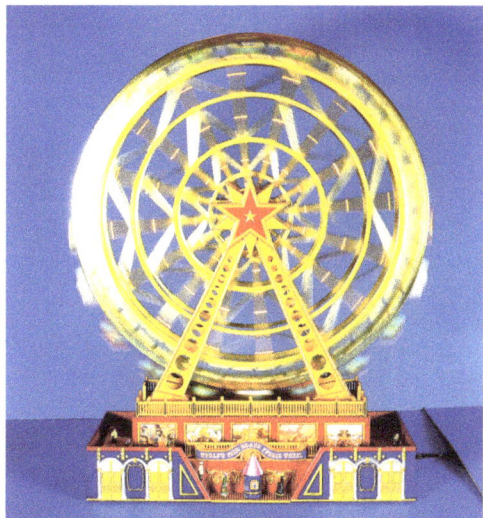

Figure 3-10: Shutter speed 1/4 second

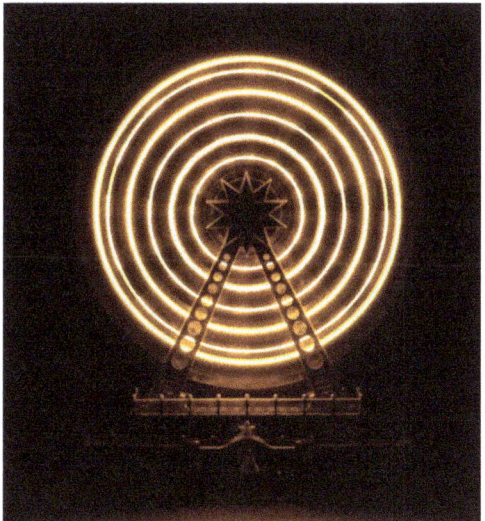

Figure 3-11: Shutter speed 1 second

You select Shutter Priority mode by setting the mode dial on top of the camera to the S indicator, shown in Figure 3-4. Then you set the shutter speed by turning the command dial—the ridged dial at the top right of the camera's back, just below the on/off switch. The LCD (or viewfinder, if selected) will display the selected shutter speed inside a yellow rectangle at the bottom center of the screen, as shown in Figure 3-12.

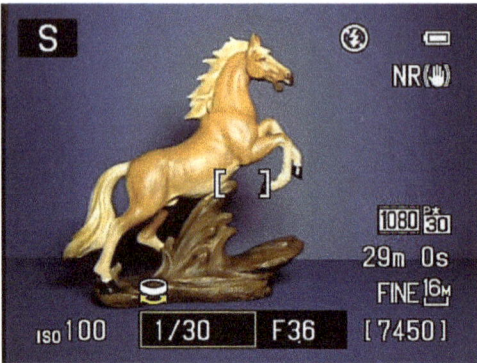
Figure 3-12: Shutter Priority setting

As you point the camera at scenes with varying lighting, the camera will select and display the appropriate aperture (such as f/3.6 in this example) to achieve a proper exposure.

Once you've pushed the shutter button halfway down, you need to watch the shutter speed number on the screen. If that number blinks, that means that proper exposure at that shutter speed is not possible at any available aperture, according to the camera's calculations. For example, with a shutter speed of 2 seconds in a well-lighted room, the shutter speed number (which may be f/8.3, the most narrow setting) may begin to blink, indicating that proper exposure is not possible. One good thing in this situation is that the camera will still let you take the picture, despite having blinked the number to warn you. The camera is saying, in effect, "Look, maybe you shouldn't do this, but that's your business. If you want an overly bright picture for some reason, help yourself." (Note: This situation is less likely to take place when the camera is in Aperture Priority mode, because in that mode, there is a wide range of shutter speeds for the camera to choose from—a range from 4 seconds to 1/4000 second in some situations, depending on factors such as ISO and continuous-shooting settings.)

When you are setting shutter speed, the fractions of a second are easy to read because they are displayed as standard fractions, such as 1/5 or 1/200. Some of the longer times are a bit harder to read; the camera displays them using quotation marks. So, for example, 2 seconds is displayed as 2", and 1.3 second is displayed as 1.3."

One feature of the shutter speed display on the Coolpix P510 is a bit confusing, at least to me. Some of the camera's shutter speeds are displayed as fractions whose denominators are decimal numbers, such as 1/1.3. I would have trouble understanding that number without doing some arithmetic, so here is a brief chart that converts these few values into terms that may be easier to comprehend:

Shutter Speed Equivalents	
2.5	1/2.5 = 0.4 = 2/5 second
1.6	1/1.6 = 0.625 = 5/8 second
1.3	1/1.3 = 0.77 = 10/13 second (approx. 0.8 sec)

Aperture Priority Mode

Aperture Priority mode is the inverse of Shutter Priority. You activate it by turning the mode dial to the A setting. Before discussing the settings for this mode, let's talk about aperture and why you would want to control it. The camera's aperture is a measure of the current width of its opening that lets in light to create the image. This width is measured numerically in f-stops. For the Coolpix P510, the range of f-stops is from f/3.0 (wide open) to f/8.3 (most narrow), though this range is limited in some circumstances, as discussed below. The amount of light that is let into the camera to create an image is controlled by the combination of aperture (how wide open the lens is) and shutter speed (how long the shutter remains open to let in the light).

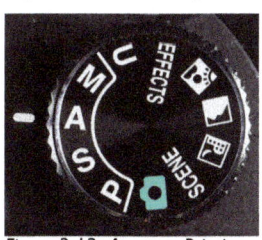

Figure 3-13: Aperture Priority

For some purposes, you may want to control the width of the aperture, but let the camera choose the corresponding shutter speed, so you can control the depth of field. Depth of field is a measure of how well a camera is able to keep multiple objects or subjects in focus at different distances (focal lengths). For example, say you have three friends lined up so you can see all of them, but they are standing at different distances—five, seven, and nine feet (1.5, 2.1, and 2.7 meters) from the camera. If the camera's depth of field is quite shallow at a particular focal length, such as five feet (1.5 meters), then, in this case, if you focus on the friend at that distance, the other two will be out of focus and blurry. But if the camera's depth of field when focused at five feet is broad, then it may be possible for all three friends to be in sharp focus in your photograph, even if the focus is set for the friend at five feet.

What does all of that have to do with aperture? One of the rules of photographic optics is that the wider the camera's aperture is, the more shallow its depth of field is at a given focal length. So in the example discussed above, if you have the camera's aperture set to its widest opening, f/3.0, the depth of field will be relatively shallow, and it will be possible to keep fewer items in focus at varying distances from the camera. If the aperture is set to the narrowest, f/8.3, the depth of field will be greater, and it will be possible to have more items in focus at varying distances.

It can be difficult to illustrate this effect with a camera like the Coolpix P510, for a couple of reasons. First, the image sensor, where the light is gathered to form the image, is relatively small, which results in the depth of field being relatively deep at all apertures. Second, the largest aperture available is f/3.0, whereas some compact cameras have lenses that open as wide as f/2.0, or even f/1.8. With such cameras it is easier to achieve a blurred background, because the depth of field can be quite shallow at such a wide aperture. With the P510, the widest aperture you can shoot with is f/3.0, and that aperture is available only when the lens is zoomed back to its extreme wide-angle setting, where depth of field is greater. If you zoom the lens in to a telephoto setting, the maximum aperture decreases steadily. At the maximum zoom range, the widest aperture available is only f/5.9, which is not far from the narrowest aperture of f/8.3.

However, by setting up a shot with fairly extreme conditions, I created the images in Figures 3-14 and 3-15 to illustrate the different depths of field that are achieved with two different apertures. For both images, the camera was about 11 inches (28 cm) away from the peacock figurine, and the poster with large print was about 9 feet (2.75 m) further past the peacock. The lens was zoomed in slightly, to 70mm, in order to compose the shot properly. I set the P510 to shoot in Aperture Priority mode. The first image was taken at f/3.9, the widest aperture available at that focal length; the second one was taken at f/7.6.

As you should be able to see, in Figure 3-14, with the wider aperture, the text on the poster is noticeably blurred because the depth of field is relatively shallow at that setting. In Figure 3-15, on the other hand, the printing is in relatively sharp focus because the depth of field is greater at the narrower f/7.9 aperture.

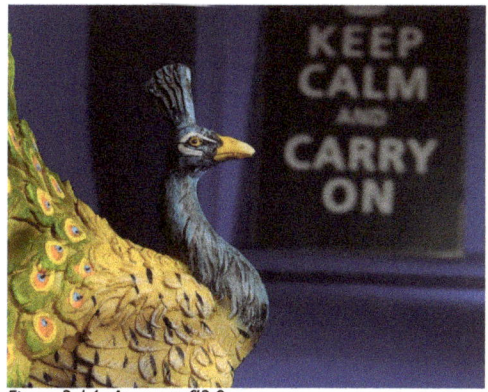

Figure 3-14: Aperture f/3.9

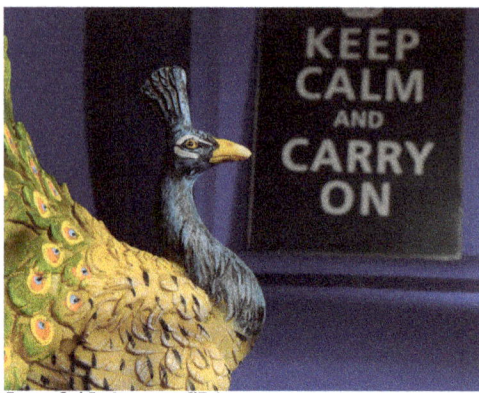

Figure 3-15: Aperture f/7.6

If you want to have the sharpest picture possible, especially when you have subjects at varying distances from the lens and you want them all to be in focus, then you may want to control the aperture, and make sure it is set to the highest number (narrowest opening) possible.

On the other hand, there are occasions when photographers prize a shallow depth of field. This situation arises often in the case of outdoor portraits. For example, you may want to take a photo of a person standing outdoors with a background of trees and bushes, and possibly some other, more distracting objects, such as a swing set or a tool shed. If you can achieve a narrow depth of field, you can have the person's face in sharp focus, but leave the background quite blurry and indistinct. This effect is sometimes called "bokeh," a Japanese term describing an aesthetically pleasing blurriness of the background.

You have undoubtedly seen images using this effect. In this situation, the blurriness of the background can be a great asset, reducing the distraction factor of unwanted objects and highlighting the sharply focused portrait of your subject.

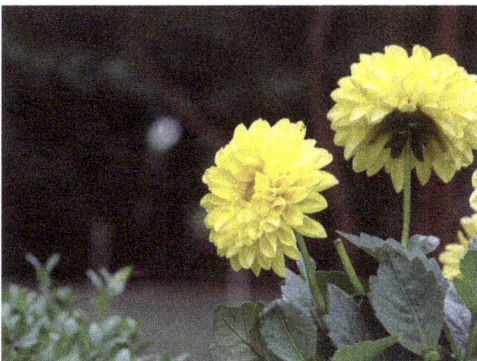

Figure 3-16: Bokeh effect

The example in Figure 3-16 shows flowers on the right, in fairly sharp focus, with the background heavily defocused; this image was shot in close-up mode with the lens very close to the foreground, resulting in a very shallow depth of field.

Having discussed some reasons for selecting the aperture yourself rather than letting the camera select it automatically, I'll outline the technical steps involved. Once you have moved the mode dial to the A setting, the next step is quite simple. Aim the camera at your subject, and use the multi selector dial (the dial around the OK button) to change the aperture. The number of the f-stop will appear inside a yellow rectangle at the bottom right of the screen. The shutter speed chosen by the camera will show up also, to the left of the aperture, as seen in Figure 3-17.

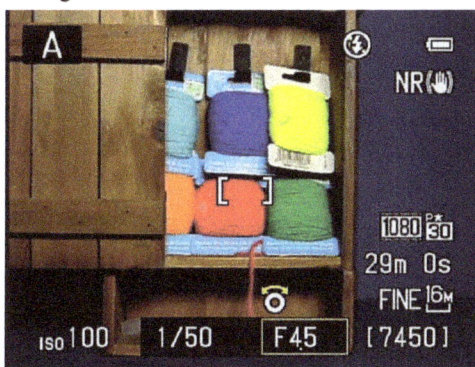

Figure 3-17: Aperture Priority setting

One more note on Aperture Priority mode that might not be immediately obvious and could easily lead to confusion: As I noted briefly above, not all apertures are available at all times. In particular, the widest-open aperture, f/3.0, is available only when the lens is zoomed out to its wide-angle setting (zoom lever moved toward the letter W). At the highest zoom levels, the widest aperture available is f/5.9. To see an illustration of this point, here is a quick test. Zoom the lens out by moving the zoom lever all the way to the left, toward the W setting. Then select Aperture Priority mode and select an aperture of f/3.0 by turning the multi selector dial all the way to the left, the direction for lower f-numbers. Now zoom the lens in by moving the zoom lever to the right, toward the T setting. The aperture will change to f/5.9. If you try to reset the aperture to f/3.0 after the zoom action is finished, you will see that the lowest aperture number you can set is f/5.9, because that is the widest aperture available on the P510 at the telephoto zoom level. (The aperture will change back to f/3.0 if you move the zoom back to the wide-angle setting.)

Manual Exposure Mode

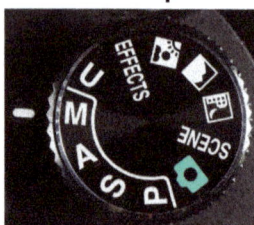

Figure 3-18: Manual exposure

The Coolpix P510 has a fully manual mode for control of aperture and shutter speed, which is one of the great features of this camera. Not all compact cameras have a manual exposure mode, which is a tremendous boon for photographers who want to exert full creative control over exposure decisions.

The technique for using this mode is not too far removed from what I discussed in connection with the Aperture Priority and Shutter Priority modes. To control exposure manually, set the mode dial to the M indicator. You now have to control both shutter speed and aperture by setting them yourself.

To set these values, first look at the camera's display and find where the shutter speed (such as 1/30) and aperture (such as

F4.5) are displayed at the bottom of the screen, as shown in Figure 3-19. You will see an icon of a horizontal dial with a yellow arrow above the shutter speed value on the left, which is inside a yellow rectangle; the dial icon means that the shutter speed value is controlled by the command dial (the wheel at the top of the camera's back, just below the power button). To the right of that value, you will see the value for the aperture, or f-stop, inside another rectangle; above that value will be an icon showing a dial that is situated vertically; that icon represents the multi selector dial, on the back of the camera surrounding the OK button.

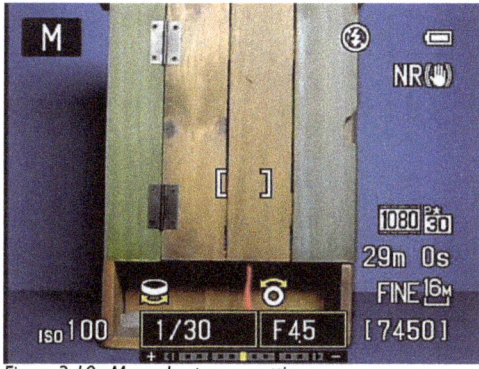

Figure 3-19: Manual exposure setting

To adjust the settings, simply turn the command dial until you have selected the shutter speed you want, and turn the multi selector dial to set your desired aperture.

As you adjust these values, watch the horizontal scale at the bottom of the screen, below the two settings. You will see the tick marks on the scale turn yellow, either to the right or left side of the scale's center point, as the values change. When the exposure is set the way the camera's meter judges to be accurate, there will be a lone yellow tick mark in the center of the scale. If the marks to the left of the center of the scale turn yellow, the exposure is too bright; if they turn yellow to the right of the center, it is too dark. If the setting becomes more extreme than the scale can indicate, a red triangle appears at the extreme left or right of the scale. (The plus and minus directions on this scale can be reversed using the Reverse Indicators item on the Setup menu, as discussed in Chapter 7.)

Of course, you don't have to center the indicator on the scale; it is there only to give you an idea of how the camera would meter the scene. You very well may want parts of the scene (or the whole image) to be darker or lighter than the metering system would indicate to be "correct." With Manual exposure mode, the settings for aperture and shutter speed are independent of each other. When you change one, the other one stays unchanged until you change it manually. The camera is leaving the creative decision about exposure entirely up to you, even if the resulting photograph would be washed out by excessive exposure or underexposed to the point of near-blackness.

One note to remember: As with Aperture Priority mode, the range of available apertures in Manual exposure mode is limited as the lens is zoomed in to greater levels of magnification. Also, the range of shutter speeds has certain limits. For example, here again, the slowest shutter speed available at ISO 800 is 2 seconds; at ISO 3200, the slowest is 1/2 second. However, in Manual mode, you are able to set the camera to its slowest shutter speed of 8 seconds, which is not available in any other shooting mode. This setting is available only when the ISO is set to 100. (If ISO is set to Auto in Manual exposure mode, the camera automatically sets the ISO to 100, so the 8-second shutter speed is available in that situation also.)

Scene Modes

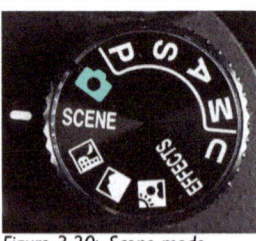

Figure 3-20: Scene mode

The Coolpix P510 offers several of what I will call Scene modes. The terminology can be a bit confusing, because the camera's menus and documentation use the word "scene" in several similar and overlapping contexts. First, there are three Scene modes that occupy individual slots marked by icons on the mode dial: Night Landscape, Landscape, and Backlighting. Next, there is another slot on the mode dial marked SCENE, as shown in Figure 3-20. When you select that setting, you can press the Menu button to the lower left of the multi selector and scroll through a list of 16 specific Scene settings: Portrait, Sports, Night Portrait, Party/Indoor, Beach, Snow, Sunset, Dusk/Dawn, Close-up, Food, Museum, Fireworks Show, Black and White Copy, Panorama, Pet Portrait, and 3D Photography.

Finally, there is a 17th entry on this list, which actually is the first entry at the top of the list: Scene Auto Selector. If you choose that option, the camera will analyze the live view using its digital circuitry and try to determine the most appropriate shooting mode to use from among these choices: Portrait, Landscape, Night Portrait, Night Landscape, Close-up, Backlighting, and Other Scenes.

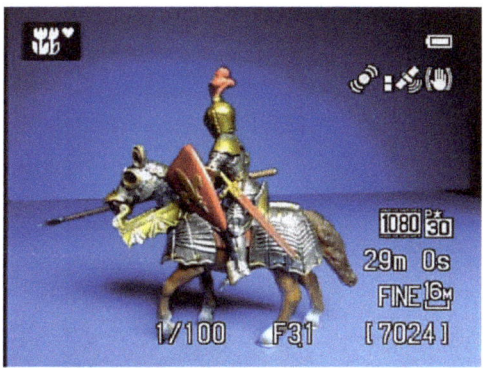

Figure 3-21: Scene Auto Selector mode

If the camera can identify what appears to be a scene calling for one of the listed settings, it displays an icon for that setting in the upper left corner of the screen. For example, in Figure 3-21, the camera appropriately identified the shot of a model knight on horseback as calling for Close-up mode, represented by the icon in the upper left of the screen.

In this mode, you can use exposure compensation and the self-timer, but you cannot select an autofocus mode. If you press the Flash button (up direction button), you are offered only two options: Auto Flash or Flash Off.

If the camera chooses a Scene mode that you don't like, you of course have the option of using the mode dial to select another mode, such as Auto, or a specific Scene mode.

Scene modes are rather different from the other shooting modes we have discussed. These modes do not have a single defining feature, such as permitting control over one or more aspects of exposure. Instead, when you select Scene mode, and then choose a particular Scene type within that mode, you are in effect telling the camera what type of environment the picture is being taken in, and what type of image you are looking for, and you are letting the camera make a group of decisions as to what settings to use to produce that result.

Some photographers may not like Scene modes because they take some creative decisions away from you and limit your options in some unfortunate ways. For example, you will find that your Shooting menu options are severely limited when the mode dial is turned to the SCENE setting or any of the Scene modes with slots on the mode dial, such as Night Landscape. That means that you cannot set the white balance, but must rely on the camera's Auto White Balance setting, which may not always properly evaluate the existing light source. In most cases, you cannot select features such as continuous shooting, and you can't choose your metering mode or your ISO setting.

Despite the limitations, though, I have found the various Scene settings to be quite useful in certain situations. Remember that you don't have to use these settings only for their labeled purposes; you may find that some of them offer a group of options that is well-suited for some shooting scenarios that you are regularly faced with. For example, you may find the Sports setting works well for shots of children at play, or that the Sunset setting, which emphasizes red hues, is great for images in a particular garden that is rich with reddish plants and flowers.

That concludes the general introduction to the Scene modes.

But there are numerous choices, and you need to know something about each option to decide whether it's one you would want to select. In general, a given Scene setting carries with it a variety of values, including things like focus mode, flash status, range of shutter speeds, sensitivity to various colors, and others. I will discuss the complete list of Scene settings, so you can make informed choices. I will first discuss the settings that have their own slots on the mode dial, followed by the settings that are grouped under the SCENE setting on that dial.

Night Landscape

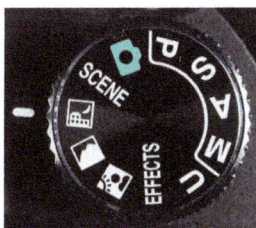

Figure 3-22: Night Landscape

This mode, symbolized by a crescent moon above a building, appears on the mode dial just below the SCENE setting. It is intended for use without flash to take shots outdoors at night in areas that are not brightly lighted. When you select this shooting mode with the mode dial, there are two sub-options that appear on the Shooting menu: Hand-held and Tripod. To choose one of these options, press the Menu button, then select Night Landscape, the bottom item on the brief menu list that appears. Then press the OK button or the right direction button, and choose either Hand-held or Tripod, as shown in Figure 3-23.

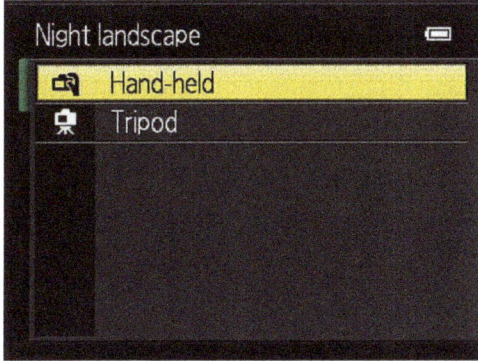

Figure 3-23: Night Landscape menu

With Hand-held, the camera will take a continuous group of pictures and combine them in the camera into a single image, to overcome the effects of the high ISO setting the camera uses to take a good exposure in dim light without flash. A single image could be degraded from the visual "noise" that results from the use of high ISO values; by combining several images, the camera can create a single image using the best aspects of each, and can digitally smooth away the noise. You should try to hold the camera as steady as possible when shooting, but it will use a relatively fast shutter speed if at all possible to avoid blur from camera shake.

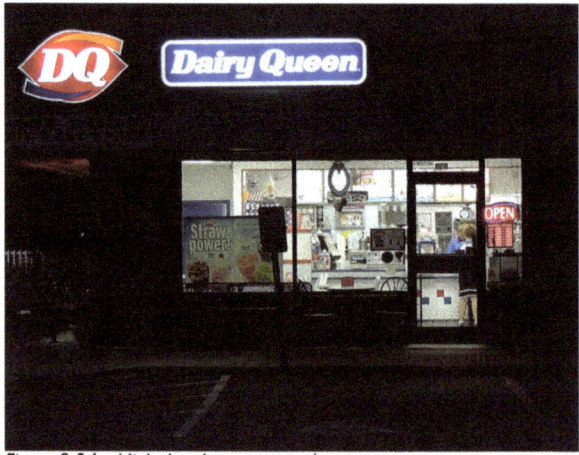

Figure 3-24: Night Landscape example

The image in Figure 3-24 was taken with the P510 handheld after dark; the only illumination was lights coming from the restaurant. The camera took a series of shots and combined them internally to create the composite image shown here, which was exposed at f/4.1 for 1/30 second at ISO 800.

If you choose the Tripod option from the menu, then the camera will use a slower shutter speed and a lower ISO setting, so as to avoid noise. The use of the tripod will avoid the effects of camera shake. Of course, this setting is useful only if you actually attach the camera firmly to a tripod.

Landscape

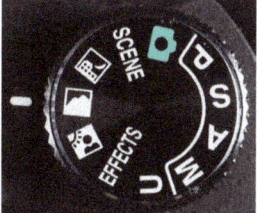

Figure 3-25: Landscape mode

This is the setting with a mountain-range icon on the mode dial next to Night Landscape. With many other cameras, including the Nikon Coolpix P500, the predecessor to the P510, this shooting mode was one of those that are selected through the Shooting menu when the dial is set to the SCENE setting. With the P510, though, the Landscape setting has been promoted to its own slot on the mode dial, perhaps in recognition of the great usefulness of this setting.

I find myself using the Landscape setting often, and I appreciate that it is very easy to twist the mode dial to choose it. When you do, you will again, as with Night Landscape mode, have the ability to select one of the two options from the Shooting menu: in this case, Noise Reduction Burst or Single Shot.

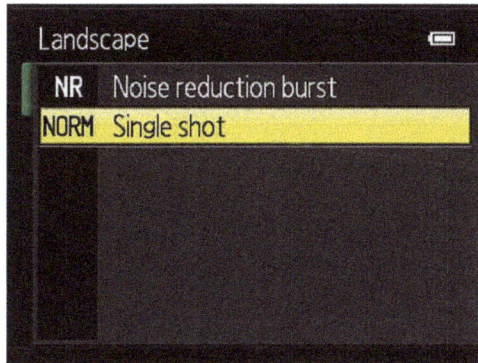

Figure 3-26: Landscape menu

If you select Noise Reduction Burst, the camera will take a rapid series of shots at a relatively high ISO setting and combine them in the camera into a final image. The camera's internal processing will combine the individual shots so as to reduce the visual "noise" that results from using higher ISO settings.

If, instead, you select the Single Shot option, the camera will operate as you would expect for a normal Landscape setting—it will take just one shot at a lower ISO setting, which likely will result in a sharper picture than one taken with the Noise Reduction Burst setting. The example in Figure 3-27 was taken with the Single Shot setting with the camera on a tripod.

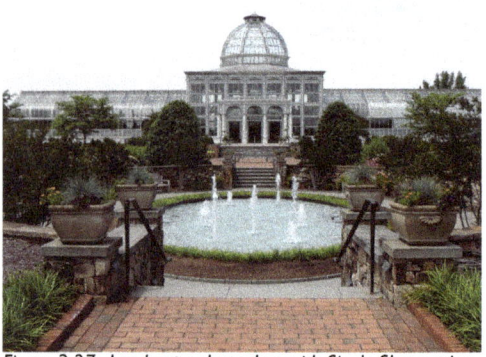

Figure 3-27: Landscape shot taken with Single Shot setting

Backlighting/HDR

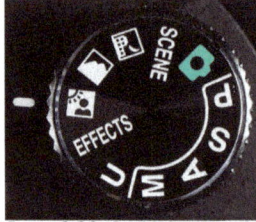

Figure 3-28: Backlighting mode

This mode, marked on the mode dial by an icon of a person with a bright light in the background to the upper left, is intended to be used in difficult lighting situations—in particular, when there is bright light present, but it is not located in a way that is helpful to the photographer. (Nikon calls this mode simply "Backlighting," but its single sub-mode is HDR, which, as discussed below, is an important feature for modern cameras, so I have added HDR to the heading here for easier identification.)

When this mode is selected, as with the two previous modes, you have two basic sub-options selectable by pressing the Menu button. In this case, the two options are HDR On and HDR Off.

If you choose the default value, HDR Off, the camera forces the built-in flash to fire in order to overcome the shadows caused by your subject's being lighted from behind.

If, instead, you choose HDR On, you have a considerably different situation. With this setting, the camera internally performs its own version of HDR, or High Dynamic Range, processing. In case you haven't encountered this phenomenon before, HDR has been a very popular photographic style for the past several years. Essentially, HDR photography involves using special techniques to deal with subjects that include areas of extreme contrast between light and dark. For example, if a building is partly lit by bright sunshine and partly hidden in deep shadow, the contrast is likely to be so great that a photograph cannot depict both parts of the building with normal exposure. Either one area of the image will be much too bright, so the highlights are blown out, or one area will be much too dark, so the details are swallowed in the shadows.

In the past, HDR was carried out in post-processing, using software such as Photoshop or special programs such as PhotoAcute or Photomatix Pro. The photographer would take multiple exposures of the scene using different exposure levels, some of them exposing the dark parts of the scene properly and some of them exposing the bright parts properly. When combined in HDR software, the images could be combined to result in a final composite image that showed all parts of the image nicely exposed. These HDR composite images often have an unnatural or surrealistic appearance, because it is obvious that a "normal" photograph could not include such a wide range of well-exposed areas.

With many modern cameras, including the Coolpix P510, the manufacturer has included programming that gives the photographer the ability to take multiple photographs that are combined inside the camera to result in an HDR-like image. With the P510, I would not say that the result can match the "true" HDR that you can obtain through software, but it certainly does make a noticeable difference. Here is how it works.

When you choose the HDR On setting on the P510, you then

must select the degree of HDR processing the camera will use: Level 1, 2, or 3, as shown in Figure 3-29.

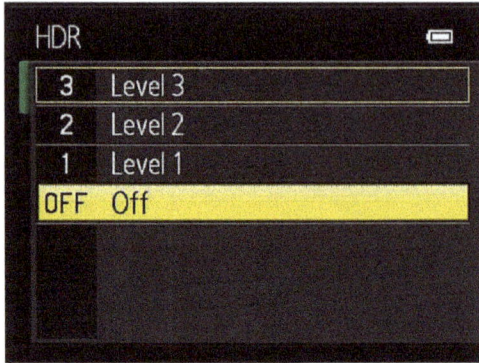

Figure 3-29: HDR menu

The higher the level, the greater the HDR effect. With all of these levels, the camera turns the built-in flash unit off. When you shoot using these settings, you should hold the camera very steady, or, ideally, place it on a tripod. After you press the shutter, you will see a yellow progress bar appear on the display and extend to the right as the camera processes the multiple images into two final ones. The first of the two final images will be an image taken with the Active D-Lighting feature turned on, to brighten shadowy areas of the image to bring out details. The second image will be an HDR composite that contains the best-exposed parts of multiple images, thereby expanding the dynamic range of the shot.

The images shown here illustrate the effects of this setting, followed by an HDR image done with software. These images show a vase sitting in deep shade next to a decorative cowboy boot in bright sunlight. The first two shots, Figures 3-30 and 3-31, were taken with the camera in Manual exposure mode, with no special settings, to show the contrast between the bright and shadowed parts of the scene.

CHAPTER 3: THE SHOOTING MODES

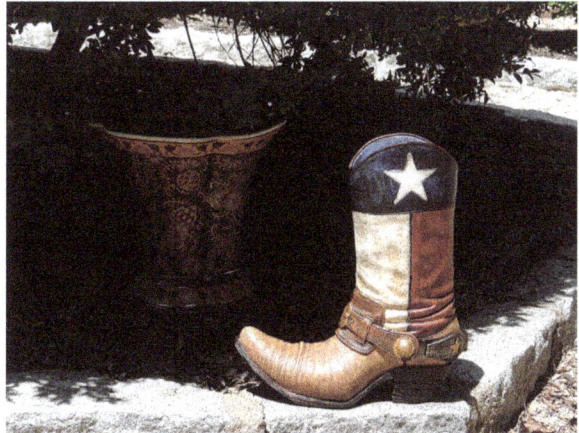

Figure 3-30: Manual exposure - exposed for boot

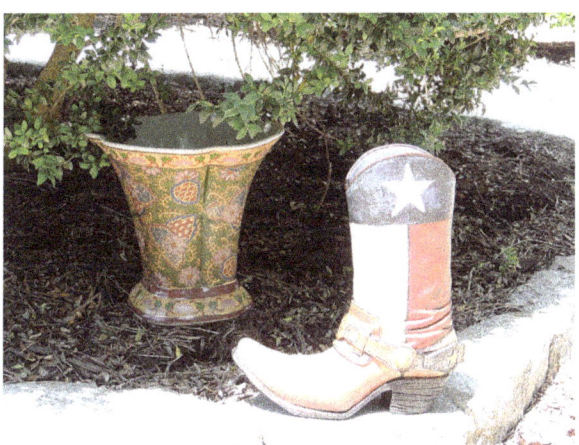

Figure 3-31: Manual exposure - exposed for vase

The next shot, Figure 3-32, was taken in Backlighting mode, with HDR turned off. In this mode, the camera always uses flash.

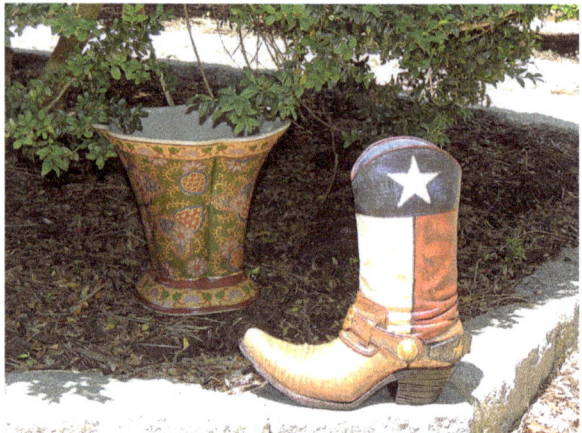

Figure 3-32: Backlighting mode - HDR off

The next image was taken with the HDR setting turned on. In this situation, the camera takes multiple images, and the first one it saves is one taken with the flash off, but with Active D-Lighting (not HDR) turned on. Figure 3-33 is the composite shot that was the result of the P510's in-camera HDR processing. This shot was taken with HDR set to Level 1.

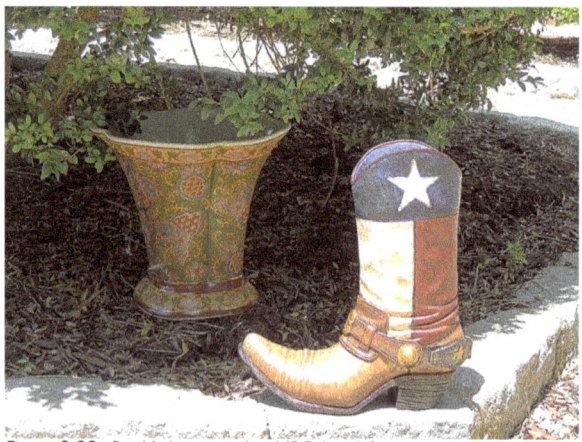

Figure 3-33: Backlighting mode - HDR Level 1

The last example, Figure 3-34, is a composite image created in Photomatix Pro, a special software program designed for creating HDR compositions. I took several images at different settings in Manual exposure mode to use as the basis for this composite. In my opinion, the P510's in-camera processing does a good job of reducing the contrast between the light and dark areas, but it cannot match the performance of specialized HDR software like Photomatix Pro, especially when, as here, you take several shots in Manual exposure mode, giving the software a wide variety of exposure values to work with.

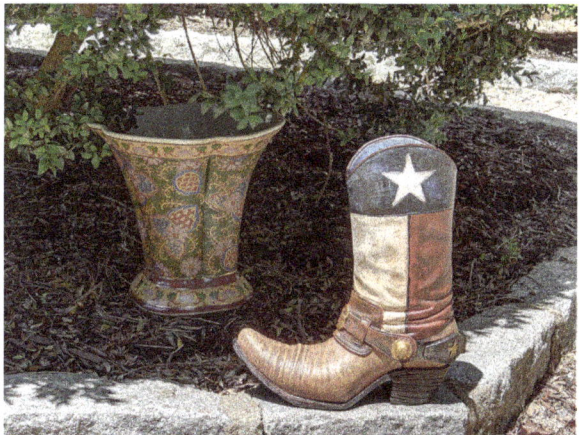

Figure 3-34: HDR composite done in Photomatix Pro software

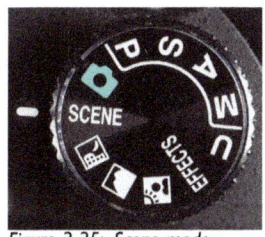

The SCENE Setting on the Mode Dial

Figure 3-35: Scene mode

Next, I'll discuss the settings that are available with the mode dial at its SCENE position. To review, this option brings up a menu with a list of 17 choices, including Scene Auto Selector and 16 specific scene types. When the mode dial is set to SCENE, you can select any one of these choices by pressing the Menu button and selecting a scene setting from the menu list, shown in Figure 3-36.

77

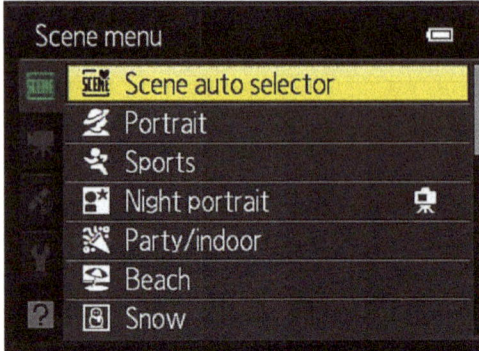

Figure 3-36: Scene menu

While that list is displayed, you can press the zoom lever on top of the camera towards the T position, where there also is a question mark on the camera's top. In this situation, as shown here, the zoom lever activates an information screen, like the one shown in Figure 3-37, that gives you a brief description of how this particular Scene setting can be used.

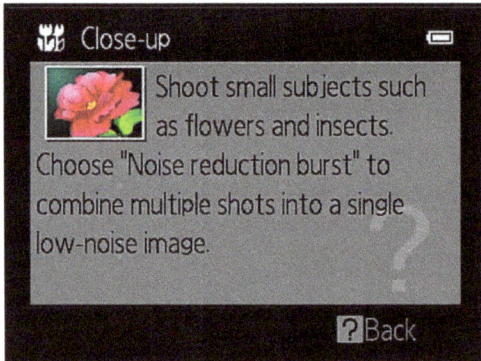

Figure 3-37: Scene mode help screen

Note, though, that when you select any of these settings, the Menu system offers few other choices; that is, when you have made a selection such as Portrait or Sunset from the SCENE setting menu, you cannot make any more choices using the menu system other than Image Size and Image Quality. The camera will make all other settings as it deems appropriate for the given selection. So, these Scene settings are convenient if you are faced with a certain type of photographic situation and you want the camera to make reasonable choices for that situation, but you have very little control over the camera's settings. Following are details about each of those types, including what sorts of settings the camera chooses for each.

Portrait

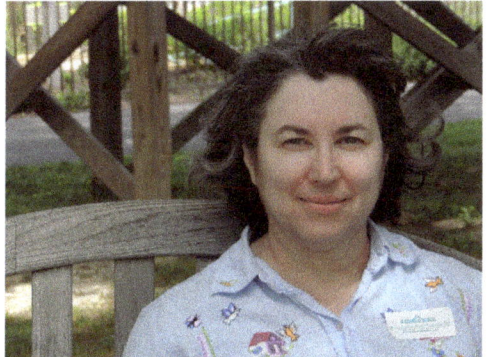

Figure 3-38: Scene mode - Portrait setting

With the Portrait setting, the camera automatically sets itself for face detection, which means it looks for human faces and focuses on the one closest to the camera. It also automatically applies skin softening, which smooths wrinkles and other harsh features on the skin. However, you cannot control the amount of skin softening or turn it off. There are no Shooting menu options with this Scene setting. However, you can pop up the flash and select a flash mode if you want. You cannot make any changes to the focus mode, but you can use the self-timer and exposure compensation.

Sports

The Sports setting is intended for subjects that move around unpredictably. The camera sets itself for continuous shooting and takes a rapid series of as many as five images at a rate of up to seven frames per second when you hold down the shutter button, depending on conditions. The flash is forced off, and focus and exposure are locked when the first image is taken, to increase the speed of the sequence of shots. You can use manual focus and exposure compensation if you wish, but you cannot use the self-timer, and the Shooting menu is not available. This mode is useful when you need to stop action in relatively bright lighting conditions.

Night Portrait

This mode is similar to Night Landscape, but, because your subject will be a person in a dark outdoor setting, the camera will use the built-in flash. The subject presumably will be close to the camera and, unlike a landscape scene, can be illuminated by the flash. The camera will select Slow Sync for the flash mode, and will not let you change it. (If you don't pop up the flash unit, the camera will display an error message until you do.) Apart from the use of flash, this mode operates in a similar way to Night Landscape. The menu lets you select either Hand-held or Tripod. If you select Hand-held, the camera may take multiple shots and combine them into a single final image. However, if you zoom the lens in to a telephoto setting, the camera may take just a single shot. You can use the self-timer (including the Smile Timer) or exposure compensation, but you cannot change the focus method. The camera uses its face detection circuitry, and attempts to find a face to focus on.

If you choose Tripod from the menu, the camera will take a single shot at a slower shutter speed. It still will use the flash.

Party/Indoor

This setting is meant for indoor photos of people and rooms. In most cases, you should pop up the flash; the flash mode is initially set to Auto with Red-eye Reduction, but you can change to another flash mode if you want to. If you don't want to use flash, you can leave the flash unit retracted, in which case the P510 will try to use a relatively slow shutter speed. In that case, you should hold the camera very steady or place it on a tripod. (Realistically, though, you probably are not going to be setting up a tripod for candid or impromptu pictures at a party.) The camera will focus on the subject at the center of the frame. In the example shown in Figure 3-39, the camera did fire the flash.

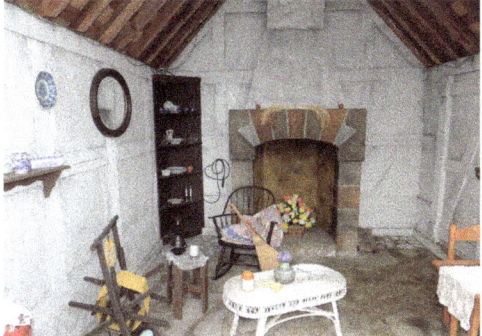

Figure 3-39: Scene mode - Party/Indoor setting

With the Party/Indoor setting, there are no Shooting menu options available. You can use exposure compensation or the self-timer, but you cannot change the focus method.

Beach

With this selection, the camera optimizes its settings for the beach, where there is likely to be bright sunlight reflected from the ground. In this environment, the camera will have a tendency to underexpose the subject because the exposure meter will be measuring the brightness of the beach. If you pop up the flash, the camera will set the flash mode to Auto in order to light the subject sufficiently, and it is quite likely that the flash will fire in order to enhance the brightness of the subject so it will be clearly visible against the glare of the background. However, you do not have to pop up the flash when using the Beach setting. You can use either macro focus or normal autofocus, but you cannot select manual focus or use Infinity autofocus. You can use the self-timer or exposure compensation.

The image shown in Figure 3-40 obviously was not taken at the beach; I took it to illustrate how the camera processes shots in this mode, in comparison to the Snow setting, discussed next.

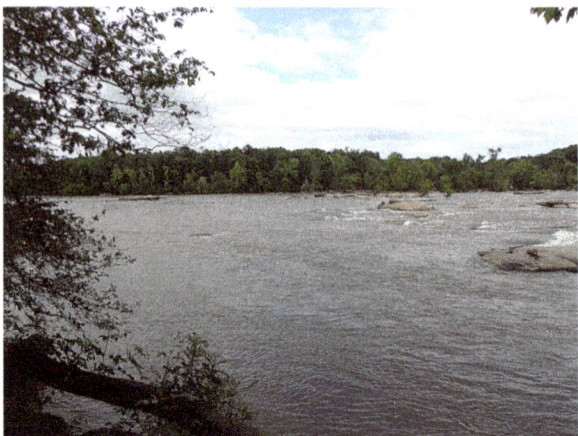

Figure 3-40: Scene mode - Beach setting

Snow

The Snow setting is similar to Beach, in that the camera may use the flash to compensate for the brightness of the snowy background, if you have chosen to pop up the flash unit. The camera appears to use a greater amount of reddish hue than the beach setting, as a balance against the bluish color temperature of a snowy scene. Other settings are similar to those for the Beach setting. As you can see from Figure 3-41, which was taken at the same place and time as Figure 3-40, there is not a great deal of difference in the processing of photos taken with the Snow and Beach settings.

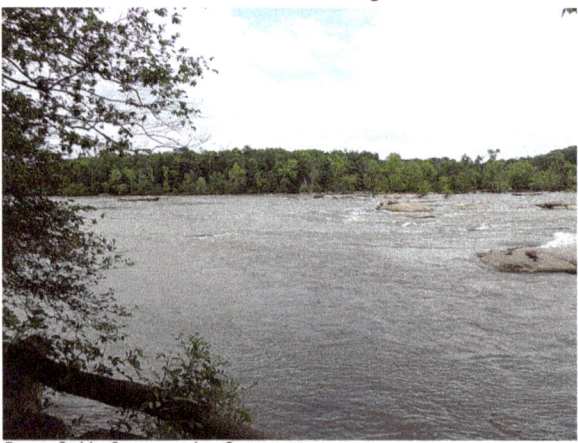

Figure 3-41: Scene mode - Snow setting

Sunset

Choose this setting to capture the rich hues of the setting (or rising) sun. The camera disables the flash, but you can use the self-timer and exposure compensation. You cannot change the focus mode from normal autofocus. The camera processes the shot to emphasize red-orange tones in the heavily slanted rays of the late afternoon or early morning sun. Of course, you don't have to limit the use of this (or any other) Scene setting according to its label; if you are photographing autumn leaves with reddish hues, red-brick buildings, or other subjects with reds you want to emphasize, consider this setting as one tool that may be of use. For example, Figure 3-42, taken with this setting, does not show a sunset, but I felt that the emphasis on reddish light was appropriate for this scene that was lit by the sun's long rays in the early morning, not long after sunrise.

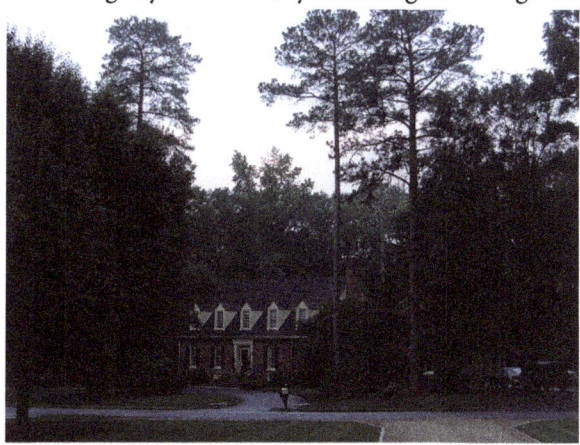

Figure 3-42: Scene mode - Sunset

Dusk/Dawn

If you are taking pictures before sunrise or after sunset, this is a setting to be aware of. With the Dusk/Dawn setting activated, the camera forces the flash off and intensifies the colors in order to add interest to images that otherwise might seem flat or washed out because of the low intensity of the available light. This Scene setting imposes the same restrictions as the Sunset mode; you cannot alter any significant settings on the camera. The primary feature of this option is that it emphasizes the purplish or bluish tones that may be present in the twilight or early morning hours. In Figure 3-43, I am including another version of the same scene I used for Sunset mode, to show the different results from using these two similar settings.

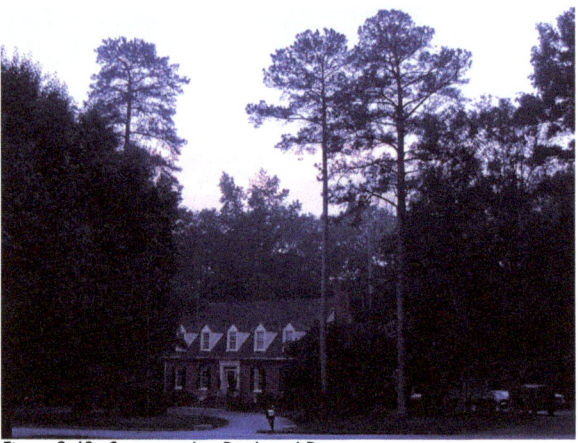

Figure 3-43: Scene mode - Dusk and Dawn

Close-up

With this setting, the camera switches into macro mode so it will focus properly on items close to the lens. As with several other Scene settings, with Close-up the Shooting menu gives you the option of choosing Noise Reduction Burst or Normal. With Noise Reduction Burst, the camera focuses in the center of the image and takes a rapid set of shots to counter the effects of high ISO noise. The camera uses continuous autofocus and the flash is disabled. You can use the self-timer or exposure compensation; you cannot, naturally enough, change the focus mode, which is set on macro.

With the Normal setting, the camera takes a single shot, and acts somewhat differently in other ways as well. If the lens is zoomed in to a telephoto position, when you switch into the Close-up setting it will automatically zoom back out to a position that allows the camera to focus on the subject. The camera also switches the AF Area Mode setting to Manual. This means that you can control exactly where the focus point is placed. To do this, you press the OK button in the center of the multi selector, then press one of the four direction buttons on the multi selector to move the focus area around the screen so that it covers the point where you want the camera to focus. If you need to use one of the direction buttons for its other function (self-timer, flash, or exposure compensation), press the OK button again, and those functions will be available. Press the OK button once more if you need to move the focus area another time. The camera also uses continuous autofocus, so it continues to adjust the focus until you press the shutter button halfway down to lock in the focus. Finally, with this setting, you can pop up the flash and select a flash mode, which you cannot do with the Noise Reduction Burst setting. The other restrictions are the same as for that selection.

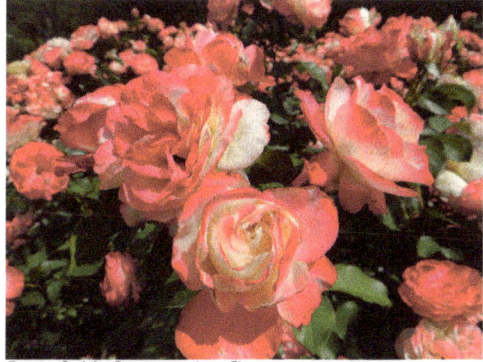

Figure 3-44: Scene mode - Close-up setting

You could, if you want, use another shooting mode, such as Program or Auto, and just select macro focusing using the focus button (down direction button). But, if you want to quickly set up the camera for close-up shooting, it can be convenient to have this Scene mode available. You should hold the camera very steady to avoid blurring the image. Use of a tripod or monopod is the best practice, but of course that is often impractical.

Food

This setting is similar to the Close-up setting, discussed above, though it does not offer Noise Reduction Burst mode; only single shots are available and there are no menu options. The camera switches to macro focus mode and zooms back if necessary so it can focus on a nearby subject. It turns on Manual for the AF Area Mode, so you can move the focus point around, and it uses continuous autofocus. The flash is disabled, but you can use exposure compensation or the self-timer. The one major difference from Close-up mode (apart from the lack of the burst option) is that, in Food mode, the camera places a scale of colors at the left side of the screen and allows you to adjust the hues of your images by moving the pointer up and down along the scale using the direction buttons. Move towards the top for more reddish hues, and towards the bottom for more bluish ones. In Figure 3-45, I used the slider to emphasize the reddish hues of the apples and butternut squash.

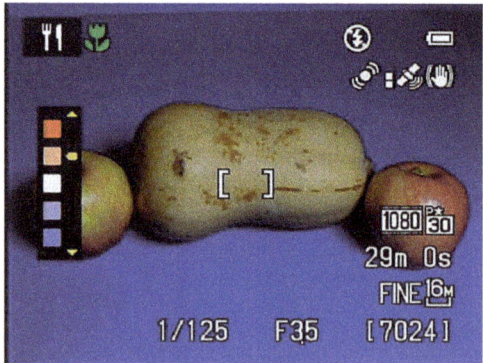

Figure 3-45: Scene mode - Food setting

This setting is suited for people who are in the habit of documenting their meals through food blogs or photographic diaries of their dining experiences. With the hue slider, you can experiment until you achieve the desired effect of emphasizing the colors of meats, vegetables, or other aspects of the meal.

Unless you want to leave a hue adjustment permanently in place, be sure to return the hue slider to the neutral position when you're done shooting, because the adjustments you make will remain in place the next time you choose the Food setting, even if the camera has been turned off in the meantime.

Museum

The Museum setting is useful when you are shooting in a museum or other place where flash is prohibited. The camera turns the flash off and will not use it even if the flash is popped up. The camera also disables the autofocus assist lamp, which could be distracting in a museum setting. You can use exposure compensation or the self-timer, and you can switch to macro focus if you want. Also, the P510 activates the Best Shot Selector function. With this option, which normally is controlled with the continuous-shooting option on the Shooting menu, the camera takes 10 shots in rapid succession while you hold down the shutter release button, and automatically saves the one shot that is sharpest and has the most detail. In this way, even though you are taking pictures in dim light with no flash, you have a good chance of getting a usable image because the camera will take multiple shots and discard the ones that exhibit motion blur. For the image shown in Figure 3-46, taken in dim lighting, the camera set the ISO to 1400 to permit the use of a reasonably fast shutter speed of 1/30 second.

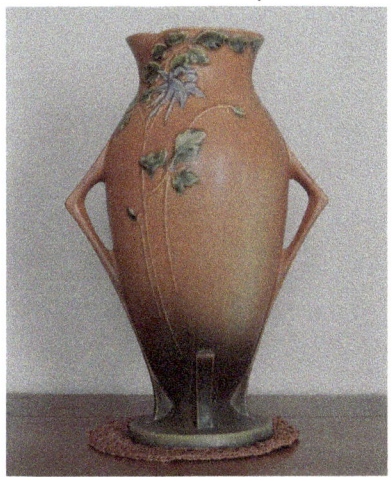

Here again, as with most of the Scene settings, don't let the name of this setting exclude it from consideration for other purposes. You might want to use it in any dimly lit area when you can't (or don't want to) use flash.

Figure 3-46:   Scene mode - Museum setting

87

Fireworks Show

With this setting, the camera sets the focus to infinity and uses a slow shutter speed so you can capture a relatively long burst of color from a fireworks display. The camera also increases the vividness of the colors. The flash is forced off and you cannot use exposure compensation or the self-timer, and you can't change the focus method. You should set the camera on a tripod if possible, or hold it firmly on a fence post or other solid object as an alternative.

Black and White Copy

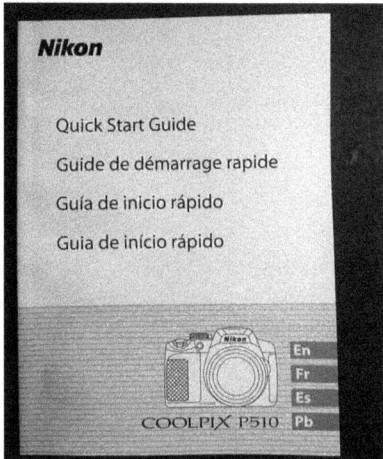

Figure 3-47: Scene mode - Black and White Copy

This setting lets you copy black-and-white text, like words on a blackboard or whiteboard, or perhaps on a poster. I consider it to be a handy way to capture a document you need to carry with you, such as a shopping list or itinerary. In effect, your P510 becomes a very portable photocopier; you can copy the item quickly and crisply, and enlarge the view on the screen.

When you choose this setting, the camera switches into a black-and-white mode and captures the image in monochrome format. The focus is initially set to normal autofocus, but you can switch into macro autofocus if you are copying something close up, such as words on a sheet of paper. You also can use the flash, exposure compensation, or the self-timer if you want.

Of course, this mode is of no use to you if you need to record any colors at all, such as colors of highlighting of the text, or of images that accompany the text. For those situations, you might want to try the Close-up Scene setting. Again, don't let its name limit your use of this mode; you might want to try it for street photography, as discussed in Chapter 9.

Panorama

This setting gives you two sub-options for taking panoramic scenes with the P510 like the ones shown in Figures 3-48 and 3-49 on the next page.

Once you have selected Panorama from the Scene menu, select either Easy Panorama or Panorama Assist from the sub-menu. With Easy Panorama, the camera does most of the work for you; with Panorama Assist, the camera gives you some guidance, but you have to handle more of the details yourself. Both of the examples included here were taken with the Easy Panorama feature.

Easy Panorama

When you select this option, you are presented with yet another sub-menu with two more options—Normal (180°) or Wide (360°). Make your selection and then aim the camera at the first part of your panoramic scene. For example, if you are shooting a panorama of a wide mountain range, you may want to aim at the far left side of the range. Press the shutter button halfway down to lock in focus and exposure; the camera will automatically zoom back to the wide-angle position, and will not let you zoom in. In addition, the flash is disabled. You can use exposure compensation, though.

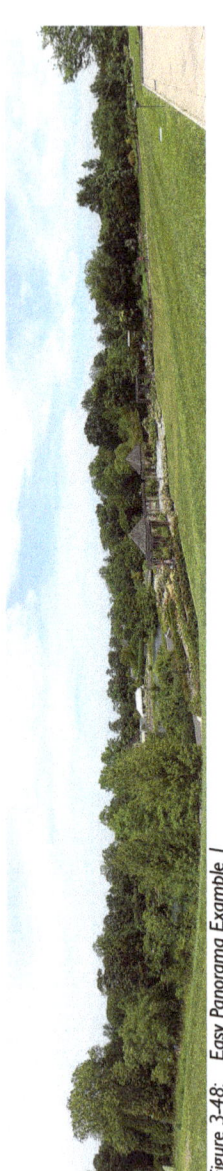

Figure 3-48: Easy Panorama Example 1

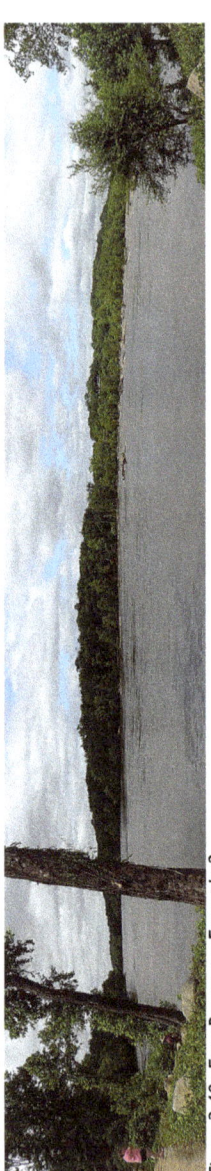

Figure 3-49: Easy Panorama Example 2

When you are satisfied with the initial view, press the shutter button and release it; you don't need to hold it down while the panorama shooting proceeds. Now hold the camera steady and level as you sweep it in the direction of your shot—in this case, from left to right—until you have covered the entire scene. The camera will detect the direction you are moving in, and it will automatically stop shooting when it detects the end point of the 180-degree shot. You should take about 15 seconds to complete this arc.

You can shoot the panorama moving either from left to right or right to left, or you can shoot it vertically, moving the camera from low to high or vice-versa. And, if you select the Wide option, you can move the camera through a complete circle to cover an entire scene. In that case, you should take about 30 seconds to complete the entire circuit.

When you are done, you can view the whole panorama on the screen by pressing the Playback button. To see the panorama scroll by on the screen, press the OK button, and it will scroll in the same direction in which it was taken.

Panorama Assist

Use this setting when you want to exercise more control over the shooting of your panorama. When you select this option from the Panorama sub-menu, you will see a pair of yellow arrows on the display pointing either up, down, right, or left, indicating the direction in which the panorama will be shot. Press one of the direction buttons if you want to change that direction. For example, if the two yellow arrows are pointing to the right, press the left direction button, and the two arrows will point to the left, indicating that the panorama will be shot from right to left.

After pressing a direction button, press the OK button to confirm. At that point, you can again use the direction buttons for exposure compensation or for choosing a flash mode, though it's hard to imagine a situation in which you would want to use flash for shooting a panorama. You also can select normal autofocus, landscape autofocus, or, oddly enough, macro autofocus using the down direction button. And, you can even use the self-timer, though I have difficulty thinking of a time when the self-timer would be useful for shooting images for a panorama.

With the Panorama Assist setting, it is a good idea to use a tripod in order to keep the multiple shots lined up properly, because you will be taking them one at a time, rather than in a continuous stream as with the Easy Panorama setting. When you have set up the composition as you want it, press the shutter button to take the first shot. Within a second or two, you will see that image appear on the camera's display, with about one-third of the image appearing translucent.

Use the translucent part of the first image to line up the next shot. That is, try to superimpose the translucent area over its real-life counterpart, as viewed through the camera's lens. When you do that, the first and second images will overlap by the proper amount. Then repeat this process for as many images as you would like to include in the panorama. When you have finished shooting your images, press the OK button to end the panorama shooting.

To actually create the panorama, you need to load the individual images onto your computer and use "stitching" software to create the panorama. You can use the software supplied with the Coolpix P510, which is called Panorama Maker 6, from ArcSoft. Following the prompts in the software, load the panorama images into the program. You will find all the files for any one panorama in a folder on your memory card with a number starting with the letter "P."

For example, I shot a panorama with several images, and they were saved in a folder on my SD card named 108P_004. Other sets of panorama images would be in folders with names such as 109P_002, and so on.

To create the panorama from these shots, first, I used the navigation panel at the left of the computer screen to open the folder that contained the panorama shots. I clicked on the files for this panorama to select them, and then I clicked on the "Next" button at the lower right of the screen. The computer then displayed the message, "Analyzing and stitching." After a few moments, the computer had produced a nicely assembled panoramic image. The program gives you the opportunity to realign the images if necessary, but, if you are satisfied with the result as it comes out at first, you can click the "Done" button and enjoy your panorama.

This Nikon-supplied panorama software works well and has the advantage of coming with the camera, but you can also use other programs, such as Adobe Photoshop or Photoshop Elements, or any one of numerous others that I have not tried.

The advantage of using Panorama Assist rather than the Easy option for shooting panoramas is that you have more control over the creation of the panorama, including the ability to zoom, to choose a focus mode, and to choose the number of images that make up the view. You also can take your time making each shot from your tripod, rather than panning the camera through its complete arc within 15 or 30 seconds. Finally, you can fine-tune the panorama in your software rather than just relying on the camera's internal processing to create the final product. But, it's very nice to have the option of creating a panorama quickly with the Easy Panorama setting when you don't have time to deal with the steps required for creating a panorama with the Panorama Assist option.

Pet Portrait

This next setting on the Scene menu is specifically designed for shooting pictures of the family dog or cat. When you choose this mode, the camera sets itself for continuous shooting and activates a feature called "Pet Portrait Auto Release." With this feature, the camera looks for the face of a dog or cat, and, if it detects one, it triggers the shutter automatically and takes three pictures in quick succession, to try to capture a good expression on the pet's face. If the camera does not display the double-bordered yellow frame that indicates detection of a face, you can just press the shutter button to take the image when you're ready. For Figure 3-50, I pressed the shutter button myself, because the camera was not aimed at the dog's face.

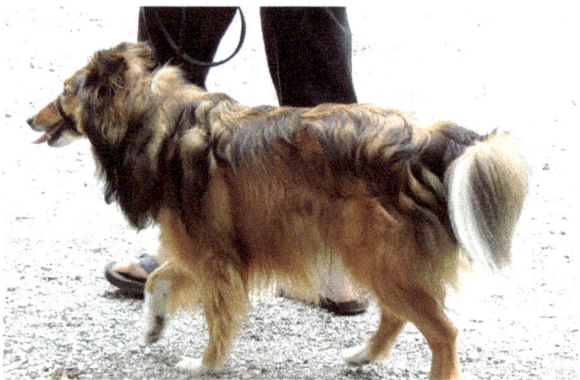
Figure 3-50: Scene mode - Pet Portrait setting

The default setting with this option is continuous shooting, but you can use single-shot exposures by pressing the Menu button and selecting Single from the Shooting menu. You also can change the Pet Portrait Auto Release setting, which is turned on by default. To turn it off, press the self-timer button (left direction button), and select the Off setting, rather than the icon of a pet's face. If you turn this setting off but leave continuous shooting turned on, then the camera will take about five shots when you press and hold the shutter button.

With the Pet Portrait setting, use of the flash is disabled, but you can use exposure compensation.

3D Photography

There's been a lot of attention paid to 3D movies and images lately, with the advent of 3D televisions and the renaissance in 3D movies. Some cameras have appeared recently with special features for creating 3D panoramas and other stereoscopic images, including the Sony NEX models and the Fujifilm FinePix

Real 3D W3. The Coolpix P500, predecessor of the P510, did not have that capability, but, with the P510, Nikon has added a setting for taking 3D photographs. Here is how to use it.

The key to this type of 3D photography is to take two photographs of the same scene that are nearly identical, but are taken from two slightly different vantage points. When you select 3D Photography from the Scene menu, the camera will prompt you with a message saying to take the first photograph, and then to move the camera horizontally to the right to take the second picture, as shown in Figure 3-51.

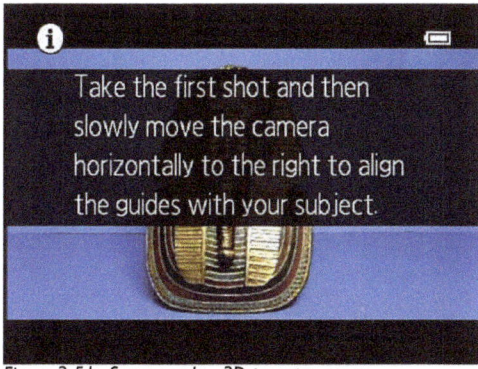

Figure 3-51: Scene mode - 3D prompt screen

After the first image is taken, the camera will superimpose a ghost image on the screen (as in Panorama Assist mode) while you move the camera to the right, as seen in Figure 3-52.

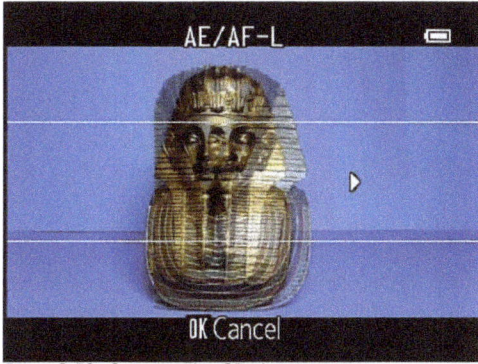

Figure 3-52: Scene mode - 3D shooting screen

You should try to line up that ghost image over the same objects in real life. Once the images are aligned, the camera will take the second picture automatically. When you move the camera, you should move it horizontally to the right. The camera needs to be facing straight ahead each time, not angled in toward the subject. If the camera does not take the picture automatically, you can press the shutter button yourself. If the second image is taken successfully, the camera will display the message, Saved 3D image, to announce the success. If the procedure fails, the camera will announce that as well.

The 3D effect will not be visible on the camera's screen; only the left image is displayed there. To view the result in 3D, the camera needs to be connected to a 3D-capable HDTV set, and the appropriate settings need to be turned on in the Setup menu, as discussed in Chapter 7.

However, if, like me, you do not happen to have a 3D-capable HDTV, you can still view your 3D images in 3D with a little bit of extra work. You can produce a stereoscopic image that can be viewed with readily available 3D glasses, with red and blue viewing lenses. The example shown here was taken with my P510 and then converted in software to this format.

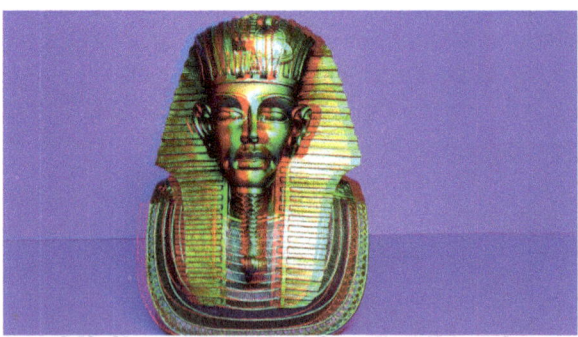

Figure 3-53: 3D image processed with Stereo Photo Maker software

To do this, I used a Windows program called Stereo Photo Maker, which can be downloaded free at http://stereo.jpn.org/eng/stphmkr. From the program's File menu I selected Open Stereoscopic image. Using this command, I opened the camera's 3D image, which has an .mpo extension. Then I went to the Stereo menu and selected Color Anaglyph. On the submenu that appeared, I chose Dubois (red/cyan).

The program produced the single image in Figure 3-53, which looks blurry, with red and blue lines characteristic of 3D images you may have seen in comic books or other printed materials. (If you're using a Mac, there are other programs available, though I haven't used them. One possibility is Anabuilder, at http://anabuilder.free.fr. You also can use Photoshop, but you'll need to experiment a bit, or find instructions on the web.)

If you follow these steps with an .mpo image produced by the P510, the resulting image should be ready for viewing, either on screen or on paper, using old-fashioned red/blue 3D glasses. (The red side goes over the left eye.) If it doesn't pop out as a 3D image when viewed through the glasses, go to the Adjustment menu and try various adjustments, including Auto Alignment, Easy Adjustment, and others, until it looks good.

Special Effects Mode

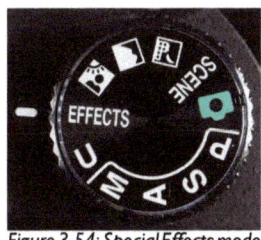

Figure 3-54: Special Effects mode

Several notches around the mode dial from the SCENE mode is the EFFECTS slot, indicating the Special Effects shooting mode. This shooting mode provides you with some very interesting ways to alter the appearance of your images. These nine settings operate in a manner similar to the Scene settings, but there are some differences. The Special Effects settings are not designed for particular types of subjects, such as portraits, landscapes, or fireworks, as the Scene settings are. Instead, the Special Effects settings offer you various manipulations to change how your image looks, regardless of the subject.

To select one of these settings, turn the mode dial to the EFFECTS position, then press the Menu button. There are only three choices on the Shooting menu when the camera is set to Special Effects mode: Image Quality, Image Size, and Special Effects. Once you have set the quality and size of the image as you want them (I recommend Fine and the largest size for most purposes), navigate to the Special Effects line on the menu. Then press the OK button or the right direction button to go to the next screen, which displays the nine choices for effects: Soft, Nostalgic Sepia, High-contrast Monochrome, High Key, Low Key, Selective Color, Painting, High ISO Monochrome, and Silhouette, as shown in part in Figure 3-55.

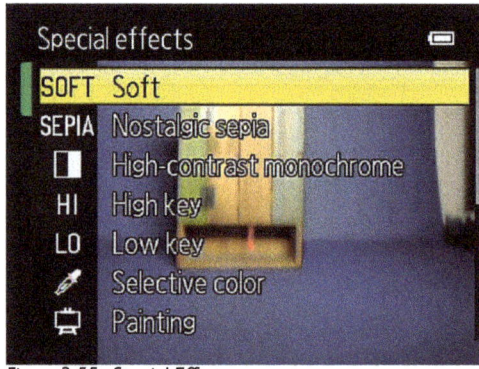

Figure 3-55: Special Effects menu

Highlight an option and press the OK button to confirm. The camera will return to the shooting screen and the display will change its appearance according to the setting you have chosen. For example, if you chose High ISO Monochrome, the display will be in black and white and will appear grainy.

As noted above, there are no other options available on the Shooting menu when you are using Special Effects mode, apart from Image Quality and Image Size. However, you can use the four buttons on the multi selector to choose exposure compensation, the flash mode, the self-timer, or the focus mode.

I will describe each of the settings along with sample images showing each one as it was used to photograph the same scene.

Soft

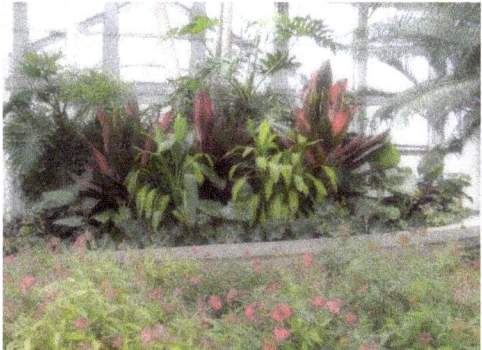
Figure 3-56: Special Effects - Soft

This setting applies a small amount of blur to the image. You could use this option when taking pictures of an aging movie star to soften facial wrinkles, or you might use it just to add a somewhat dreamlike or fantasy aura to the image.

Nostalgic Sepia

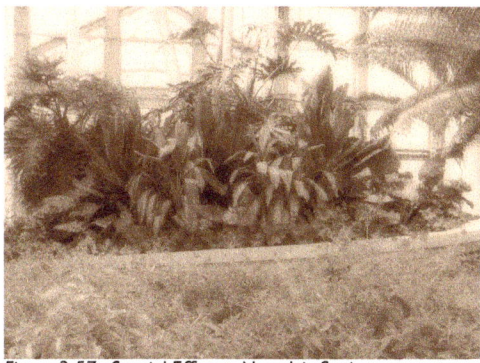
Figure 3-57: Special Effects - Nostalgic Sepia

With the Nostalgic Sepia setting, the camera produces a monochrome image with a sepia (brownish) tone and softens the contrast somewhat to give the look of an antique photograph.

High-contrast Monochrome

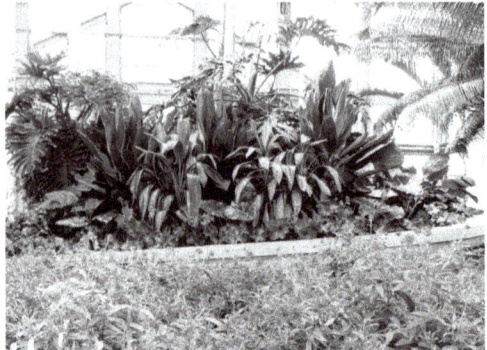

Figure 3-58: Special Effects - High Contrast Monochrome

This effect, which yields a black-and-white image with enhanced contrast, is likely to have a stark, harsh appearance. You might want to use it for street photography when you want to produce images with a realistic or journalistic look.

High Key

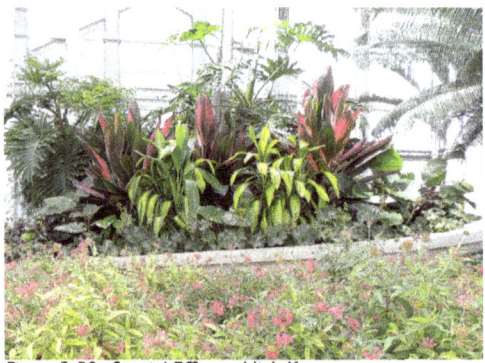

Figure 3-59: Special Effects - High Key

"High key" is a technique in which a studio photographer uses bright lighting throughout the scene, striving for a very bright overall look with light colors and few shadows. This technique often is used in advertising photography. With the P510, this single setting cannot necessarily remake your image to look like a traditional high key shot, but the camera does boost the exposure to produce a brighter-than-normal image.

CHAPTER 3: THE SHOOTING MODES

Low Key

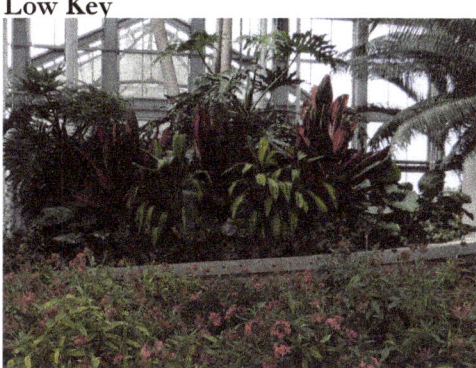

Figure 3-60: Special Effects - Low Key

"Low key" lighting, of course, is the opposite of "high key." With this approach, the photographer welcomes shadows and dark areas in the photograph. Here again, the P510 cannot produce a true "low key" image all by itself; what it can do is reduce the exposure and otherwise process the photograph to look more dark and shadowy than normal.

Selective Color

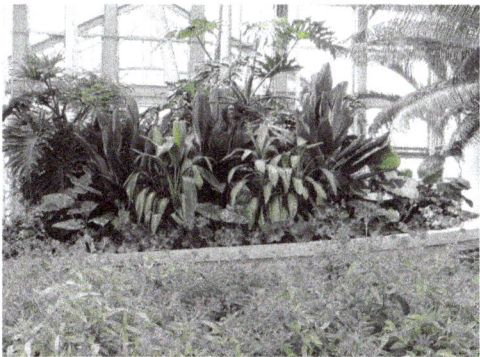

Figure 3-61: Special Effects - Selective Color

This setting is unlike all of the other Special Effects options, because it gives you the ability to control its operation. When you first choose this option from the menu screen, the camera displays a message telling you to press OK to select a color. Then, when you press the OK button, the camera displays a yellow indicator beside a vertical spectrum of 12 colors plus one entry for no color, as shown in Figure 3-62.

101

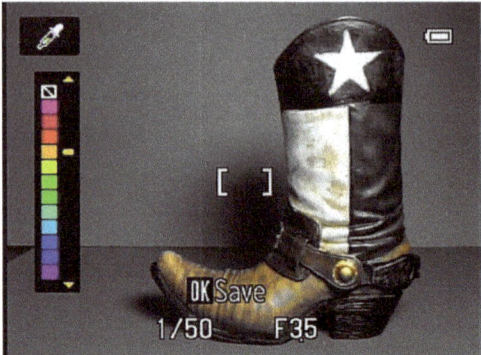

Figure 3-62: Selective Color selection screen

Use the up and down direction buttons to move the indicator to the block in the spectrum for the single color you want to retain in the image. Figure 3-63 shows the image that resulted from the color selection in Figure 3-62.

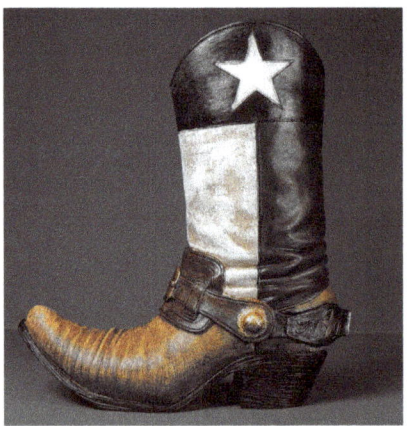

Figure 3-63: Image shot with Selective Color setting

Note that the topmost block in the spectrum has a negative symbol in it; if you select that block, the camera retains all colors, and does not use the Selective Color function. The result in that case is an ordinary image, with no special processing at all. It will look as if you took the image using Program or Auto mode. You might want to consider leaving the Special Effects mode setting on Selective Color, with this top option selected. That way, if you accidentally turn the mode dial to the EFFECTS position, any shots you take will not have the exotic processing of the settings such as Soft, Nostalgic Sepia, and the like.

Painting

If you select the Painting setting from the Special Effects menu, the camera applies a distinctive form of processing that results in heightened emphasis on colors and imbues the image with a pastel-like look, as shown in Figure 3-64. It is somewhat like one of the more exotic types of HDR processing, and also is akin to posterization, in which the number of different colors used in the image is decreased to make it look as if the image was created from just a few poster paints; the result has an unrealistic but dramatic effect.

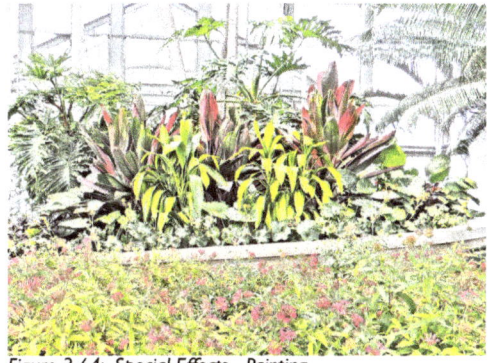
Figure 3-64: Special Effects - Painting

I recommend using this setting when you want to achieve a distinctly artistic effect, perhaps to create a colorful poster or greeting card. Sometimes the images can be improved by using some negative exposure compensation to reduce the washed-out appearance that results from excessive brightness. For example, the image in Figure 3-65 was shot with the Painting effect, but with -2.0 EV of exposure compensation.

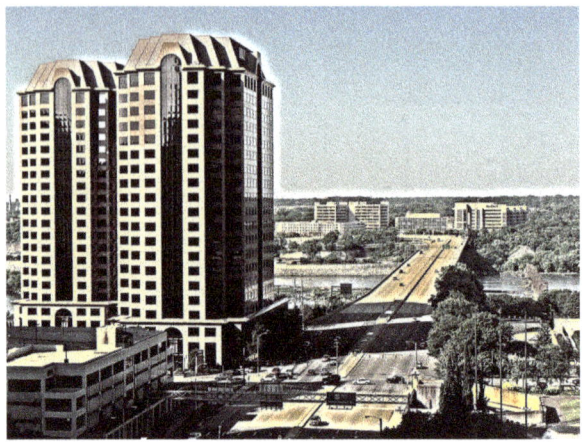

Figure 3-65: Special Effects - Painting Example 2

High ISO Monochrome

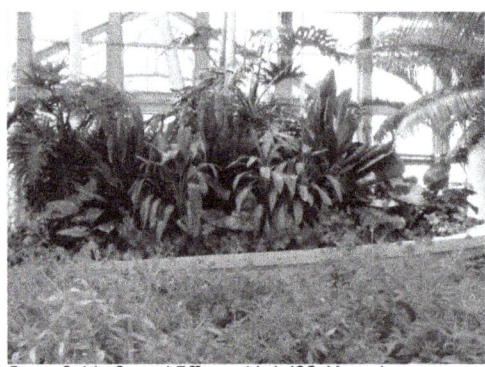

Figure 3-66: Special Effects - High ISO Monochrome

With the High ISO Monochrome setting, Nikon has made it clear in the setting's name what sort of special processing is involved; the camera uses a very high ISO setting—ordinarily much higher than would be needed to capture the image, and uses monochrome rather than color processing. In fact, with this setting, the camera sets ISO to what Nikon calls Hi 2, which is the equivalent of ISO 12800, a setting that cannot be achieved through the ISO menu item.

Although this setting can be useful when you are shooting in very dimly lighted conditions, in my opinion its real use is for creative purposes, when you want to have the gritty, grainy effect that is produced by the visual noise from high ISO settings. I enjoy using this setting when I don't want a great deal of realism, and the subject calls for an impressionistic look. With this setting, the flash is forced off and cannot be used.

Silhouette

Finally, the Silhouette setting is fairly self-explanatory. This option is useful when you want to photograph a subject, often one with a distinctive, sharply-outlined shape, against a bright background, so the details of the subject are lost in shadow. You could consider this setting to be the opposite of the Backlighting shooting mode, in which the camera strives to pull details out of the shadows and reduce the contrast between the bright and dark areas of the image. Here, as seen in Figure 3-67, the camera lets the natural lighting prevail, so the classic silhouette effect is achieved.

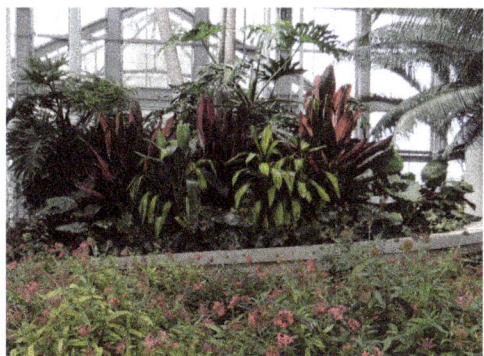

Figure 3-67: Special Effects - Silhouette

With the Silhouette setting, as with High ISO Monochrome, you cannot use the built-in flash.

User Setting Mode

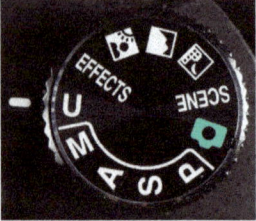

Figure 3-68: User Setting mode

The last slot on the mode dial to be discussed is the U setting, which allows you, the user, to store a full set of your favorite or most often-needed settings for instant recall. When you turn the mode dial to the U setting, you take advantage of a very powerful and convenient feature of the Coolpix P510. You can set up the camera exactly as you want it, with a shooting mode, zoom amount, white balance, ISO, and other settings, and then recall all of those settings instantly just by turning the mode dial to the letter U. The only shooting modes that you can save settings for are Program, Aperture Priority, Shutter Priority, and Manual; you cannot save them for the Auto, Scene, Effects, or Movie modes.

Here is how this works. First, set up the camera with all of the settings you want to be able to recall. For example, suppose you are going to do street photography. You may want to shoot with a fast shutter speed, say 1/250 second, at ISO 1600 in black-and-white, using continuous shooting with autofocus, at the 16:9 aspect ratio with a large image size and Fine quality.

Your first step is to make all of these settings. Turn the mode dial to S for Shutter Priority, and turn the command dial to set a shutter speed of 1/250 second. Then press the Menu button to summon the Shooting menu, and go to the menu item for Image Quality and choose Fine. For Image Size, select 4608 X 2592 pixels, which, as indicated to the left of those numbers, translates to a 16:9 aspect ratio with an image size of 12 megapixels. Then navigate in the menu system to the Picture Control selection, and select the Monochrome option. Set the ISO menu option to 1600. Next, select the Continuous item on the Shooting menu and navigate to the next screen; on that screen, go down to the second option, marked with an H on a stack of frames, for high-speed shots. You also may want to push the zoom lever all the way to the left, for wide-angle shooting.

Once all of these settings are made, press the Menu button to call up the Shooting menu, and scroll down (or scroll up and wrap around to the bottom) to select the Save User Settings item, shown in Figure 3-69, and then press the OK button or the right direction button; you will see a confirming message saying Done. Be sure you have all the settings the way you want them before you press OK or the right button, because the camera does not ask you to confirm your choices; it just says "Done." I was a bit taken aback the first couple of times I used this feature, because in most other cases there's a chance to back out before you make your choices final; not here.

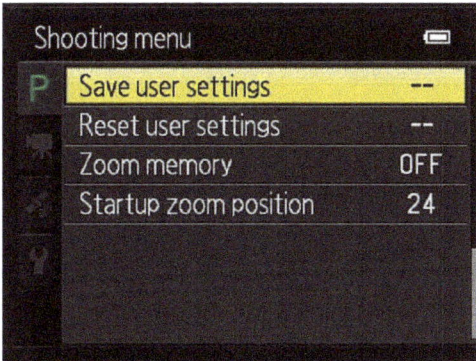

Figure 3-69: Menu item to save user settings

Now, to check how this option worked, try making some very different settings, such as Manual exposure with a shutter speed of one second, Picture Control set to Standard, continuous shooting turned off, the zoom lever moved all the way to the T for telephoto, ISO set to Auto, and Image Size set to the maximum, 4608 X 3456 pixels. Then turn the mode dial to the U setting, and you will see that all of the custom settings you made have come back, including the zoom position, shutter speed, black-and-white shooting at ISO 1600, and everything else. This is really a wonderful feature, and more powerful than similar features on some other cameras, which can save menu settings but not settings such as shutter speed and zoom position.

The lone flaw I find with this mode is that there is only one slot for it on the mode dial, and therefore only one group of settings that can be saved at a time. But it's much better than nothing. I suggest you experiment to find one custom settings group that is the most useful to you, and save it to the U mode for instant recall. Of course, you can change the settings that are stored as often as you like. You may want to jot down in a notebook some of your favorite groups of settings for various situations, so you can program the most appropriate set into the U slot when you're setting out for a particular type of shooting session.

Chapter 4: The Shooting Menu

Much of the power of the Nikon Coolpix P510 resides in the many options included in the Shooting menu, which provides the user with control over the appearance of the images and how they are captured. Depending on your own preferences, you may not have to use this menu too much. You may prefer to use the various Scene or Special Effects mode settings, which choose many of the options for you, or you may prefer, at least on occasion, to use Auto mode, in which the camera makes its own choices. However, it's nice to know that you do have this degree of control available if you want it, and it is very useful to understand what types of items you can exercise control over.

The Shooting menu is quite easy to use once you have played around with it a bit. As I discussed earlier, the menu options change depending on the setting of the mode dial on top of the camera. For example, if the mode dial is set to the green camera icon, for Auto mode, the Shooting menu options are very limited, because Auto mode is for a user who wants the camera to make almost all of the decisions without input from him or her. If the mode dial is set to one of the dedicated Scene types with its own slot on the dial (Night Landscape, Landscape, or Backlighting), the Shooting menu is re-named after the currently active mode.

For example, if you select the Night Landscape mode from the mode dial and then press the Menu button, the menu that appears on the display is labeled Night Landscape, rather than Shooting. These menus, as in Auto mode, are abbreviated versions of the Shooting menu; they include only a few items from the normal Shooting menu, usually Image Quality and Image Size. In addition, they may include a specific menu item for the mode that is in effect. In this case, there is a Night Landscape menu item, which lets you select either Hand-held or Tripod for shooting.

When the mode dial is turned to the SCENE setting, pressing the Menu button brings up another version of the Shooting menu, in this case called the Scene menu. This menu provides a way to select either Scene Auto Selector or any one of the 16 specific scene types (Portrait, Panorama, Sports, etc.). In addition, at the very bottom of the Scene menu, just after the entries for Panorama, Pet Portrait, and 3D Photography, the camera presents you with the options for choosing Image Quality and Image Size. (The Image Quality and Image Size menu options are grayed out and unavailable for selection when Panorama or 3D Photography is selected for the Scene type.) When the EFFECTS slot on the mode dial is selected, the Shooting menu presents the Special Effects menu, which lets you choose only which effect to select, along with Image Quality and Image Size.

A basic point to bear in mind is that, although the Menu button presents you with some choices in all shooting modes, in the more automatic modes, including Auto and the various Scene types, there are only a few options, apart from options specific to a given mode, such as choosing a Scene type. It is only when the mode dial is set to the P, S, A, or M setting for the Program, Shutter Priority, Aperture Priority, or Manual exposure mode, that the wide variety of Shooting menu options is available.

For the following discussion, I'm assuming you have the camera set to Program mode (shooting mode dial turned to the P setting), because in that setting you potentially have access to all of the power of the Shooting menu. (Though some menu

CHAPTER 4: THE SHOOTING MENU

options will be unavailable in certain situations.)

So turn the mode dial to P for Program mode, then enter the menu system by pressing the Menu button.

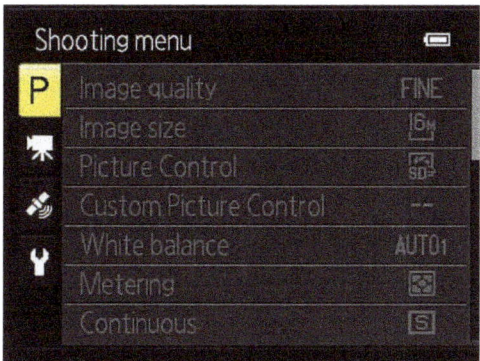

Figure 4-1: Menu icons highlighted

In the menu system, when the camera is in shooting mode, besides the Shooting menu (or Scene or Special Effects menu), there are the Movie menu, designated by a movie camera icon in the column at the left of the menu, the GPS Options menu, marked by a satellite icon, and the Setup menu, marked by a wrench icon. These icons are shown in Figure 4-1. When the camera is in Playback mode the three choices are the Playback, GPS Options, and Setup menus. For now, I will discuss only the Shooting menu, which is designated by a capital letter or icon at the left standing for the current shooting mode: P, S, A, or M, or an icon for one of the more automatic modes.

On the Shooting menu (in Program mode), you'll see a fairly long list of options. Each option (such as Picture Control) occupies one line, with its name on the left and its current setting (such as the Standard icon) on the right. You have to scroll through three screens to see all of the options. If you find it tedious to scroll using the up and down direction buttons, you can rotate the multi selector dial on the camera's back, which may help you speed through the menus a bit more quickly. Also, depending on which menu option you are trying to get to, you may be able to reach it more quickly by revers-

111

ing direction with the direction buttons or multi selector dial, and wrapping around to reach the option you want. In other words, if you're on the top line of the menu, you can scroll up to reach the bottom option. Or, if the highlight is already near the bottom option, you can scroll down to go back to the options at the top of the menu. The first menu screen is shown in Figure 4-2.

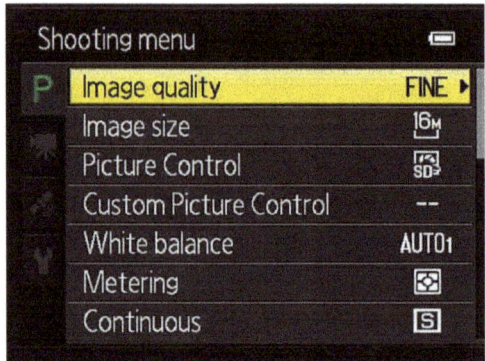

Figure 4-2: First screen of Shooting menu

Once you have highlighted the menu item you want, you can make any sub-selections by pressing the OK button or the right direction button, which will take you to the next screen (if one exists) for that menu item. To go back to a previous menu screen, press the left direction button; to exit the menu system, press the Menu button. Note that it's important to press the OK button to confirm your choice of a particular menu item selection; just highlighting it and then exiting from the menu screen will not activate that item.

If you like to use shortcuts, here is a way to navigate the menu system with fewer button-presses. Press the menu button to display the menu screen, and then use the up and down direction buttons or the multi selector dial to move up or down the list to the item you wish to set. In many cases, the menu item has a secondary screen where you make the actual setting; to get to that screen, you ordinarily press the right direction button or the OK button to move to that screen. However, to short-cut that process, once the yellow highlight rectangle is on the menu item you want to adjust, just turn the command dial (the ridged wheel at the upper right of the camera's back), and the value will adjust without having to move to the secondary screen. You do not have to press the OK button to confirm the selection; just turn that wheel and the adjustment is made. This technique works for many important settings, including Image Quality, Image Size, Picture Control, White Balance, Continuous shooting, ISO, and others. It does not work for items such as Custom Picture Control, Save User Settings, and others that do not have a list of settings to make on the secondary screen.

On occasion you will find that you are unable to select a certain menu option. That is, although it will appear on the menu screen, you will not be able to navigate to it and select it. This situation occurs when there is an option in effect that is not compatible with the menu option you are trying to select. For example, if you have selected Multi-shot 16 by using the Continuous menu option, the Image Quality setting is fixed at Normal and the Image Size setting is fixed at 5 megapixels (2560 X 1920 pixels), so neither of those settings can be changed (or even selected) in the menu system. Or, if you have selected the option to shoot in monochrome from the Picture Control menu setting, you will not be able to get access to the White Balance menu option.

With the mode dial set to P you should have access to just about every option on the Shooting menu. If you find that you can't select certain menu options, check to make sure you have set other options to compatible settings. For example, use the Continuous option on the Shooting menu to select Single-shot exposures rather than a continuous setting, and set ISO to Auto. If you have trouble getting to some menu options and can't figure out what setting is causing the problem, you can go the Setup menu (marked at the left by the wrench icon) and scroll down (or scroll up and wrap around) to the Reset All option, the next-to-last option on the menu. Using that operation will reset all of the camera's basic shooting functions to their default values. In this way, you will undo whatever setting is causing a conflict with the setting you are trying to make. (You also will undo any custom settings you have made, so be sure you don't mind taking that step.)

Starting at the top line of the Shooting menu, I will discuss below each option on the menu's three screens.

Image Quality

There are two basic settings to make when you are deciding on your overall image "quality" in the broadest sense: Image Quality, discussed here, and Image Size, discussed below. The Image Quality option lets you select how much "compression" the camera applies. That is, the camera "compresses" the data by squeezing out a certain amount of information, preserving enough to recreate the image, but trimming it down so the file does not take up too much storage space.

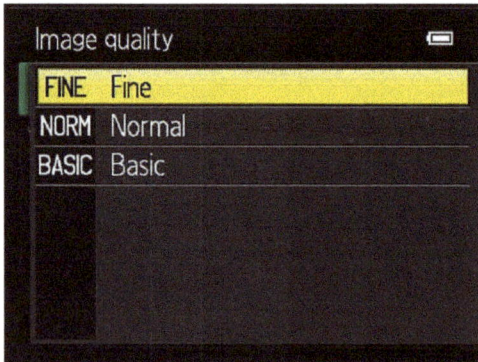

Figure 4-3: Image Quality menu option

The three options are Fine, Normal, and Basic. Each option uses up roughly twice as much storage space as the next lower option. So, for example, if you choose Fine for your quality setting, the camera can store 470 of the largest-sized images on a 4 GB memory card. If you choose Normal, it can store 840 of those images. If you choose Basic, it can store 1,480 images. Of course, there is a trade-off of quality against storage space. If you are planning to make large prints, you should choose Fine.

It is worth noting that the Coolpix P510 does not offer RAW as an option for image quality. Virtually all DSLRs and quite a few advanced compact cameras today offer the RAW format, which preserves the maximum image data and gives the photographer considerable flexibility in processing images in software. However, using RAW has its disadvantages, including very large file sizes and incompatibility with some post-processing software (at least until software updates are provided). Using a RAW format also requires that the images be processed in software; you cannot use them straight from the camera. The P510 provides a great deal of flexibility in producing excellent JPEG images, and you should have no problem in using this camera to make excellent prints or other photographic products.

Image Size

The next option on the Shooting menu, Image Size, works hand-in-hand with Image Quality to determine the overall quality of your images. With the Coolpix P510, Image Size actually has two components, which can be selected separately on some other cameras: resolution and aspect ratio. On the P510, these two components are not named, but their numerical values are listed on the Image Size menu. (The aspect ratio values are listed only for the settings that deviate from the normal aspect ratio of 4:3.)

The resolution of the image is the number of pixels it contains, given in a formula that contains the horizontal pixel count followed by the vertical pixel count. For example, the largest Image Size setting available on the P510 is 4608 X 3456, meaning the image has 4608 pixels horizontally and 3456 vertically. When you multiply these two numbers together, the result is about 16 million pixels, also written as 16 megapixels or 16M. So, as in Figure 4-4, you will see the figure 16M on the menu screen when you select this largest value for Image Size.

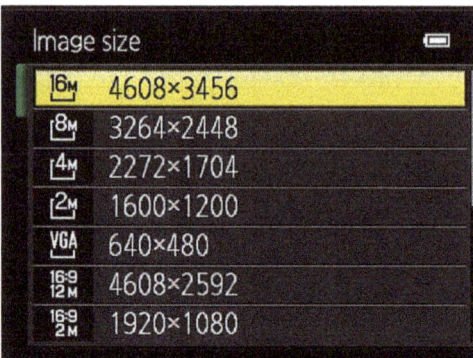

Figure 4-4: Image Size menu option

You can also determine the aspect ratio of the image from the Image Size setting. For example, the 4608 X 3456 setting yields an image 4 units wide for every 3 units tall, for a 4:3 aspect ratio. Most of the Image Size settings for the P510 are in that ratio, which is a standard one for digital images, being the same shape as the camera's LCD display. However, if you scroll down through the second screen on the Image Size menu, you will see a few entries that note a different aspect ratio. Specifically, just below the setting for VGA (640 X 480), there is the entry for 4608 X 2592 pixels. At the far left on the line for this entry, rather than the number of megapixels, which is shown for the previous entries, the menu shows the notation 16:9, meaning this Image Size setting is in a 16:9 aspect ratio: 16 units wide for every 9 units tall. This aspect ratio is another fairly common one, which corresponds to the shape of a widescreen HDTV set, and therefore often is called "widescreen."

Further down on the Image Size menu, another entry, 4608 X 3072, is labeled as 3:2, meaning its aspect ratio has 3 horizontal units for every 2 vertical ones. This is a common aspect ratio, which corresponds to the standard print size in the United States of 6 by 4 inches (15 by 10 cm).

Finally, the last entry on the Image size menu, 3456 X 3456 pixels, is in an aspect ratio of 1:1, resulting in a square image.

With the Image Size menu setting, you have two choices to

make. First, you can choose your images' resolution, or number of pixels (megapixels). The larger the number of pixels, the larger you can make clean-looking enlargements on paper, and the more options you have for cropping the image to highlight particular details from the exposure. Second, although most of the choices on the menu are in the standard 4:3 aspect ratio, you have the option of selecting an aspect ratio of 3:2, 16:9, or 1:1 if you want. Of course, you should bear in mind that you can always just shoot with the maximum image size of 4608 X 3456 and then crop the image down in software later; in that way, you can use any aspect ratio you want, including those listed here or any other. But, if you want to use a 1:1 aspect ratio for creative reasons, or you want your landscape photo to have the 16:9 widescreen look and you don't want to be bothered with changing the aspect ratio in software, you can go ahead and select an Image Size setting that corresponds to your desired aspect ratio, so the final result will come straight out of the camera. In addition, you will have the advantage of seeing how the final image will be composed as you set it up on the camera's display screen or in the viewfinder.

Figures 4-5 through 4-8 were all taken at the same time and place; the only differences among them is that they were taken with different Image Size settings, resulting in different aspect ratios, as indicated in the captions.

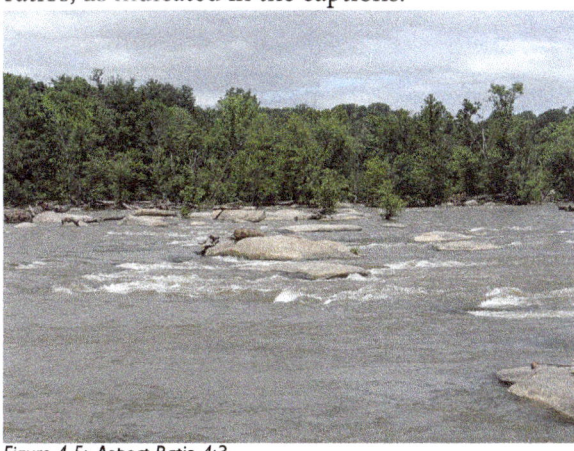

Figure 4-5: Aspect Ratio 4:3

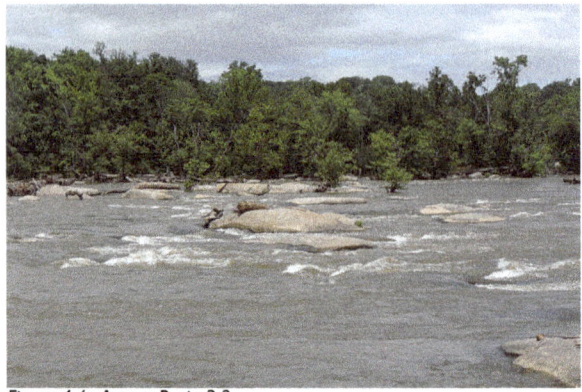
Figure 4-6: Aspect Ratio 3:2

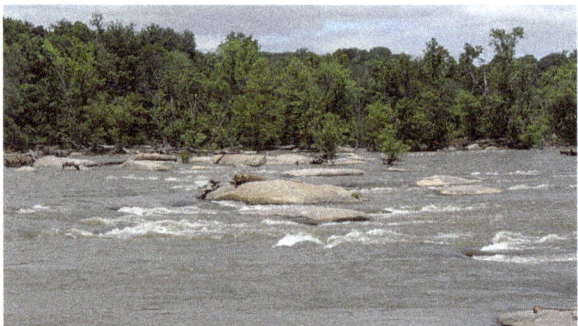
Figure 4-7: Aspect Ratio 16:9

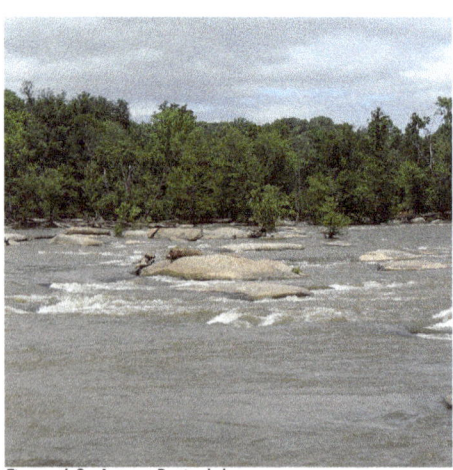
Figure 4-8: Aspect Ratio 1:1

Picture Control

This next menu option provides you with a list of four choices for the appearance of your images through different types of in-camera processing: Standard, Neutral, Vivid, and Monochrome. With each of these options, the camera provides varying degrees of adjustment to three basic parameters: sharpening, contrast, and saturation.

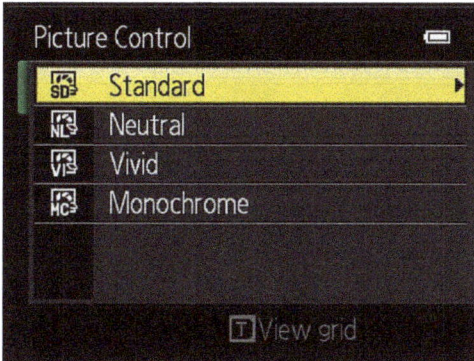

Figure 4-9: Picture Control menu option

Following are descriptions of the individual settings, with a sample photo of the same scene included for each one, illustrating the general appearance given by the different choices:

Standard

With this setting, as shown in Figure 4-10, you should see a standard rendering of the image, with no emphasis on any particular aspect. The camera does some internal processing of the captured image to make it appear suitably sharp and contrasty for normal purposes. This is the setting you should use for everyday shooting when you have no interest in producing a specific effect.

Neutral

With the Neutral setting, illustrated in Figure 4-11, the camera does minimal internal processing of the image. Therefore, the image may appear less sharp and contrasty, and have less color

119

intensity, than you would like. The intent with this setting is for you to process the image after the fact in software such as Photoshop. With minimal internal processing, the camera is leaving the fine-tuning of the image up to you.

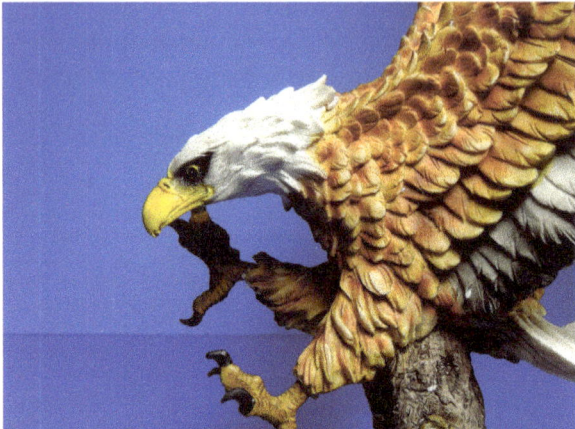

Figure 4-10: Picture Control Standard

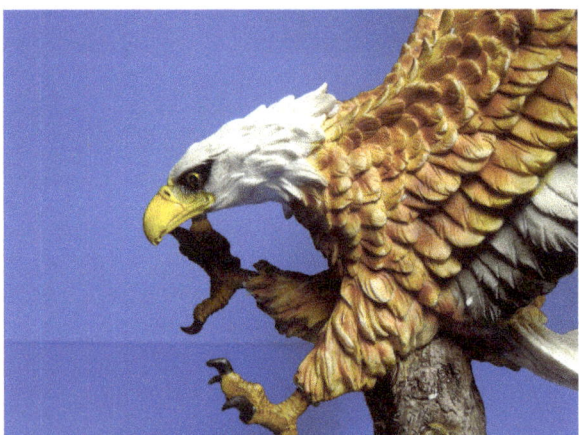

Figure 4-11: Picture Control Neutral

Vivid

Use this setting to increase the saturation, or intensity, of the colors in the image, as seen in Figure 4-12. The Vivid setting also provides some increase in sharpening and contrast, with the result that the image may "jump" off the page at the viewer with increased impact.

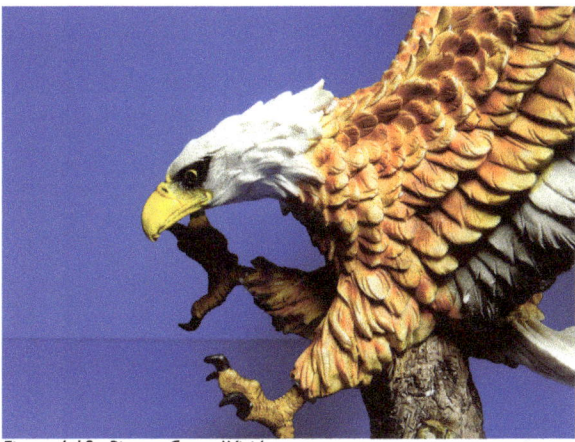

Figure 4-12: Picture Control Vivid

Monochrome

The Monochrome setting gives you a quick way to set the camera to take black-and-white images. Of course, as with many aspects of digital photography, you can always convert color images to monochrome using software such as Photoshop or Photoshop Elements, but it is convenient to be able to view your images in black-and-white on the camera's display before pressing the shutter button, and you may not want to devote your time and effort to converting images on the computer. The Monochrome setting is shown in Figure 4-13.

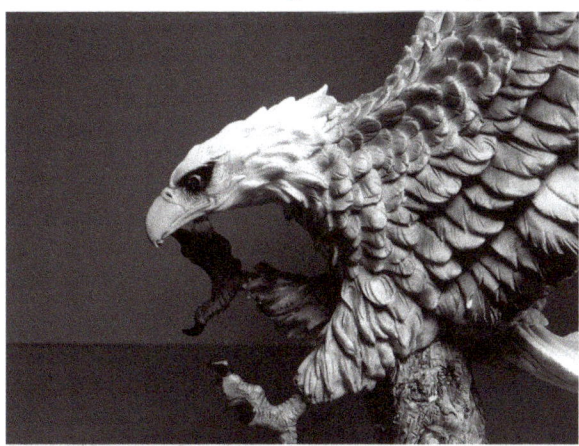

Figure 4-13: Picture Control Monochrome

Adjustments to Picture Control Settings

Once you have selected Standard or Vivid from the Picture Control menu, the camera will display a secondary menu screen with four lines: Quick Adjust, Image sharpening, Contrast, and Saturation, as shown in Figure 4-14.

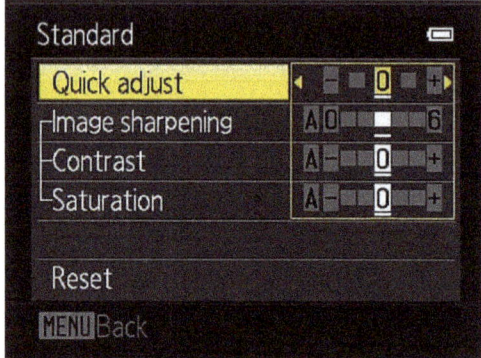
Figure 4-14: Picture Control Adjustments

You can highlight any one of those four lines using the up and down direction buttons. When the line is highlighted, use the multi selector dial or the left and right direction buttons to change the settings. If you change the Quick Adjust value, you will see that the three values below it—Image sharpening, Contrast, and Saturation—also move, but not all in the same amounts. Nikon has programmed the Quick Adjust feature to move the other three values in what Nikon considers to be "balanced" amounts, so that sharpening, contrast, and saturation may be adjusted upward or downward in amounts that work well with the adjustments to the other values.

If, instead of using the Quick Adjust menu option, you move the highlight down to the specific line for Image sharpening, Contrast, or Saturation, you can adjust any one of those values individually. To take an example, suppose you especially like the punchy, aggressive look of images taken with the Vivid setting, but you don't want to have the colors quite so intense. You can set Picture Control to Vivid, and then, on the secondary screen, adjust the Saturation value down to a low level, to reduce the intensity of the colors.

If you select Neutral from the Picture Control menu, the secondary screen does not include the Quick Adjust option, but it does let you adjust Image sharpening, Contrast, and Saturation individually.

If you select Monochrome from the Picture Control menu, the secondary adjustment screen, seen in Figure 4-15, is even more different from the screens for those other settings, all of which include Saturation processing that affects colors.

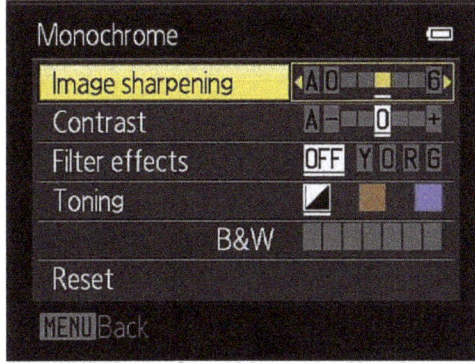

Figure 4-15: Picture Control Adjustments - Monochrome

With the Monochrome setting, adjustments are available for Image sharpening and Contrast, but not for Saturation, and there is no Quick Adjustment option. However, the Monochrome setting includes two other options: Filter Effects and Toning. Contrast and sharpening work just the same as with the other Picture Control settings, as discussed above.

The third sub-option, Filter Effects, is a simulation of the use of a glass filter over the lens. If you select Filter Effects, you have four options on the adjustment screen: Off, Y, O, R, and G, which stand for yellow, orange, red, and green. These settings are intended to mimic the effects of colored filters, which are often used with film cameras when taking photographs with monochrome films. The yellow, orange, and red filters can provide increasing levels of contrast that may, for exam-

123

ple, darken the sky and enhance the appearance of a landscape scene. The green filter setting is intended to soften skin tones for use with portraits.

The Toning options give you the ability to add a color cast to your monochrome shots. The three Toning choices on the Monochrome menu are B&W(none), Sepia (brown), and Cyanotype (blue). Once you have selected either Sepia or Cyanotype, if you press the down direction button, the cursor will move to a scale below the three options that includes gradations of intensity for the selected color tone. Move the cursor right for more intensity, or left for less.

One more note: When you first select Picture Control from the Shooting menu and have the yellow highlight rectangle on one of the main selections—Standard, Neutral, Vivid, or Monochrome—you can press the zoom lever on top of the camera towards the T (telephoto) position to display a grid, as shown in Figure 4-16, that shows the relative amounts of contrast and saturation (but not sharpening) that is currently set for each of the four options. (Monochrome, of course, has no saturation setting, so its grid is separate from the others.)

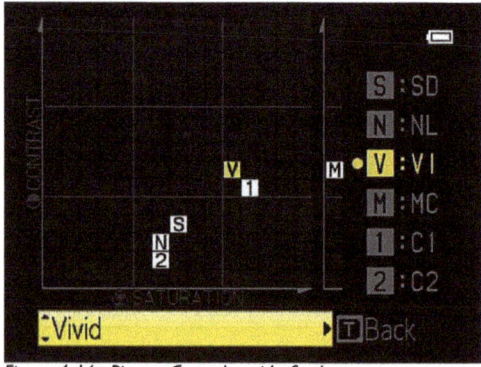

Figure 4-16: Picture Control - grid of values

This grid may be useful if you want a quick, graphic indication of how widely apart these parameters have been set. I do not find a need to use this grid myself, but it is there if you want to use it.

Custom Picture Control

The Custom Picture Control option lets you take one of the four available Picture Control settings (Standard, Neutral, Vivid, or Monochrome) and tweak the three available parameters (Image sharpening, Contrast, and Saturation) to create a new setting that is crafted to your individual taste and that can be saved for later recall as an added selection for the Picture Control menu option.

To use this feature, select Custom Picture Control from the Shooting menu, then press the OK button or the right direction button to bring up the menu with the four choices, as shown in Figure 4-17, and select one of them.

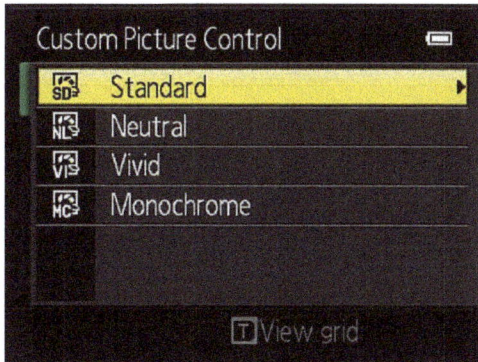

Figure 4-17: Custom Picture Control menu option

When the adjustment screen appears, adjust the available parameters, which are the same as for the Picture Control item, discussed above. As discussed there, the options are somewhat different for some of the settings: Monochrome, for example, has no Saturation adjustment, but does have Filter Effects and Toning adjustments.

Here is an example. Let's say you have found a group of adjustments to the Neutral setting that produces an appearance that you want to be able to use whenever you take photographs of a certain waterfall. Just go to the Custom Picture Control menu item, press OK or the right direction button, and then, on the next screen, select Edit and Save. You then are taken to a screen with the four basic Picture Control settings. Select Neutral, and, on the next screen, make your adjustments to sharpening, contrast, and saturation. When you are done, press OK, and you are taken to a screen that lets you save this setting to the Custom 1 or Custom 2 slot. Highlight one of those options and press the OK button to confirm that selection. Then, whenever you want to recall that setting, go to the Picture Control menu item, where Custom 1 (or Custom 2) will now appear as an option below Monochrome, as shown in Figure 4-18.

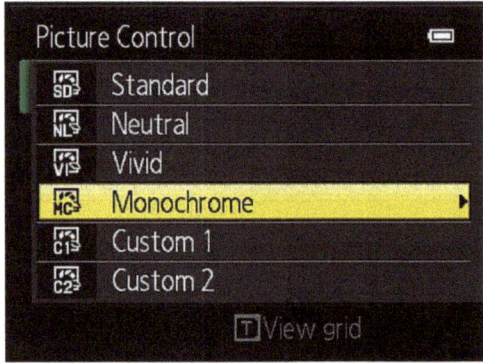

Figure 4-18: Picture Control with Custom settings added

If you later want to delete the Custom 1 or 2 option, use the Custom Picture Control item, and select Delete instead of Edit and Save.

White Balance

One issue that arises in all photography is that film, or a digital camera's sensor, reacts differently to colors than the human eye does. When you or I see a scene in daylight or indoors under various types of artificial lighting, we generally do not notice a difference in the hues of the things we see depending on the light source. However, the camera does not have this auto-correcting ability. The camera "sees" colors differently depending on the "color temperature" of the light that illuminates the object or scene in question. The color temperature of light is a numerical value that is expressed in a unit known as kelvins (K). A light source with a lower kelvin rating produces a "warmer" or more reddish light. A light source with a higher kelvin rating produces a "cooler" or more bluish light. For example, candlelight is rated at about 1,800 K; indoor tungsten light (ordinary light bulb) is rated at about 3,000 K; outdoor sunlight and electronic flash are rated at about 5,500 K; and outdoor shade is rated at about 7,000 K.

What does this mean in practice? If you are using a film camera, you may need a colored filter in front of the lens to "correct" for the color temperature of the light source. Any given color film is rated to expose colors correctly at a particular color temperature (or, to put it another way, with a particular light source). So if you are using color film rated for daylight use, you can use it outdoors without a filter. But if you happen to be using that film indoors, you will need a color filter to correct the color temperature; otherwise, the resulting picture will look excessively reddish because of the imbalance between the film and the color temperature of the light source.

With a modern digital camera, you do not need to worry about filters, because the camera can adjust its electronic circuitry to correct the "white balance," which is the term used in the context of digital photography for balancing color temperature.

The Coolpix P510, like most current digital cameras, has a setting for White Balance, which lets you choose the proper color correction to account for any given light source. Here is how to make this setting through the Shooting menu.

Once you have highlighted the White Balance setting, which is the fifth item down on the first menu screen, press the OK button or the right direction button to bring up the list of the following choices for the White Balance setting, each of them represented by an icon or a word or abbreviation: Auto (normal) [AUTO1]; Auto (warm lighting) [AUTO2]; Preset Manual [PRE]; Daylight [sun]; Incandescent [round light bulb]; Fluorescent [rectangular light bulb]; Cloudy [cloud]; and Flash [lightning bolt]. The first 7 of these are shown in Figure 4-19.

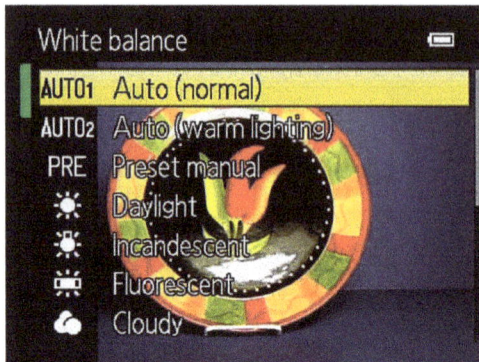

Figure 4-19: White Balance menu option

The labels for these settings should be largely self-explanatory, although you need to know a few details about how each one works. To select a setting, highlight the choice you want, and press the OK button to confirm. If you select either Auto setting, you are done; there are no further adjustments available. With each of the other selections, though, you can fine-tune the setting, as described below.

If you highlight Daylight, Incandescent, Cloudy, or Flash, you can then press the right direction button to bring up a screen with a scale at the left going from -3 at the bottom to +3 at the top, as shown in Figure 4-20.

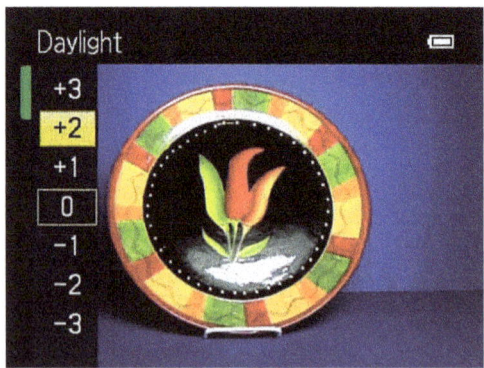

Figure 4-20: White Balance adjustment

You can use the up and down direction buttons or the multi selector dial to move the yellow selection block up and down this scale to select a value. If the value is positive, the white balance is biased toward a bluish tint, and if it is negative, it is biased toward a reddish tint.

If you highlight the Fluorescent option, pressing the right direction button brings up the further choices of 1, 2, or 3. These three sub-varieties of Fluorescent range from white to neutral to daylight. There are no other adjustments available with the Fluorescent setting.

Finally, if you select Preset Manual, you can set the white balance manually. Use this option when you are faced with mixed lighting from multiple sources, or from a reddish or otherwise unusual light source. To make this setting, highlight Preset Manual, then press the right direction button. The next screen will present the options to Cancel or Measure, as shown in Figure 4-21.

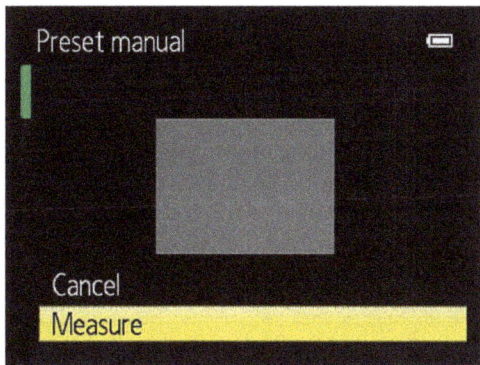

Figure 4-21: White Balance - Preset measurement

Highlight Measure, and then aim the square in the middle of the screen so it will be filled by a white or gray surface that is illuminated by the light source you will be using. Then press the OK button, and the camera will measure the white balance and store the setting. To use this setting now or in the future, turn back to the Preset Manual option at any time, even after the camera has been turned off and back on.

Note: You can take advantage of the Preset Manual setting as a nice way to add a color tint to a scene for creative effect if you want. For example, you can set the white balance manually using a red or orange surface for the measurement, which will result in a pronounced blue tint for any pictures taken under the same light source that you used when setting that white balance value. Just be careful to turn the white balance setting back to Auto or another more normal setting when you don't want that special effect for your images.

Before I leave this topic, I'm going to include a group of images showing how the various white balance settings affect the colors of your shots. All of these, shown in Figure 4-22, were taken under the same indoor lighting, which was balanced primarily for daylight; the only thing that changed from shot to shot was the white balance setting, as indicated.

The gray card that you see in each shot at the base of the model lighthouse is a photographic "gray card," a tool used to set a custom white balance. When the white balance is set properly, the card should appear gray, as it does in the shots with the Preset Manual and Daylight settings. In my opinion, the Auto 1 and Auto 2 settings did not do a perfect job of measuring the white balance, possibly because I had a mixture of light bulbs turned on. This means that you probably should not rely too heavily on the Auto White Balance settings, particularly with artificial light. The chances are that these settings will do better in outdoors settings, but indoors you may want to use the Preset Manual setting if the colors of your subjects need to be very accurate. Or, you could use the Incandescent option or one of the three Fluorescent settings, but take some test shots to be sure the colors are accurate. Also, don't forget that you can make further adjustments to the preset settings, to tweak them for more or less bluish and reddish tints.

CHAPTER 4: THE SHOOTING MENU

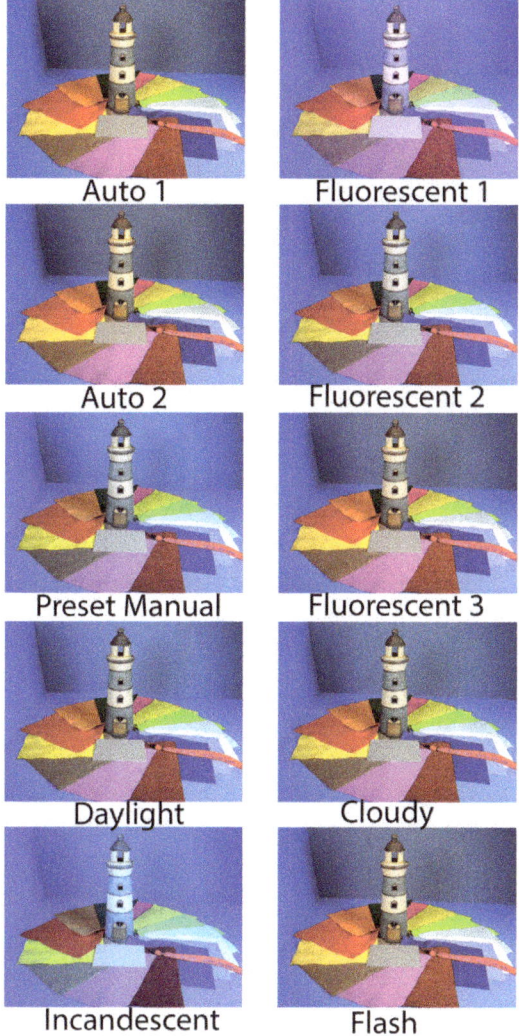

Figure 4-22: White Balance chart

Metering

This next option on the Shooting menu lets you choose among the three patterns of exposure metering offered by the Coolpix P510: Matrix, Center-weighted, and Spot. The menu selection screen is shown in Figure 4-23.

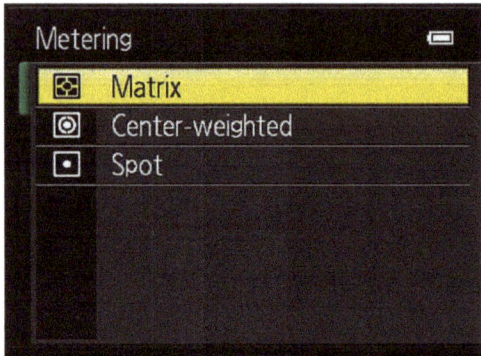

Figure 4-23: Metering menu option

This setting tells the camera's automatic exposure system what part of the scene it should evaluate when deciding how to set the exposure. If you choose Matrix, the default option, the camera uses the entire scene that is visible on the LCD. If you choose Center-weighted, as shown in Figure 4-24, the camera still considers all of the light from the scene, but it gives additional weight to the center portion of the image, on the theory that your main subject is in or near the center. The camera displays two large arcs to mark the area that is being emphasized. With Spot, as illustrated in Figure 4-25, the camera considers only the light in the part of the scene covered by the small circle that appears in the center of the screen.

When you set the metering method to Spot, you can see the effects of the exposure system quite dramatically by setting the camera to the Program exposure mode and aiming the small circle at various points, some bright and some dark, and seeing how dramatically the brightness of the scene in the LCD changes. If you try a similar experiment by moving the camera around to aim at differently lit areas in Matrix mode, you will still see changes, but much more subtle and gradual ones.

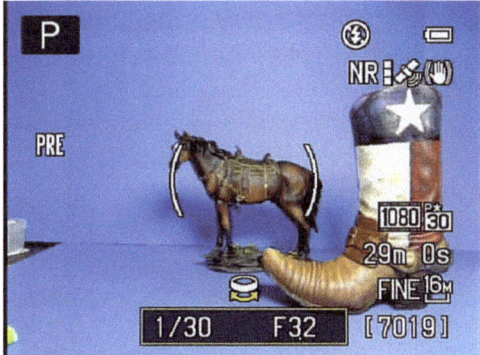

Figure 4-24: Center Weighted metering

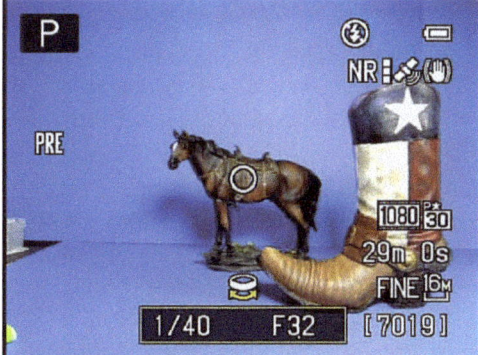

Figure 4-25: Spot metering

My personal preference is to use the Matrix metering method for outdoor shots with relatively even lighting conditions, such as landscapes, groups of people, and general views of buildings, monuments, and the like. I use Spot metering on occasion, primarily when I am photographing an object whose brightness level contrasts fairly sharply with the background. For example, if I am photographing a black camera against a white background, I may use Spot metering on the camera in order to avoid throwing off the metering system because of the expanse of bright white in the scene. I have not found many occasions to use the Center-weighted method, though it is certainly worth experimenting with.

Continuous shooting

With some cameras, including the Coolpix P500, the predecessor to the P510, there is a button you can press to turn on continuous (sometimes called "burst") shooting. With the P510, the numerous options for continuous shooting have been relocated to the Shooting menu, under the item called "Continuous." When the camera is set to a shooting mode in which burst shooting is available, this menu item provides you with an impressive array of options. Before describing them, I will provide a brief introduction to the concept of continuous shooting.

With film cameras, continuous shooting involves the use of a special motor to advance the film rapidly, and often the use of an extra-large cassette to hold a large quantity of film. This sort of equipment is bulky and expensive, and, of course, shooting and developing large numbers of exposures is itself quite expensive. With digital cameras like the Coolpix P510, expense is no longer a factor. Continuous shooting is literally available at your fingertips whenever you want to take advantage of it.

The usefulness of rapid bursts of exposures is clearer in some contexts than in others. For example, when you're shooting sports, it's worthwhile to fire off a swift sequence of shots in order to catch the perfect instant when a baseball player tags a runner heading for home plate, or to catch a soccer ball as it bounces off a player's head towards the goal. But continuous shooting also can be helpful in more ordinary shooting, such as pictures of children at play. You have a better chance of capturing a fleeting smile or cute gesture if you keep the exposures rolling. And, even when your subject is not moving, it can be advantageous to take multiple shots. For example, when you're taking a portrait, there may be subtle changes in the subject's expression, or in the way sunlight falls on a cheek. Taking a series of shots gives you some insurance against coming away from the photo session with no winning images.

Now let's look at the bounty of continuous-shooting options

that the P510 provides. To get access to these options, the camera has to be in the Program, Aperture Priority, Shutter Priority, or Manual exposure mode. Select the Continuous menu item, press the right direction button or the OK button, and the next screen will display the first 7 of the 9 available settings, as shown in Figure 4-26.

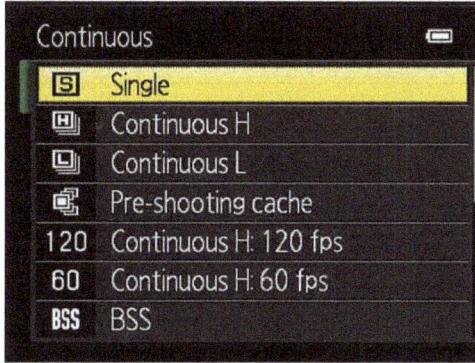

Figure 4-26: Continuous menu option

All 9 of the settings (except the first, for single shots, and the last, for intervals) offer various ways to take multiple shots while you hold down the shutter button. In each case, the exposure, focus, and white balance settings are fixed when the first image is taken, and they will not vary for later shots, even if the conditions would require different settings. You cannot use the flash for any of the multiple-shot settings except for the last one, the Interval Timer option. You cannot use the self-timer either. Be careful of this limitation; when you select a continuous-shooting mode and then activate the self-timer, the continuous shooting will be deactivated for that exposure, and you may not realize this until you find that your press of the shutter release button resulted in only one image.

By the way, as I discuss in Chapter 6, playing back continuous shots in this camera can be somewhat confusing. In Playback mode, you will see a stack-of-frames icon at the top of the image, indicating that this is one of a continuous set, or, using Nikon's terminology, the "key" image of a "sequence." There also will be a message at the bottom of the screen indicating that you have to press the OK button to display the full set of images. Then, when you press the OK button, you can move through the set of continuous shots using the normal navigation tools—the left and right buttons and the multi selector dial. To return to the main playback screen, press the up direction button. You can then keep navigating through the various individual shots and sequences on the memory card.

Here is the rundown of your wide variety of choices for continuous shooting with the Coolpix P510. The first option at the top of the continuous-shooting menu is an icon with an S, for single shots. This is the default option. In effect, choosing this first option turns off continuous shooting.

The second option on the menu is the first option for multiple shots. It is marked by an icon that looks like a stack of rectangular frames with the letter H inside, representing high-speed continuous shooting. When you select this option, the camera will shoot up to 5 shots at a speed of up to 7 frames per second, depending on factors such as image size, image quality, amount of lighting present, and the like. You can use any settings for the image quality and size, including the maximum Fine at 4608 X 3456 pixels.

The next icon, marked by an L for low-speed shooting, provides a capability similar to that for high-speed shooting, except that there is a trade-off of increased capacity versus slower speed. That is, you can take up to 30 images, but at a speed of no more than about one frame per second.

The next icon down the list looks like a stack of frames branching out into two directions. Selecting this icon activates a very interesting and useful feature of the Coolpix P510, which is called Pre-shooting Cache. When you choose this option, the camera actually captures several images before you press the shutter button to take pictures.

In practice, this option has its limitations, though it is still a welcome innovation. When you press the shutter button halfway down to evaluate exposure and focus, the camera will take up to 5 images before you press the button the rest of the way down, and up to 15 more as you hold the button down to take the images. The pre-shooting cache icon on the display turns green while images are being recorded to the cache; once you press the shutter button all the way down, the last 5 of those cached images are saved to the memory card, along with up to 15 shots taken while the shutter is pressed all the way down. The maximum rate is a speedy 15 frames per second, but the catch is that the image is fixed at a rather small size of 3 megapixels, or 2048 X 1536 pixels, and at Normal quality.

Pre-shooting Cache is a tool to use when you are monitoring a scene and waiting for just the right moment to catch a particular action or expression that may come up very quickly, and possibly will fade away quickly as well. When it looks as if the action is about to happen, you can press the shutter button halfway down to get ready, and, if the action comes up faster than expected, you won't miss it because of slow reactions. You can then press the shutter button all the way down to capture the rest of the sequence. If you don't mind a reduction in the resolution of your images, this is an interesting option to have available.

Be sure to note one possible pitfall here: If you press the shutter button down halfway but never press it all the way to take any pictures, the contents of the pre-shooting cache will be discarded and no pictures at all will be recorded. You have to press the shutter button down all the way at some point in order to "lock in" the pre-shooting images. Note also that, when you have finished shooting, you may see an hour-glass icon on the screen, indicating that the camera needs time to process the contents of the cache as well as the contents of the other images you have taken.

The next choice on the menu screen, Continuous H: 120 fps, is represented by a stack of icons accompanied by the number 120, representing the extremely rapid shooting rate of 120 frames per second. With this setting, the camera emphasizes both speed and volume, giving you up to 60 images at this super pace, but at a drastic reduction in quality, down to VGA quality or 640 X 480 pixels, which is the resolution of an old-fashioned computer monitor. Images shot using this option may look fine on your computer, but they will be quite grainy and will not be suitable for any degree of enlargement. Still, if you need to analyze a golf swing or otherwise shoot a sequence of many pictures over a period of about one-half second, this is the choice for you. Here again, you will almost certainly see the hour-glass icon after shooting, as the camera processes the large quantity of image information that it sucked in like a vacuum cleaner.

The next option, Continuous H: 60 fps, is similar to the previous one, except that the numbers are different: This option is marked by an icon with the number 60, for 60 frames per second, and the camera takes up to 60 shots at a somewhat larger resolution of 1 megapixel, or 1280 X 960 pixels. Use this option if you need a super-speedy sequence of numerous shots, but need a bit better quality.

The final option on the first screen of the Continuous menu is called Best Shot Selector, marked by the BSS icon. This option is a very useful one, though it is quite different from those discussed above. With the BSS feature, the camera does not emphasize speed. Rather, it takes up to 10 shots at a rather leisurely pace, one after another. When it's done, it "examines" them internally to determine which one is the sharpest, with the most details. The camera then discards all but that "best" shot, and displays it as if it were the only shot taken.

The BSS feature is intended for use with non-moving objects, such as taking a portrait inside a dimly-lit room without flash. (In fact, you cannot use flash when you're using BSS, just as you cannot with most other continuous-shooting options.) The idea is to give you several chances to capture an image that is not marred by blur from camera motion. You can set the image quality and size to their highest levels if you like, and you can control all other settings. (Though, as with all of the continuous-shooting options, the focus, exposure, and white balance will be fixed with the first shot.) Also, you may recall that the Museum setting in the Scene shooting mode uses the BSS feature, though you cannot make many other settings if you choose the Museum option, because of the limited settings available when using the Scene mode.

The first item at the top of the second screen of the Continuous menu is the somewhat unusual feature called Multi-shot 16, marked by an icon that looks like a frame subdivided into smaller squares. When you press the shutter button with this setting activated, the camera takes a series of 16 images at a speed of about 30 frames per second, and places them all into a single image, arranged in 4 rows of 4 pictures each. So, you end up with something that looks like a proof sheet, as shown in Figure 4-27.

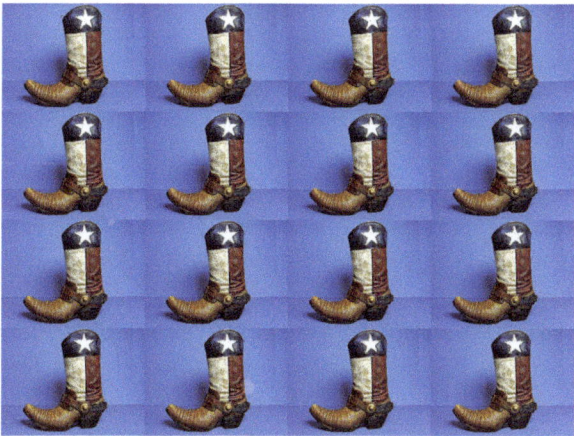

Figure 4-27: Multi-shot 16 example

Of course, there may be some variations among the images if the subject moved at all during the half-second it took to capture all the images. This feature seems like a novelty, but you may find a good practical application for it, such as studying the motion of a subject over a short period of time, and this feature might be useful for analyzing some sports actions. The image quality is fixed at Normal, and the image size is limited to 2560 X 1920 pixels, or about 5 megapixels. (That is the image size for the whole, composite image; the 16 individual images are very small and would not be useful in themselves.)

Finally, the last entry on the continuous-shooting menu is Interval Timer shooting, which gives the Coolpix P510 a limited capability for time-lapse shooting. When you select this option, the camera displays a small menu with 4 options for the interval between shots: 30 seconds, 1 minute, 5 minutes, or 10 minutes, as shown in Figure 4-28.

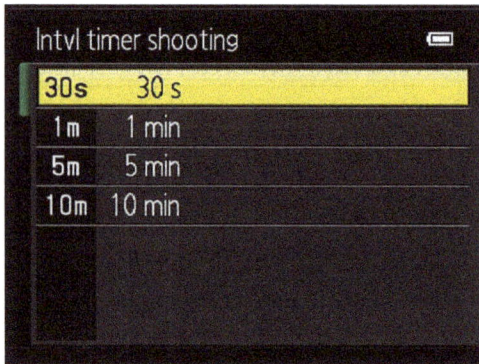

Figure 4-28: Interval Timer settings

When you press the shutter button all the way down, the camera takes the first image, then blanks out the display. The green light around the power button will blink slowly while interval shooting is active. Shortly before the interval has elapsed, the display will come back to normal brightness, and at the specified time the camera will take the next shot, and so on. If you want to interrupt the sequence of shots before it is complete, you can press the shutter button and the sequence will end.

You cannot take a great many shots with this technique; the maximum numbers for each of the intervals are as follows: for 30 seconds, 600 images; for one minute, 300 images; for five minutes, 60 images; for 10 minutes, 30 images. (That is, the intervals can last for a total of 300 minutes, or five hours.) These images are stored on your memory card in specially designated folders with the letters INTVL in their names. For example, an image might be labeled as 101INTVL-008.

Despite its limited capacity for numbers of images, the Interval Timer option can give you some excellent opportunities for creative photography. For example, you can aim the camera at a site where construction work is taking place, and record all work that is done in five hours. You can then play back these images as a time-lapse movie, using appropriate software such as Adobe Premiere Elements or iMovie. If you used an interval of one minute, resulting in 300 images, you could play back those 300 images at 30 frames per second (the standard video rate in the United States), which would take just 10 seconds to play. So, 5 hours of action would be collapsed into a 10-second sequence. You probably have seen time-lapse sequences of this sort on television, when the program shows weather patterns unfolding at rapid speeds, or shows a speeded-up view of a crowd gathering for an event, etc.

When you use interval shooting, you need to set the camera on a sturdy, steady tripod; the slightest motion of the camera will be magnified and quite obvious when the sequence is played back. Also, you need to be able to keep the camera powered on for 5 hours continuously. The camera does turn off its display between shots, so you might be able to squeeze through, especially if you're shooting for less than the full 5 hours. However, to be safe, you should use the AC adapter designated for this camera, model number EH-62A, which is discussed in Appendix A. Finally, it's generally a good idea to use Manual exposure mode and to set the white balance and ISO to definite settings rather than to Auto settings, so that there is no distracting flickering among the images when the camera adjusts these settings automatically.

ISO Sensitivity

The initials ISO stand for International Standards Organization. When I first started in film photography, this standard was known as ASA, for American Standards Association. The ISO acronym reflects the more international nature of the modern photographic industry. The original use of the ISO/ASA standard was to designate the "speed," or light sensitivity, of film. So, for example, a "slow" film might be rated ISO 64, or even ISO 25, meaning it takes a considerable amount of exposure to light to create a usable image on the film. Slow films yield higher-quality, less-grainy images than faster films. There are "fast" films available, some black-and-white and some color, with ISO ratings of 400 or even higher, that are designed to yield usable images in lower light. Such films can often be used indoors without flash, for example.

With digital technology, the industry has retained the ISO concept, but it applies not just to film, but to the light sensitivity of the camera's sensor, because there is no film involved in a digital camera. The ISO ratings for digital cameras are supposed to be essentially equivalent to the ISO ratings for films. So if your Coolpix P510 is set to its minimum level, ISO 100, there will have to be a fair amount of light to expose the image properly, but if the camera is set to the highest numerical level of ISO 3200, a reasonably good (but "noisier" or "fuzzier") image can be made in very low light.

The upshot of all of this is that, generally speaking, you want to shoot your images with the camera set to the lowest ISO possible that will allow the image to be exposed properly. (One exception to this rule is if you want, for creative purposes, the grainy look that comes from shooting at a high ISO value.) For example, if you are shooting indoors in low light, you may need to set the ISO to a high value (say, ISO 800) so you can expose the image with a reasonably fast shutter speed. Otherwise, if the camera uses a slow shutter speed, the resulting image would likely be blurry and possibly unusable.

To summarize: Shoot with low ISO settings (usually 100 with the P510) when possible; shoot with high ISO settings (say 400 or higher, up to 1600 or even 3200) when necessary to allow a fast shutter speed to stop action and avoid blurriness, or when desired to achieve a creative effect with graininess.

With that background, here is how to set ISO on this camera. Press the Menu button and move to the ISO Sensitivity line, then press the right direction button to get to the screen that lets you select either ISO Sensitivity or Minimum Shutter Speed. For now, select ISO Sensitivity and press the right button again to get to the ISO Sensitivity options. The first of the two ISO menu screens is shown in Figure 4-29.

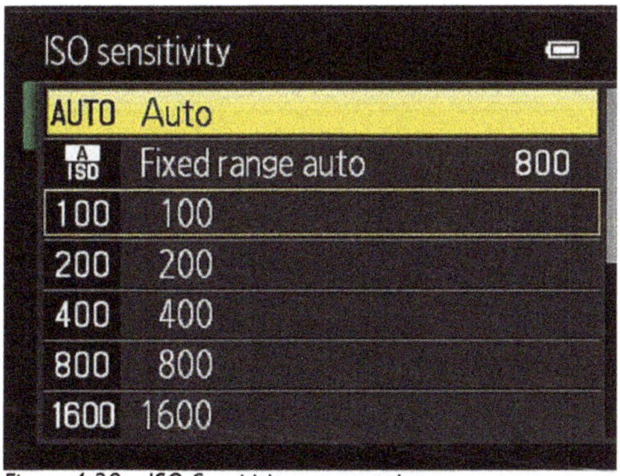

ISO sensitivity		
AUTO	Auto	
A ISO	Fixed range auto	800
100	100	
200	200	
400	400	
800	800	
1600	1600	

Figure 4-29: ISO Sensitivity menu option

With the first option, Auto, the camera will set the ISO level at 100 in relatively bright light, and it will raise the level as high as 1600 as the light grows dimmer. The second option on the list, Fixed Range Auto, has two choices, reached by pressing the right direction button. You can choose from two ranges, 100-400 or 100-800, if you want to constrain the camera's ISO choices to a fairly narrow range of possibilities. You can use this approach if you want the camera to use a certain amount of flexibility, but you want to make sure the ISO value does not go high enough to cause noticeable "noise" in your images. Finally, you can choose any one of the individual ISO values, if you want to specify exactly what ISO setting the camera uses. The choices are 100, 200, 400, 800, 1600, 3200, and 6400, which Nikon labels as Hi 1 on the menu screen. (There is one higher level, called Hi 2 by Nikon, which is equivalent to ISO 12800; it cannot be selected from the ISO menu; it is activated only when the camera is set to High ISO Monochrome in the Special Effects shooting mode, described in Chapter 3.)

Minimum Shutter Speed

Going back to the first branch on this set of menu screens, you can use the Minimum Shutter Speed setting to specify the slowest shutter speed that the camera will use when the camera is set to the Program or Aperture Priority mode and any of the Auto ISO settings are in effect, before the camera starts to increase the ISO sensitivity.

To understand this setting, it's helpful to consider an example. Suppose the camera is in Program mode and the ISO Sensitivity setting is Auto. Press the Menu button, use the multi selector dial or the up and down direction buttons to highlight ISO sensitivity on the display, and press the right direction button to get to the next screen. Then highlight Minimum Shutter Speed, press the right direction button, and select 1/30 second from the list of values on the screen shown in Figure 4-30.

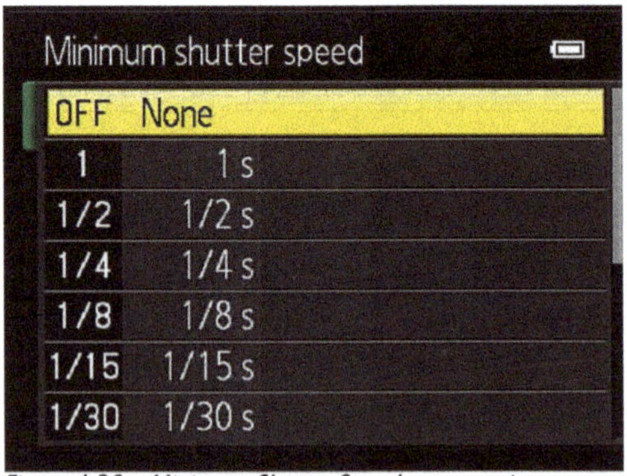

Minimum shutter speed	
OFF	None
1	1 s
1/2	1/2 s
1/4	1/4 s
1/8	1/8 s
1/15	1/15 s
1/30	1/30 s

Figure 4-30: Minimum Shutter Speed menu option

With those settings, the camera will attempt to expose the image properly using a shutter speed no slower than 1/30 second, your Minimum Shutter Speed setting. If the Auto ISO setting increases to its maximum limit and the image is still too dark, then the camera will drop to a slower shutter speed in order to achieve a good exposure. So, in effect, this setting forces the camera to try to keep the shutter speed at 1/30 second or faster, but if that's not possible, the camera will then change to a slower shutter speed. You may want to use this setting to avoid using slow shutter speeds that are likely to result in blurred photos because of camera motion, or to capture images of moving subjects, such as children playing. If you use a setting such as 1/125 second (the fastest setting possible) for Minimum Shutter Speed, along with an ISO setting such as Auto, which allows the ISO to go as high as 1600, you are likely to be able to take all of your exposures using the 1/125 second shutter speed, preserving your ability to avoid camera shake and to capture ordinary action.

Here is one more note on the Auto ISO options. If you select any of the Auto ISO settings in Manual exposure mode, the camera will set the ISO to 100. You can select any other numerical ISO value if you want, but you cannot select Auto for the ISO setting in that shooting mode. In Auto shooting mode and all varieties of the Scene shooting mode, Auto ISO is automatically set, and you cannot adjust it. The same is true of the Special Effects shooting mode, although, as noted earlier, if you choose the High ISO Monochrome setting, the camera sets the ISO to Hi 2, which is the equivalent of ISO 12800.

Also, there are some restrictions on the available ISO settings in conjunction with other settings on the camera. For example, with certain continuous shooting options, ISO is automatically set to Auto, and Active D-Lighting is not available when ISO is set to a value greater than 800. The details of these limitations are set forth at pages 80-81 of the Coolpix P510 Reference Manual.

Exposure Bracketing

Exposure bracketing is a function that lets you take three pictures with one press of the shutter button, with three different exposure settings, thereby giving you an added chance of getting one good, usable image. In addition, using exposure bracketing is an excellent way to take three pictures that can be combined later in software to produce an HDR (High Dynamic Range) composite, which shows clear details and highlights throughout the image by taking the best-exposed parts of each shot.

To use bracketing, the camera must be set to the Program, Aperture Priority, or Shutter Priority mode. Navigate down in the Shooting menu to the second line on the second menu screen. Then press the OK button or the right direction button to get access to the next screen, which will present you with four choices: ±0.3, ±0.7, ±1.0, and Off, as shown in Figure 4-31.

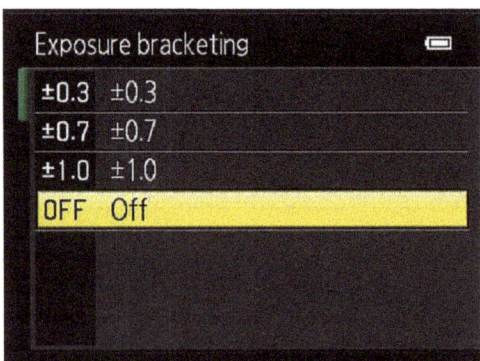

Figure 4-31: Exposure Bracketing menu option

Use the multi selector dial or the direction buttons to highlight your choice, then make the selection by pressing the OK button. When you exit back to shooting mode, the camera's display will include a notation such as BKT±0.7, unless you left bracketing turned off. (Press the Display button if necessary to show this detail on the screen.) This notation means that the camera will take three exposures separated by the indicated amount of exposure value (EV, a standard measure of brightness). Adding a single unit of EV, +1.0, has the same effect as opening the aperture by one full f-stop.

When you are ready to shoot, press and release the shutter button and hold the camera steady (or use a tripod) while it takes the three exposures. The first picture taken is always at the metered level, or 0 change in exposure value (EV); the second is at the lower EV (darker), and the third is at the higher EV (brighter). If you have added exposure compensation, the bracketed exposures are taken at three levels relative to the adjusted exposure.

Note that the flash cannot be used when bracketing is in effect. If you press the Flash button (up direction button) when bracketing is turned on, nothing will happen. If the flash was previously set to forced on (Fill Flash), the camera will turn it back off when bracketing is selected.

Be sure to cancel exposure bracketing when you are done using this feature; otherwise, it will stay in effect even after you turn the camera off and back on again.

AF Area Mode

This next option on the second screen of the Shooting menu gives you several options for controlling how the autofocus frame is set up, when the camera is in autofocus mode. Once this menu option is highlighted, press the OK button or the right direction button to get to the next menu screen, and then use the multi selector dial or the up and down direction buttons to select from the six possible options shown in Figure 4-32, as follows:

Face Priority

With this option, the camera looks for human faces. If it detects what it believes are faces, it puts a double-bordered frame on the closest face, and single-bordered frames on other faces, as shown in Figure 4-33. When you press the shutter button halfway, the camera then will focus on the main face and set the exposure and white balance. This is a good option to choose when you're at a picnic or other group function and you need to take a quick snapshot with as many faces in focus as possible. In other situations, you may want to take more time and select the focus point and other options yourself.

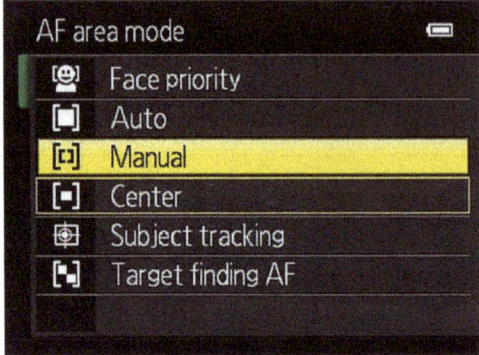

Figure 4-32: AF Area Mode menu option

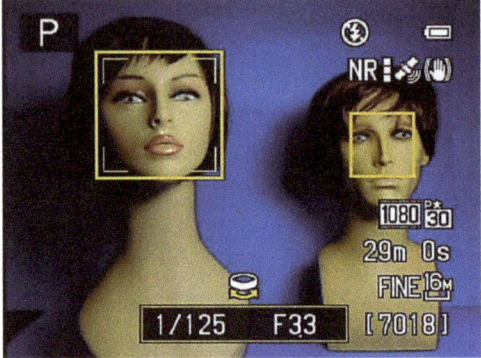

Figure 4-33: AF Area Mode Face Priority

Auto

With this option, which is the camera's default choice, the P510 chooses one or more of its nine possible focus blocks as the main focus point(s). When you press the shutter button down halfway to lock in the focus, the camera will select the point or points closest to the camera and display green rectangles on the screen to show which point(s) it chose for focusing, as shown in Figure 4-34. This focusing mode is good for shots of general scenes in which you are not trying to focus on individual people's faces.

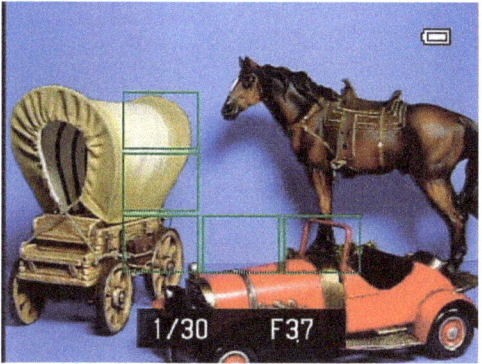

Figure 4-34: AF Area Mode Auto

Manual

If you select Manual for the AF Area Mode, the camera displays a focus frame in the center of the screen, with arrows pointing in each direction outside the frame. You can now use the four direction buttons or the multi selector dial to move the focus frame to any of 99 possible locations around the screen, as shown in Figure 4-35.

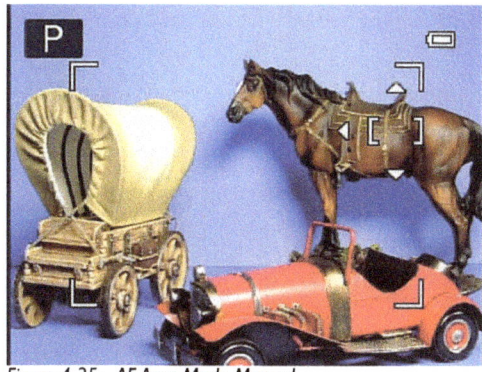

Figure 4-35: AF Area Mode Manual

This is a great option to use if you are shooting a scene with items at varying distances from the camera, and you want to direct the camera's focus on an item that is not in the center of the scene. Of course, this type of focusing is useful only if you have time to select this option and move your focus frame to the location where you want it. If you don't have time, it may be easier simply to place the center of the frame over the item you want to focus on, press the shutter button halfway down to lock the focus, and then move the camera back to compose the image as you want it.

If you do have the time to use the Manual option for AF Area Mode, here is how to use it. Once you have located the focus frame where you want it using the buttons or dial, press the shutter button to lock focus and then take the picture. The focus frame will stay in this location even after the camera is powered off and back on, so be sure to reset it to the center when you no longer need it in an off-center position.

If you need to use one of the four direction buttons on the multi selector for another purpose while using Manual AF Area Mode, press the OK button to return the direction buttons to their other functions (flash mode, focus mode, self-timer, and exposure compensation); then, after using a button for another function, press OK again to return the buttons to controlling the location of the focus frame.

Center

With this option, as shown in Figure 4-36, the camera places an autofocus frame in the center of the screen. You can then place this frame over the area of the scene that you want to be in sharpest focus. You can't move this frame around the screen. However, if the point you want to focus on doesn't happen to be in the center of the image, you can lock focus on it by pressing the shutter button halfway while aiming at it, and then keeping the button held halfway down while you move the camera back to compose the shot as you want; the focus will be locked on the target you chose.

CHAPTER 4: THE SHOOTING MENU

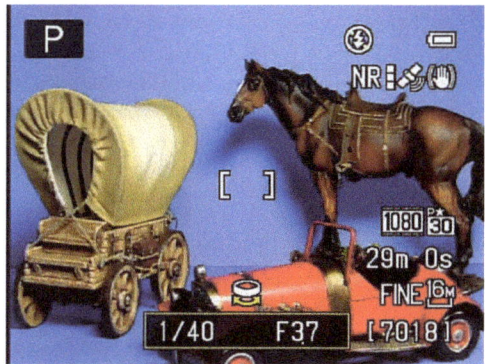

Figure 4-36: AF Area Mode Center

Subject Tracking

This next AF Area Mode option is designed for situations in which you need to track a moving subject, such as a sports competitor or a child at play. Once you have selected this mode, you will see a small, white, square-shaped bracket in the center of the screen, with the words OK Start below it, as shown in Figure 4-37.

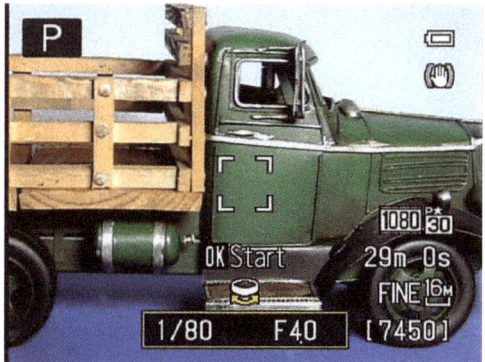

Figure 4-37: AF Area Mode Subject Tracking

Aim this square bracket at the subject you want to track, and press the OK button. The frame will change to a double set of yellow brackets, which the camera will try to keep centered over the subject, even as the subject (or the camera) moves.

When you press the shutter button down halfway to check ex-

151

posure, the frame will turn green to confirm exposure, and the tracking will stop. Press the shutter button all the way down when you are ready to take the picture.

Target Finding AF

Finally, the P510 has one more available option for the AF Area Mode setting. This one, Target Finding AF, is the setting that the camera uses when it is set to the Auto shooting mode. According to Nikon, with this setting the camera tries to determine the "main subject" in the scene and focuses on that subject. To identify the main subject, the camera looks for human faces and for objects that match the camera's programmed criteria, which include factors such as color, size, and position. If the camera cannot identify a main subject, it focuses on the object closest to the camera.

In my experience, this option does not provide any advantages over the other choices for AF Area Mode. I have not found that the results with Target Finding AF are different from the results with the Auto setting for AF Area Mode. In fact, because it is not clear exactly what criteria the camera uses in trying to identify the main subject, the Target Finding AF setting introduces a level of uncertainty that I find somewhat disconcerting. If you use the Auto shooting mode, the camera will automatically use this setting for focusing. If you shoot in other modes, I recommend that you use the Auto setting for AF Area Mode if you want a high level of automation. However, I prefer to use the Center or Manual setting in many cases.

Autofocus Mode

This feature, whose menu screen is shown in Figure 4-38, lets you decide whether the camera will focus just once, when you press the shutter button halfway, or will focus continuously before you press the button halfway.

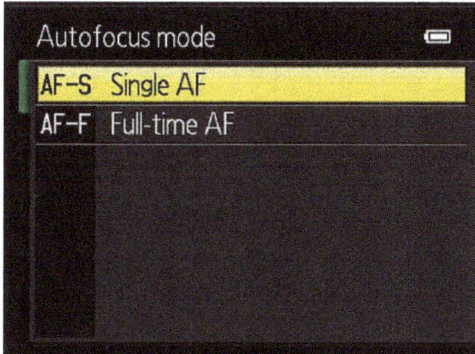

Figure 4-38: Autofocus Mode menu option

Choose Single AF if you want to conserve the battery and wait until you are ready to take the picture before the camera uses its autofocus mechanism; choose Full-time AF if you want the camera to focus continuously. Although the Full-time option will use up your battery more quickly, it has the advantage of keeping the image in focus as you move the camera or your subject moves around; in that way, when you are ready to capture the image, the camera can make the last focusing adjustments quickly when you press the shutter button.

Note that this option does not apply for shooting movies; you need to select an autofocus mode from the Movie menu to cover that situation.

Flash Exposure Compensation

This option works in similar fashion to standard exposure compensation, discussed in Chapter 2. That is, you can dial in an amount of flash exposure compensation up to 2 EV units, in increments of 1/3 EV. When you do that, you are telling the camera, in effect, "Okay, you go ahead and calculate the correct exposure with the flash, but then add in (say) 1 1/3 EV extra, to make the picture brighter."

To make use of this setting, go to its entry on the second menu screen and press the OK button or the right direction button to get to the adjustment screen. At that screen, turn the multi selector dial or use the up and down direction buttons to dial in up to +2.0 EV or -2.0 EV, to make your flash exposures that much brighter or darker, as shown in Figure 4-39.

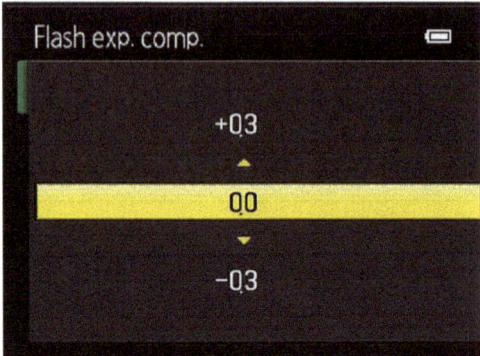

Figure 4-39: Flash exposure compensation

You have to press the OK button to confirm your selection when the value you want to choose is highlighted in the yellow bar in the middle of the screen. When you have activated a positive or negative amount of flash exposure compensation, that value will appear on the camera's display in the upper right-hand corner. That value will remain in effect even after the camera has been powered off and back on, so be sure to cancel it when you no longer need the compensation.

Noise Reduction Filter

Noise reduction is an electronic feature built into the P510's programming to compensate for visual noise in your images, which can be caused by long exposures or by the use of high ISO settings. By default, this option is set to Normal, which causes the camera to use a moderate amount of noise reduction. If you want to have larger or smaller amounts of noise reduction applied in every case, you can switch the setting to High or Low. You cannot turn noise reduction completely off.

What you do with this setting is really a matter of personal preference about processing your photos. If you are going to be using Photoshop, Photoshop Elements, or similar software to process the images on your computer, you may want to leave Noise Reduction Filter set to Low, so you can minimize the amount of processing done in the camera. However, if you will be using the shots straight from the camera and you are shooting with long shutter speeds or high ISO settings, you may well want to turn this setting up to High to avoid the graininess that comes from visual noise.

Active D-Lighting

This is a very useful option that can help you avoid problems with excessive contrast in your images. Such problems arise because digital cameras cannot easily process a very wide range of dark and light areas in the same image—that is, their "dynamic range" is limited. So, if you are taking a picture in an area that is partly lit by bright sunlight and partly in deep shade, the resulting image is likely to have some dark areas in which the details are lost in the shadows, or some areas in which the highlights, or bright areas, are excessively bright, or "blown out," so, again, the details of the image are lost. One approach to this problem is to use High Dynamic Range, or HDR, techniques, in which multiple photographs of the same scene with different exposures are combined into one composite image that is properly exposed throughout the entire scene. I discussed that technique in Chapter 3, in connection with the Backlighting shooting mode.

The Active D-Lighting setting gives you another way to approach the problem of uneven lighting. This option uses special processing in the camera to boost details in the dark areas and reduce over-exposure in the bright areas, resulting in a single image with better exposure than would be possible otherwise. If you turn this option on, the camera performs digital processing as it records the image, resulting in some degree of restoration of details in the shadows and in the highlights, to even out the lighting. The Shooting menu, as shown in Figure 4-40, provides three levels of this processing: High, Normal, and Low, as well as Off, the default setting.

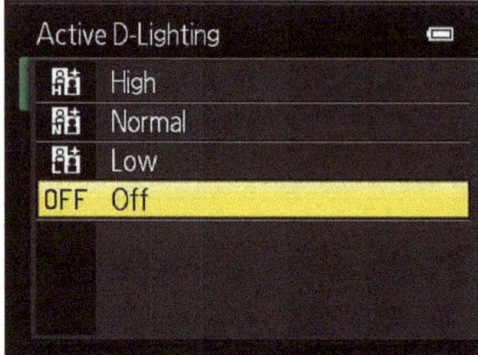

Figure 4-40: Active D-Lighting menu option

In the first image here, Figure 4-41, Active D-Lighting was turned off; in Figure 4-42, it was turned on to the High setting.

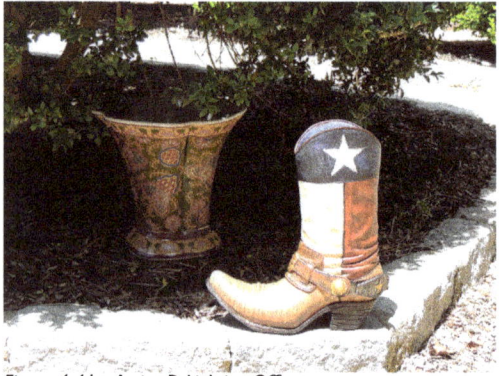

Figure 4-41: Active D-Lighting Off

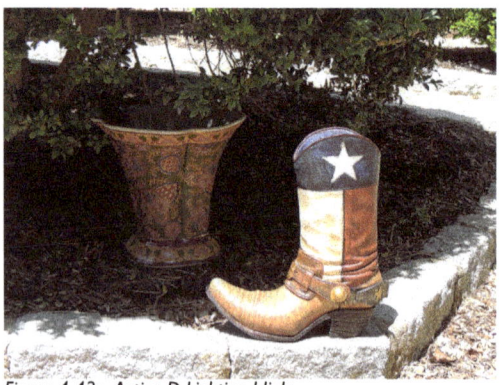

Figure 4-42: Active D-Lighting High

As you can see, with Active D-Lighting turned on, the camera brought out more detail in the shadowed areas and reduced the overexposure in the brighter parts of the image.

Note that the Coolpix P510 has a related feature called simply D-Lighting, which is used in Playback mode for images that have already been taken. I'll discuss that feature in Chapter 6.

Save User Settings

I discussed this feature in Chapter 3, in connection with the User Setting shooting mode, marked by the letter U on the mode dial. To save your current shooting settings for instant recall with the U slot on the dial, navigate to the Save User Settings option on the Shooting menu and press the right direction button or the OK button to save the settings. Be sure you have the settings exactly as you want them before you press the button, because the camera does not ask you to confirm your choice; it just announces "Done" once you press the button.

Reset User Settings

This option on the Shooting menu lets you reset the settings that are saved to the User Setting mode (U slot on the mode dial) to the default settings without having to go through the menus to adjust each one. For example, choosing this option sets the shooting mode to Program, the flash mode to Auto, exposure compensation to 0.0, the zoom lens to its wide-angle position, and all items on the Shooting menu to their default settings. Note that this option affects only the settings saved for the User Setting mode; if you want to reset all settings for the camera for all modes, you have to use the Reset All menu option, which is found on the Setup menu, as discussed in Chapter 7.

Zoom Memory and Startup Zoom Position

The last two items on the Shooting menu are closely related, so I will discuss them together. First, I will discuss Zoom Memory. This very useful option lets you control whether the zoom lever zooms the lens in continuous increments, or in distinct, separate steps. By default this option is turned off, so you can zoom continuously in any amounts, zooming either in or out.

If you turn the Zoom Memory setting on using this menu option, you are then taken to a screen, shown in Figure 4-43, that shows a list of focal lengths, from full wide-angle to full telephoto: 24mm, 28mm, 35mm, 50mm, 85mm, 105mm, 135mm, 200mm, 300mm, 400mm, 500mm, 600mm, 800mm, and 1000mm.

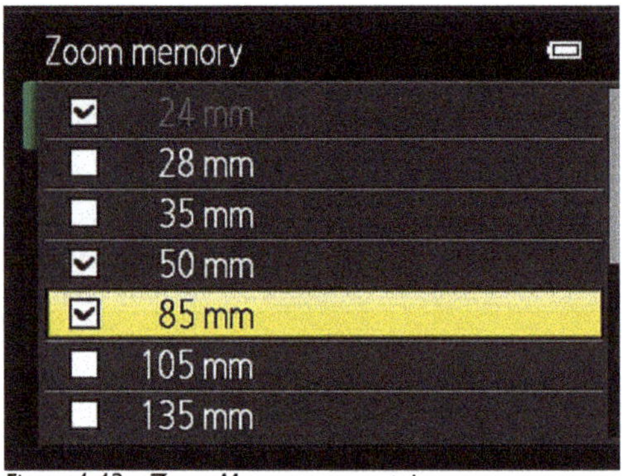

Figure 4-43: Zoom Memory menu option

Each focal length has a check-box to its left. Move the selection rectangle up and down over this list using the up and down direction buttons or the multi selector dial. As each focal length is highlighted, you can press the OK button to check or un-check its box. If the box is checked, then the camera will include that focal length in the zoom memory.

When you have finished checking the boxes for the focal lengths that you want to have included in the zoom memory, exit from the menu screen by pressing the Menu button or by half-pressing the shutter button. Now, when you press the zoom lever, each press will take the lens to the next one of the focal lengths that was checked on the Zoom Memory menu screen.

For example, suppose you turned on the Zoom Memory option and checked the boxes for 50mm, 200mm, and 1000mm. Then, if you are starting from the full wide-angle position of 24mm, when you press the zoom lever to the right, the lens will zoom in to 50mm. If you press it again, the lens will zoom to 200mm, and one more press will take it all the way to 1000mm. You will not be able to zoom the lens to any other positions. The same will be true when you zoom back out by pressing the zoom lever in the other direction. It does not matter if you use a very quick press of the lever or hold the lever in position; it will zoom only to the next level that has its box checked on the Zoom Memory menu screen.

As I noted above, the Zoom Memory option is closely related to the Startup Zoom Position option, which is directly below it on the menu screen. With that option, shown in Figure 4-44, you select a focal length where the zoom lens will start when you turn the camera on.

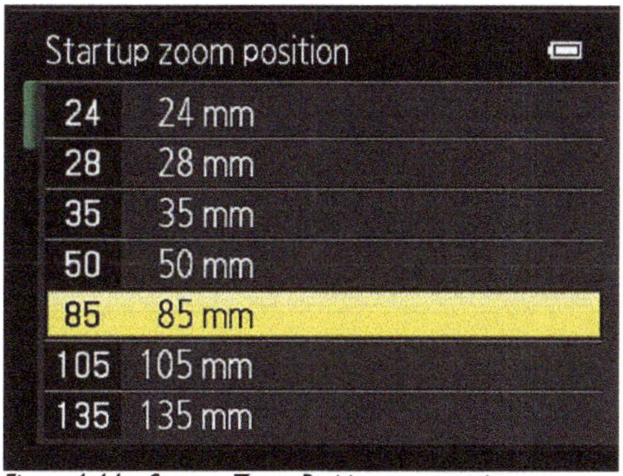

Figure 4-44: Startup Zoom Position menu option

In this case, the choices of focal lengths are more limited: 24mm, 28mm, 35mm, 50mm, 85mm, 105mm, or 135mm. You select this menu option, then move to the next screen and position the yellow rectangle on the focal length you want to select. Press the OK button to confirm. Then, when you turn the camera on the next time, the lens will automatically zoom to that focal length.

Here is how these two settings are related. When you select a focal length for Startup Zoom Position, you will see that that focal length is automatically checked on the menu screen for Zoom Memory, and its menu item is grayed out, meaning that you cannot alter it. In other words, you cannot un-check the box for that focal length, because the camera is going to start up at that focal length. For example, suppose you select 50mm on the Startup Zoom Position menu screen, and 35mm, 200mm, and 1000mm on the Zoom Memory screen. The next time you turn on the camera, the lens will zoom automatically to the 50mm position. If you press the zoom lever to zoom out, the lens will zoom out to 35 mm. If you then press the lever to zoom in, the lens will zoom back to 50mm, the startup position. From there, it will zoom to 200mm, then 1000mm.

These two menu options, working together, give you a great deal of control over how your lens zooms. Of course, you don't necessarily need to have that degree of control; you may be quite content to use the default settings, having the startup position of 24mm and allowing the lens to zoom to any setting, without using the Zoom Memory option. However, it can be quite convenient to know what focal length you are using for a given shot. If you turn Zoom Memory off, the camera's display will not show you what focal length it is using; if you turn it on, you will see the focal length displayed at the top of the display.

Chapter 5: Other Controls

The Coolpix P510, like many compact cameras, does not have a large number of physical controls. It relies to a great extent on its system of menus to give you the ability to change settings. But, because the P510 is near the upper end of the scale of high-quality compact cameras, it has more actual controls than most cameras of this size, since more advanced photographers generally prefer to be able to make settings with a button or a dial whenever possible, for speed of access. In this chapter, I'll discuss each of these controls and how they can be used to best advantage. I'll start with the controls on the top of the camera, as shown in Figure 5-1.

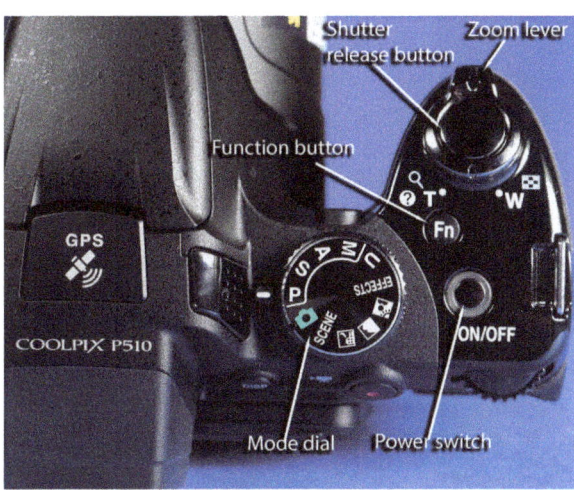

Figure 5-1: Controls on top of camera

Power Switch

The power switch, located at the right side of the camera's top, has only one function—to turn the camera on and off. When the camera is turned on, the green light around this button illuminates. When the camera enters standby mode to save power, the green light starts to blink, and does so for about three minutes. During that time, you can press the power button, the Playback button, the shutter-release button, or the Movie button, or you can turn the mode dial, to cancel standby mode and restore the camera to full power.

Shutter Release Button

The shutter release button is the single most important control on the camera. When you press it halfway down in most shooting modes, the camera evaluates exposure and focus (unless you're using manual focus). Once you are satisfied with the settings, you press the button all the way down to record the image. When the camera is set for continuous shooting, you hold this button down while the camera fires repeatedly.

You also can press this button down halfway to exit from playback mode to shooting mode, so you can take more pictures. You also can press it to exit from any menu screen. Note, though, that you have to press the OK button to confirm your selection on the menu screen before pressing the shutter button; otherwise, your setting on the menu screen will not be saved. And, you can press the shutter release button to re-awaken the camera from standby mode, which it enters after a period of inactivity. You have to press this button (or the Playback, power, or Movie button) or turn the mode dial while the green light around the power button is flashing.

Mode Dial

The mode dial, located at the right side of the camera's top, is central to the operation of the camera. Its main function is to change the camera from one shooting mode to another. In addition, as noted above, when the camera has gone into standby mode and the power light starts blinking, you can cancel standby mode and return the camera to full power-on mode by turning the mode dial (or by pushing one of the major buttons on the camera).

Zoom Lever

The zoom lever is a small ring with a handle, surrounding the shutter release button. The lever's main function is to change the focal length of the lens between its wide-angle setting of 24mm and its telephoto setting of 1000mm. If you have the camera set for digital zoom, the lever will boost the focal length to a maximum of 2000mm. (That impressive-sounding zoom amount is illusory, though, because the quality will be degraded by the electronic enlargement of the image.) If you move the lever sharply to either side, the zoom range will adjust quickly; if you move it more gradually, the range will change more slowly.

Note that, when you first turn the camera on, the lens always starts out zoomed to whatever position has been selected with the Startup Zoom Position option on the Shooting menu, as discussed in Chapter 4. And, the behavior of the zoom lever will change depending on the settings for the Zoom Memory menu option, discussed in that chapter also. As a brief reminder, if Zoom Memory is turned on, pressing the zoom lever will move the lens to the next zoom level that was selected through the Zoom Memory menu option. If that feature is turned off, pressing the lever will zoom the lens continuously through its full range of focal lengths.

In playback mode, moving the zoom lever to the left (pointing to the W setting) produces index screens with increasing numbers of images, and moving the lever to the right enlarges the current image. These functions are discussed in Chapter 6.

When the mode dial is on the SCENE setting and a Scene type is highlighted on the menu, you can move the zoom lever to the right, so it points at the question mark, to produce a screen giving some tips about the Scene type. Move the lever to the right again to make the tips vanish. This help function also is available when you have highlighted one of the Picture Control menu options on the Shooting menu.

Function Button

Nikon has provided the user with an extremely useful and powerful control in the form of the Function button, the small, recessed button marked with the Fn designation, just behind the shutter release button.

As discussed in Chapter 4, many of the most important settings on the Coolpix P510 are buried in the Shooting menu, including Image Size, ISO, White Balance, continuous shooting, and others. It can be quite inconvenient to change these settings when you have to press the Menu button, navigate to the Shooting menu, and then move to the proper line on the menu before you can make a change.

With this small button, you have the option of programming any one of seven of the most useful settings of the camera into a physical control. (You do this programming using the Fn Button item on the Setup menu, as discussed in Chapter 7.) The options that are available for choice are Image Size, Picture Control, White Balance, Metering, continuous shooting, ISO, and AF Area Mode. When you press the Function button, a menu for the item that is programmed into the button pops up on the screen, as shown in Figure 5-2, letting you quickly change the setting.

You can move through that menu using the up and down direction buttons or by turning either the command dial or the multi selector dial; you have to press the OK button to confirm your selection once it is highlighted.

CHAPTER 5: OTHER CONTROLS

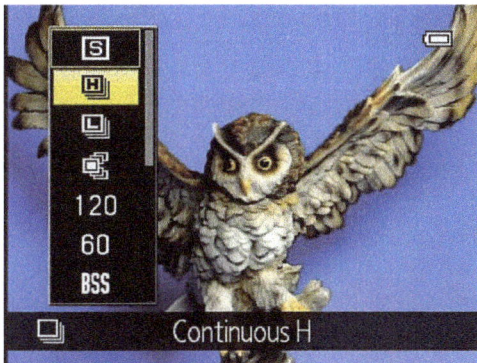

Figure 5-2: Function Button menu

The default choice, as shown here, is continuous shooting, which I tend to prefer as the item assigned to this button. If I am in a situation in which I want to fire off a burst of shots, it is very convenient to just press the Function button and be able to quickly switch to one of the burst modes for a short time. Then, when that situation has passed, I can just as quickly press the button again and reset the camera to single-shot mode. However, it also can be very useful to be able to adjust ISO quickly. Of course, the value you choose to assign to this button will depend on your own particular circumstances. If you like to experiment with various different image-processing settings, you might want to program Picture Control as the setting. In any event, it is great to have this option available.

The Function button has one other capability, completely apart from its giving you access to one menu item. When the camera is in playback mode and you are viewing an image in the normal, full-frame mode (not on an index screen, that is), if you press the Function button the camera will switch to a screen that displays the GPS coordinates (latitude and longitude) where that image was taken, and the route information logged by the GPS system, if any. Another press of the button returns the camera to the display of the image. Of course, if the GPS information was not recorded for the image, because it was taken indoors or when the GPS was not activated, no location information will be displayed, though the location screen

165

will still appear, with blanks for the data. I'll talk more about GPS functions and show a copy of this screen in Chapter 7.

Next, I'll discuss the controls on the left side of the camera, as shown in Figure 5-3.

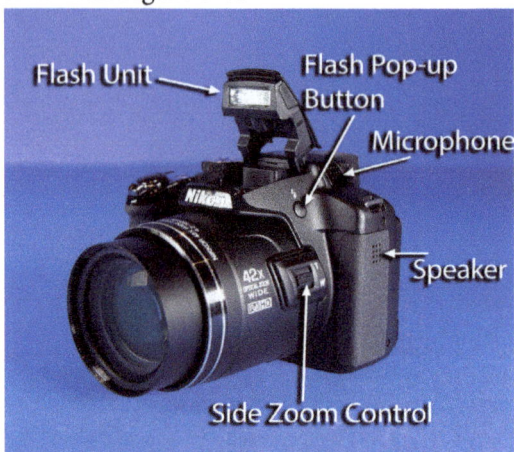

Figure 5-3: Controls on front left of camera

Flash Pop-up Button

This small round button on the left side of the flash housing has just one simple purpose—to release the built-in flash unit so it will pop up and be available for use. If you expect you will be using the flash, you need to press this button to make the unit available; if you don't press the button, the flash will not pop up, and cannot fire. If you select a shooting mode that requires use of the flash, such as Night Portrait, the camera will display a message prompting you to raise the flash. When you are done with the flash unit, press it gently back down until it clicks into place.

Note that the requirement that you press this button to pop up the flash has one clear advantage: When you are in a museum or other location where photography is permitted but the use of flash is prohibited, you can just leave the flash unit stowed away and you can be sure it will never pop up by itself and send out a flash that proves to be embarrassing or gets you ejected from the area. (With some compact cameras, the flash is always available to fire, and you have to remember to set the flash mode properly to avoid having it go off unexpectedly.)

Side Zoom Control

One of the novel and welcome features of the Coolpix P510 is the existence of a second zoom switch, which is located on the left side of the lens barrel as you hold the camera in shooting position. One reason for having this alternative control available is to free up your right hand to hold the camera firmly, rather than having to reach up to the standard zoom lever on top of the camera. With the super-powerful zoom range of the P510, you need to hold the camera as steady as possible when zooming in to the longer ranges.

Note that the functioning of the Side Zoom Control is governed by the Zoom Memory setting on the Shooting menu, just as with the zoom lever on top of the camera. That is, when Zoom Memory is turned on, pressing this control will take the lens only to the particular focal lengths that have been selected for that menu option.

Another helpful aspect of the Side Zoom Control is that its function is assignable. That is, you can use this switch to control one of two other functions besides ordinary zooming, depending on your particular preference. To do this, you use the Setup menu, as discussed in Chapter 7. The first possibility other than standard zooming is to assign the Side Zoom Control to adjust manual focus. If you do so, you still can use the up and down direction buttons of the multi selector to control manual focus, but you then have the option of using the side switch as an alternative. You may like the feel of this control for fine-tuning the focus rather than pressing the up and down buttons.

The other option available for assigning to this switch is a function that Nikon calls "snap-back zoom." Here is how this function works. When you have zoomed the lens in to a powerful telephoto setting, you can "snap" the focal length back to a wider view in a preset amount by a quick press of the side switch down towards the wide-angle (W) position. Another quick press will snap the lens back another definite step towards wide-angle. Then, at any time, as long as you have not used any other controls on the camera in the meantime, you can give a quick press upward on the Side Zoom Control, which will snap the lens all the way back to the original telephoto position.

So, in essence, with the snap-back setting, when you have the camera zoomed in for a magnified, telephoto view, you can experiment with different telephoto settings. You can "snap" the lens back out to a wider view once or twice (or more, depending on how far in the lens was zoomed), and then, once you've checked out those views, which can help you get a sense of your ultimate subject by seeing a wider view, you can snap the camera back to its original telephoto setting without having to use trial and error; that setting has been preserved precisely for you in the camera's "snap-back" memory.

I did not see much need for the snap-back function at first. However, when I was trying to photograph a bird at a long distance using the superzoom lens, I found this feature very useful. When the lens was zoomed all the way in, I found it hard to locate the bird. I eventually realized that I could quickly snap the lens back to a wider view until I found the bird in my field of view. Once I had the bird centered again, I could press the Side Zoom Control back up to snap the zoom back to the full-power telephoto view. So, to help you stay oriented when using the very long focal lengths available with the P510, the snap-back control can be quite useful.

AF Assist/Self-timer Lamp

The small lamp on the front of the camera, shown in Figure 5-4, has multiple functions. Its reddish light blinks to signal the operation of the self-timer and smile detection when the Smile Timer is used, and it also turns on in dark environments

CHAPTER 5: OTHER CONTROLS

to assist with autofocusing.

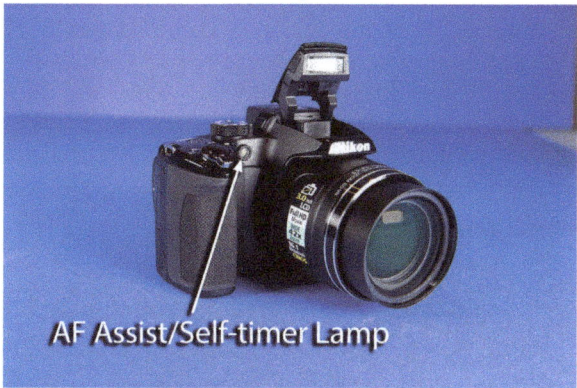

Figure 5-4: AF Assist/Self-timer lamp

You can control the use of the lamp for autofocusing through the Setup menu, as discussed in Chapter 7. You might want to disable it when taking photographs during a religious ceremony or in another environment where this rather bright light could be uncomfortably distracting.

The next controls to be discussed are those located on the camera's back, most of them to the right side of the LCD screen, as shown in Figure 5-5.

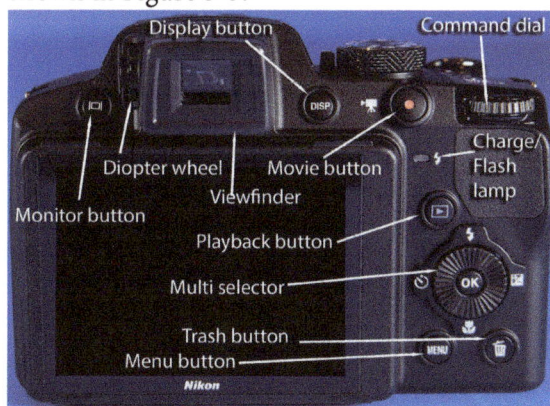

Figure 5-5: Controls on back of camera

Playback Button

This button, marked with a small triangle, is used to put the

169

camera into playback mode, which allows you to view your images on the LCD (or in the viewfinder) and gives you access to the Playback menu. It also can be used in slightly different ways, depending on the context. That is, you can use this button instead of the power button to turn the camera on, placing it immediately into playback mode. You might want to do this if you know you're only going to view your recorded images, and won't be using shooting mode.

If you turn the camera on using the Playback button, pressing it again will not turn the camera off; it will just switch the camera into shooting mode. When the camera is in playback mode, you can always press the shutter button down halfway to change into shooting mode.

When the camera goes into power saving mode and the light around the power button starts to blink, you can press the Playback button, among others, to stop the camera from powering off.

Monitor Button

This button to the left of the viewfinder has just one function—you press it to switch your view between the 3-inch (7.5-cm) LCD screen and the electronic viewfinder. The default view is the LCD display, with its large, high-resolution screen. But when you're taking photos in bright sunlight it can be very hard to view the image on this screen. Also, some photographers prefer to hold the camera against their forehead and look through the viewfinder, at least in some situations. So, it's good to have two options.

Note that the Coolpix P510 does not provide any automatic switching between the viewfinder and the LCD screen when your head approaches the viewfinder, as some cameras do; the only way to switch views is by pressing this button. And note that the camera remembers the setting of this button even when powered off. So, if you are surprised when you turn on the camera and nothing appears on the LCD, it may just be that the Monitor button has activated the viewfinder display.

Diopter Adjustment Wheel

The small wheel on the left side of the viewfinder is used to dial in optical correction to the viewfinder, so you can see a sharply focused image in the viewfinder window. Just press the Monitor button to activate the viewfinder display, and then turn this little wheel in either direction until the image is at its clearest for your eyesight. In some cases, if you wear glasses, you may be able to dial in enough of an adjustment that you can take your glasses off and still see the image clearly through the viewfinder. (I am a glasses wearer, and this works for me, though I usually just keep my glasses on.)

Display Button

The button marked DISP, directly to the right of the viewfinder, switches among the various displays of information on the camera's LCD or viewfinder, in both shooting and playback modes. In shooting mode, there are three displays available that are called up by successive presses of the Display button.

The display screen that I consider to be the most important, seen in Figure 5-6, shows the live view overlaid with icons for shooting mode, flash mode, shutter speed, aperture, image size and quality, images remaining, and a few other items.

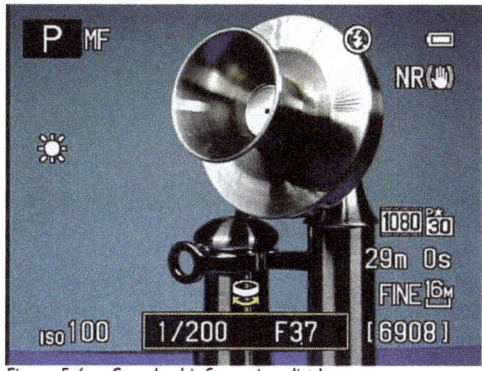

Figure 5-6: Standard information display screen

171

Another press of the Display button produces a similar screen, illustrated in Figure 5-7, which includes the same shooting information with a frame overlaid that shows the area of the image that would be used for shooting a movie.

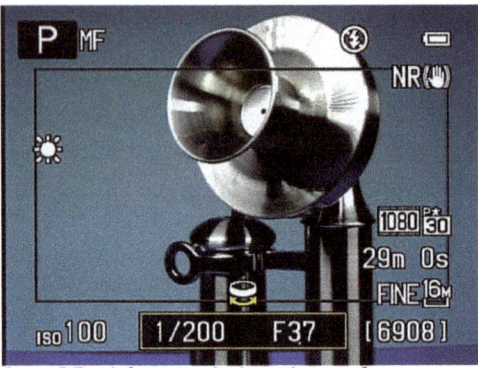
Figure 5-7: Information display with movie frame

Another press of the button produces a view of the image alone, with no information except for a lone icon showing battery status and the GPS reception icon if GPS data recording is turned on through the GPS options menu.

Through the Monitor Settings item on the Setup menu, you can add a histogram and a framing grid to the shooting information display if you want to. The histogram is discussed in Chapter 6, in connection with the histogram that displays in playback mode.

In playback mode, there also are three screens available through presses of the Display button. The first option is photo information, which shows the recorded image overlaid with icons and figures showing the date and time the picture was taken, its identification number, image quality and size, and what image number is being shown, out of how many total images. The battery status icon also is shown. The second view is a detailed display of shooting information, which includes a small version of the image along with a histogram that represents the various brightness values in the image along with details about shutter speed, aperture, exposure compensation,

ISO value, and image number. The third and final view is of the image only, with just the battery status icon added.

Movie Button

The red Movie button, at the top of the camera's back just below the mode dial, has one obvious purpose: to start and stop recording of your videos. Press it in once and release it to start recording; press it again to stop recording. I will discuss your movie recording options in Chapter 8. You also can press this button to cancel standby mode, when the monitor turns off in connection with the camera's power-saving function.

Flash/Charging Lamp

This very small lamp sits just below the Movie button, to the left of a lightning bolt icon. It provides information about the status of the charging of the camera's battery, as well as the status of the built-in flash unit.

When you are charging the camera's battery by connecting the camera to a power outlet, this lamp blinks slowly with a green light throughout the charging process. When charging of the battery is complete, this lamp turns off.

This lamp also indicates the status of the built-in flash unit when that unit is popped up. When you press the shutter release button halfway down, this lamp will light up in solid red if the flash will fire for the next shutter press. If the lamp flashes red, that means that the flash will not fire, because it is still charging. If the lamp does not light up at all, that means that the flash will not fire, because the situation does not call for it to fire (because it is in Auto Flash mode and the light is not dim enough to need flash, for example).

Command Dial

This wheel, sticking out near where your right thumb is likely to grip the camera at the top of the right side of the camera, has several functions. It is used to adjust shutter speed in the

Shutter Priority and Manual exposure modes. In the Program exposure mode, this dial is used to activate the Flexible Program function, which causes the camera to choose an alternative pair of shutter speed and aperture values. If you use the Toggle Av/Tv Selection option on the Setup menu, these functions of the command dial are switched with those of the multi selector dial, so the command dial controls aperture rather than shutter speed, and the command dial no longer controls the Flexible Program feature.

In playback mode, you can turn the command dial to magnify and shrink an image once you have pressed the zoom lever to begin enlarging it.

In addition, when you are navigating in the menu system, the command dial can help you speed your menu adjustments considerably. When you have navigated to a menu option that has a list of possible settings, such as ISO, White Balance, Image Size, and others, instead of having to move to the next screen to make those settings, you can just turn the command dial, and the various settings will appear at the right side of the selection bar on the menu screen. You can spin through the values until you find the one you want, and the setting will be made with no further button-presses needed.

Also, the command dial can be used to adjust values in the on-screen menus after you have pressed one of the direction buttons to bring up a menu on the display. That is, the command dial can be used to adjust exposure compensation after the right direction button has been pressed to put that scale on the display; it can be used to select a focus mode after the down button has been pressed to put the focus mode menu on the display; it can be used to set the mode for the self-timer after the left button is pressed; and it can be used to select a flash mode after the up button is pressed. This dial also can be used to select an item from the pop-up menu that appears on the screen when the Function button is pressed.

One nice feature of the Coolpix P510 is that it puts an icon on the screen representing the command dial when there is a value that can be adjusted by the dial. For example, as discussed in Chapter 3, in Shutter Priority mode, the icon, which looks like a white disk with a yellow arrow underneath it, is positioned above the value for shutter speed. This means that you can turn the command dial to adjust that setting.

Menu Button

The Menu button, to the lower left of the multi selector, is quite straightforward in its basic function. Press it to enter the menu system, and press it once more to exit back to whatever mode the camera was in previously (shooting mode or playback mode). There are several different menus available, depending on what mode the camera is in. The main menu systems are for Shooting, Playback, GPS Options, and Setup, but there also are more specific menus for various shooting modes, including Scene, Special Effects, Night Landscape, Landscape, and others, as well as a separate menu for Movie mode. I discuss the menu systems in Chapters 4, 6, 7, and 8.

Trash Button

To the right of the Menu button is a round button marked with a trash can icon. This is the Delete button, which can also be called the Trash button. Its operation is quite simple; this control has no other function other than to delete images and videos. When the camera is in playback mode, press the Trash button and the camera will display a short menu of choices: Current Image, Erase Selected Images, or All Images, as shown in Figure 5-8.

Use the multi selector dial or the up and down direction buttons to highlight your choice. If you select Current Image and press the OK button, the camera will display one more message, asking you to confirm. You can cancel out of this (or any) deletion message by pressing the Menu button. When you are using the Trash button to delete images in this way, note that, if the image displayed is the key image for a sequence of continuous shots (see discussion of continuous shooting in Chapter 4), choosing Current Image will delete all images in the sequence. (If the images in the sequence are displayed individually, only one image at a time will be deleted.)

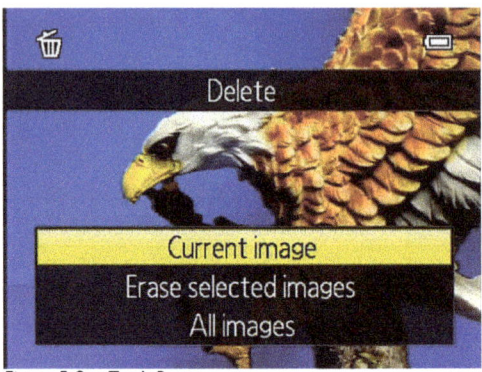

Figure 5-8: Trash Button screen

If you choose Erase Selected Images and press OK, the camera will display an index screen showing thumbnail versions of all recorded images. Navigate through them with the left and right direction buttons or the multi selector dial, and press the up button to mark (or down button to unmark) any image you want to delete. Check marks will appear on images marked for deletion. You can enlarge any of the thumbnails to get a better view of it by turning the zoom lever towards the telephoto position; turn it back the other way to reduce the image back to the thumbnail size. When all selected images have been marked, press the OK button, and the camera will ask you for one final confirmation before deleting the selected images.

If you choose to erase All Images, the camera will delete all images that are not protected using the Protect function, as discussed in Chapter 6.

The Trash button also is used to delete voice memos from images with voice memos attached, as discussed in Chapter 6. In addition, this button can delete movies, as discussed in Chapter 8.

When the camera is in shooting mode, if you press this button, the camera will ask if you want to delete one image. The camera will then display the last image that was recorded, and present a Yes/No choice. If you select Yes, that image will be deleted and the camera will return to shooting mode.

Multi Selector and its Buttons and Dial

The most prominent set of controls on the back of the camera is contained within the perimeter of the multi selector, the circular area with raised edges that function as the four direction buttons. Each of these four buttons also has another purpose designated by an icon on the button. In the center of the multi selector is the OK button, and the round, ridged wheel functions as a rotating dial. I will discuss each of these controls in turn.

Multi Selector Dial

The ridged wheel that surrounds the OK button, known as the multi selector dial, is a very important control. It is easy to operate, because you can easily catch it on your thumbnail or just engage it with the flesh of your thumb and spin it freely. One of its most significant duties is to control the aperture setting when you are shooting in Aperture Priority mode or Manual exposure mode. If you turn on the Toggle Av/Tv option on the Setup menu, then the functions of this dial and the command dial are reversed, and the multi selector dial controls shutter speed for Shutter Priority mode and Manual exposure mode. In addition, if that menu option is activated, the multi selector dial controls the Flexible Program feature, which ordinarily is controlled by the command dial.

In addition, when you are navigating in the menu systems, this dial moves up and down the lists of menu options, and it can be used to highlight an item from the pop-up menu that appears on the screen when the Function button is pressed. When the camera is in playback mode, the dial navigates through your individual images, and it also moves through the screens of images when index screens are displayed.

OK Button

This button in the center of the multi selector is one of the P510's most-used controls. It serves as a selection, confirmation, or "set" button when you choose certain options. For example, whenever you highlight a desired menu option, you press the OK button to confirm and set your selection. Similarly, when you press the focus mode button (down direction button) and then highlight a focus mode on the pop-up menu (autofocus, macro focus, infinity, or manual focus), you press the OK button to confirm that choice. You also can use this button to get access to sub-menus. For example, when you highlight Image Quality on the Shooting menu, you can then press the OK button to bring up the sub-menu with the list of choices: Fine, Normal, and Basic. Then, you can press the OK button again to make the actual selection.

In playback mode, when the first frame of a movie is displayed on the screen, the OK button is used to start the movie playing. The button also is used to select any one of the playback controls that appear at the top of the screen during movie playback. (You use the direction buttons to highlight one of these controls, such as play, stop, or rewind, and then press OK to choose that function.) The button is also used to "open up" a sequence of continuous shots so you can view them individually.

Direction Buttons

Each of the four edges—up, down, left, and right—of the multi selector dial is also a "button" that you can press to get access to a setting or operation. This may not be immediately obvious, and sometimes it can be tricky to press in exactly the right spot, but these four direction buttons are very important to your control of the camera. You use them to navigate through menus and screens for settings, whether moving left and right or up and down.

You also use them in playback mode to move through your images and, when you have enlarged an image using the zoom lever, to scroll around within the magnified image.

Besides these navigational duties, the direction buttons have several miscellaneous functions in connection with various settings. When you are navigating in the menu system, you can use the left direction button to move back one screen in the system. When you are on the main screen of a given menu system (Shooting, Playback, Scene, etc.), pressing the left direction button moves the yellow selection block to the left column of the screen, which contains the icons that identify the currently available menus. For example, when you are on the main screen of the Shooting menu, pressing the left direction button takes the selection block to the column that contains a letter or icon for the Shooting menu, a movie camera icon for the Movie menu, a satellite for the GPS options menu, and a wrench for the Setup menu. You can navigate up and down through these icons to select the icon for the menu you want to use. You can then press the OK button to select that menu.

The right direction button also can be used to move to the sub-menu screens within the menu system. In most cases, you can press either the OK button or the right direction button to move to the sub-menu screen that contains further options for a given menu item.

The up direction button also has a non-obvious extra function. When you are viewing a "sequence" of continuous shots, as discussed in Chapters 4 and 6, pressing the up button returns the camera to normal playback mode, in which you view only the "key" image from the continuous set (assuming the Sequence Display Options setting on the Playback menu is set to show key images rather than individual images from sequences).

Finally, each of the four direction buttons has its own separate identity, as indicated by the icon that appears on each of the buttons, as discussed below.

Up Button: Flash Settings. When the camera is in shooting mode, pressing the top button brings up a small menu showing the options for setting the behavior of the flash unit. (If the flash unit is not popped up, the camera will display a brief message telling you to raise the flash.) Depending on the shooting mode, these options may include Auto, Auto with Red-eye Reduction, Off, Fill Flash, Slow Sync, and Rear-curtain Sync, or possibly just two of those. In some cases, such as when you have selected one of the dedicated Scene modes on the mode dial (Night Landscape, Landscape, or Backlighting), pressing the top button will not bring up any flash menu at all, even if the flash unit is popped up; the camera makes all flash decisions for you in those modes. Once the menu with options has appeared, you need to press the up and down direction buttons or turn the command dial or multi selector dial to highlight your choice, and press the OK button to select it.

Right Button: Exposure Compensation. When not acting as the right direction button, this control serves as the exposure compensation button. As I discussed in Chapter 2, you press this button to bring up an EV scale on the screen, and then press the up and down buttons on the multi selector or turn the command dial or multi selector dial to adjust the value. You do not need to press the OK button to select the value; just let the pop-up menu disappear and the setting will take effect.

Down Button: Focus Mode. In shooting mode, press this button to bring up the small menu of options for the camera's focus mode: autofocus, macro focus, infinity, and manual focus. After you press the down direction button, use the up and down buttons or turn the multi selector dial or the command dial to navigate to the icon for your desired mode, then press the OK button to confirm. You have to move quickly, because the menu disappears after a few seconds.

Left Button: Self-timer; Smile Timer; Pet Portrait Release. This final button is labeled with an icon showing the dial of a timer. Press this button in shooting mode and the camera displays a small menu of the available choices for setting the self-timer.

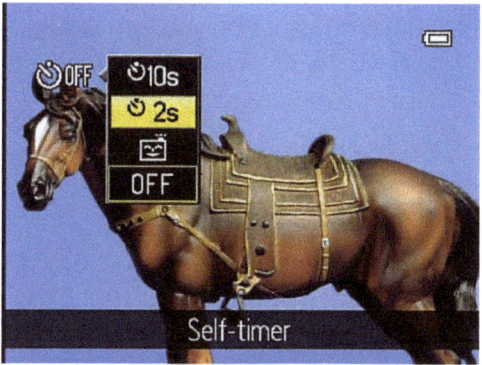

Figure 5-9: Self-timer screen

Those choices may include 10 seconds, 2 seconds, Smile Timer, and Off, or, in some cases, such as with most Scene modes and all Special Effects settings, all of these except the Smile Timer. If you set a delay of either 10 seconds or 2 seconds, the camera will delay the specified amount of time before taking the picture, after you press the shutter button. Choose 10 seconds if you need a substantial delay so you can get into a group picture after pressing the shutter button; choose 2 seconds if you just need to avoid touching the camera during the exposure, to minimize the camera shake that can accompany a shutter press. You might need to use the 2-second delay when you're taking extreme close-ups, because any camera motion could be magnified by the closeness to the subject. Or, the 2-second delay could help when you're shooting in a dim light and a slow shutter speed is needed, because any camera motion during the long exposure could blur the image.

Unfortunately, with the Coolpix P510 you cannot use continuous shooting in conjunction with the self-timer, so you are limited to having the camera take just one shot after the self-timer delay period runs out. If you need another shot, you will have to press the shutter button again. However, the self-timer does function with movie recording, so you can turn on a delay with the self-timer, and then press the red Movie button to start a movie recording after the specified delay.

When the camera is set to the Auto, Program, Aperture Priority, Shutter Priority, or Manual exposure mode, or to the Portrait or Night Portrait Scene setting, the Smile Timer is added to the options on the self-timer menu.

The Smile Timer is a special feature that fires the shutter automatically when the camera detects a smile. This function works together with the camera's face detection system, which is automatically turned on when the Smile Timer is selected.

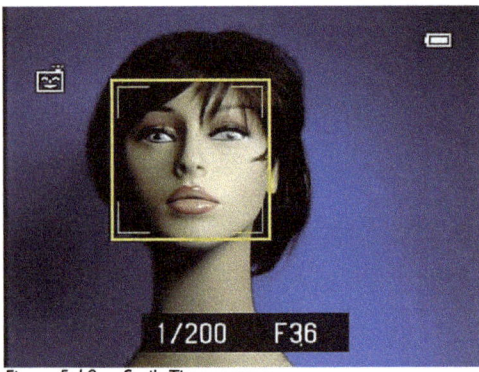

Figure 5-10: Smile Timer screen

When this option is turned on, whenever the camera detects faces, it focuses on the face closest to the center of the image and places a yellow double border around that face, as shown in Figure 5-10; the self-timer lamp starts blinking to indicate that a face has been detected. The shutter will be triggered automatically if the face inside the double border smiles. Once that happens, the lamp will blink rapidly to indicate that a picture of a smile has been taken.

This feature is really more of a novelty than a particularly useful function, in my opinion, though it may be of use in some situations, such as when you need to encourage a child to smile by telling him or her that the smile will automatically trigger the camera. Also, the Smile Timer is unique because it acts as a sort of remote control for the camera; each time the subject smiles, the camera is triggered again. So, if you are taking self-portraits, you can stand in front of your P510 on its tripod, and control the camera's operation with your smile as it takes repeated portraits.

In the Pet Portrait setting in Scene mode, the left button has a special function of turning on or off the Pet Portrait Auto Release function. As was discussed in Chapter 3, when that feature is turned on, the shutter is automatically triggered when the camera detects the face of a cat or dog. In that situation, neither the self-timer nor the Smile Timer is available.

Finally, there are a few other controls that are located in their own particular areas, described below.

USB and HDMI Ports

These small openings under a little door on the right side of the camera, shown in Figure 5-11, have several functions.

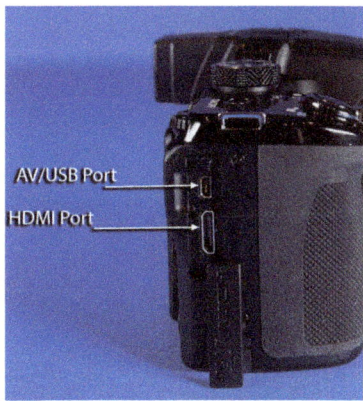

Figure 5-11: Ports on side of camera

The smaller one at the top, the USB port, is where you plug in the charging cable when you charge the battery inside the camera. It also is where you connect the camera to a computer to import photos using the supplied USB cable, and where you connect the camera to a non-HDTV set to view photos or videos using the supplied audio-video cable (the one with red, white, and yellow plugs at one end).

The larger port is where you plug in an HDMI cable (which you need to purchase as a separate option) to view photos or videos on an HDTV set. The end going into this port is a mini-HDMI connector; the end going to the HDTV should be a standard HDMI connector. These cables are available through Amazon. com, at Radio Shack, on eBay, and elsewhere.

Tilting LCD Screen

The last item to be discussed in this chapter is not really a "control," but it does allow some physical adjustment, so I will discuss it here. This is the tilting, or articulated, LCD display on the back of the camera. This screen, even without its tilting ability, is a notable feature of the camera. It has a diagonal span of 3 inches (7.5 cm), and provides a resolution of 921,000 dots, giving a very clear and sharp view of your images before and after you capture them.

With its ability to move up and down vertically, the monitor gives you a considerable amount of added flexibility for your shooting.

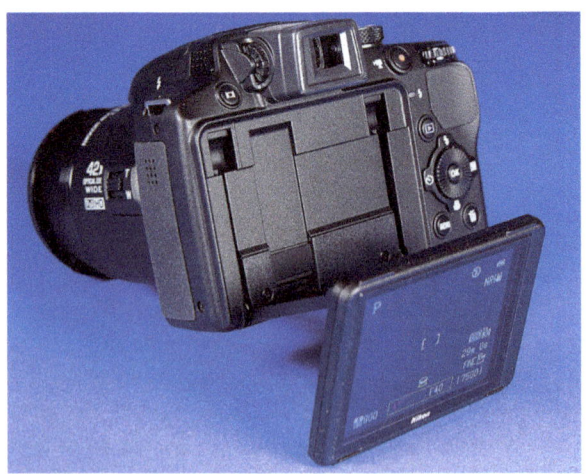

Figure 5-12:   LCD screen set for overhead shots

CHAPTER 5: OTHER CONTROLS

If, as shown in Figure 5-12, you pull it back and fold the screen underneath the camera so it aims downward, you can hold the camera high above your head and view the scene as if you were an arm's-length taller, or were standing on a small ladder. If you attach the camera to a monopod or other support and hold it up in the air, you can extend the camera's vertical height even further and still view the LCD screen quite well. You can activate the self-timer before raising the camera up in the air to take the photo.

On the other hand, if you need to take images from a very low vantage point, near ground level, you can fold the screen so it tilts upward towards your eye, as shown in Figure 5-13, and hold the camera down as far as you need to get a mole's-eye view of the world.

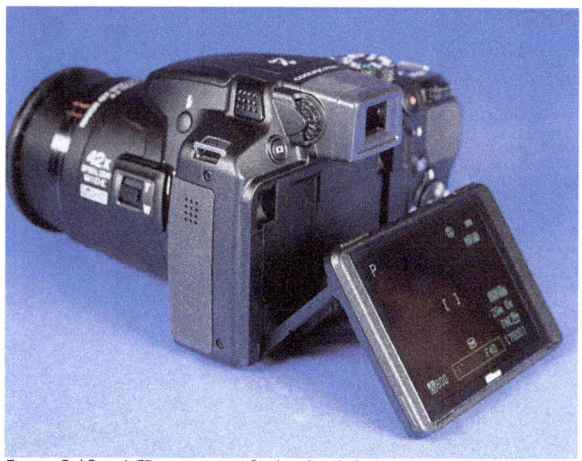

Figure 5-13: LCD screen set for low-level shots

Also, as I discuss further in Chapter 9, the tilting display can be quite useful for street photography, because it lets you fold the screen upward so you can look down at the camera while taking long-zoom photos of people on the streets without drawing undue attention to yourself.

185

Chapter 6: Playback

If you're like me, you take the images you've created and import them into your computer, where you manipulate them with software, then post them on the web, print them out, e-mail them, or do whatever else the occasion calls for. In other words, I don't spend a lot of time viewing my pictures in the camera. But that doesn't mean it's not a good thing to know about. Depending on your needs, there may be plenty of times when you take a picture or record a movie and then need to examine it closely in the camera. Also, the camera can serve as a viewing device like an iPod or other gadget that is designed, at least in part, for storing and viewing photos. So it's worth taking a good look at the various playback functions of the Coolpix P510.

Normal Playback

Let's start with a brief rundown of the basic playback techniques. First, you should be aware that, when you take a new photo, your image stays on the screen for a couple of seconds for review. If your major concern with viewing images in the camera is to check them right after they are taken, this feature is somewhat helpful, but the review time is very brief, and there is no way to adjust its duration. You can turn this feature off using the Monitor Settings item on the Setup menu.

If you want to control how your images are viewed, you need to work with the settings that are available in playback mode.

For plain vanilla review of images in playback mode, the process is simple. Press the Playback button, marked by a right-facing triangle, to the right of the LCD screen on the camera's back. Once you press that button, the camera is in playback mode, and you will see the most recent image saved to the memory card that is in the camera (or, if no card is inserted, to the internal memory). To move back through older images, press either the left direction button or the up direction button or turn the multi selector dial (the dial that surrounds the OK button on the camera's back) to the left. To move through the increasingly more recent images, use the right direction button or the down direction button, or turn the multi selector dial to the right. To scroll through your images rapidly, hold down the left or right (or up or down) direction button.

Index View and Enlarging Images

In playback mode, you can press the zoom lever on top of the camera to view an index screen of your images or to enlarge a single image. When you are viewing an image, press the zoom lever once to the left (towards the W setting), and you will see a screen showing four images, one of which is outlined by a yellow frame, as shown in Figure 6-1.

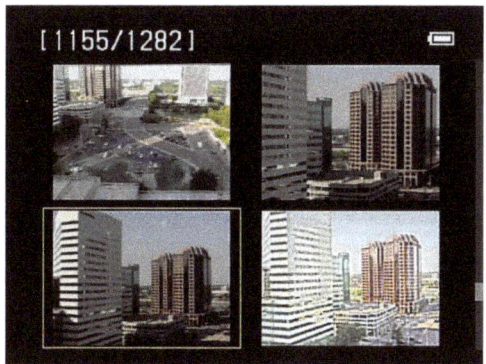

Figure 6-1: Playback index screen

You can then press the OK button to bring up the outlined image as the single image on the screen, or you can move through your images with the 4-image index screen by pressing the four direction buttons or by turning the multi selector dial.

If you press the zoom lever to the W mark once more, the camera will display an index screen of 9 images; another press brings 16 images; and a last press brings a 72-image index screen (assuming in each case that you have that many images; if not, there will be blank spaces on the screen). You can maneuver through any of these screens to select a single image for viewing. If you want to reduce the number of images per screen, just press the zoom lever to the right (towards the T position) repeatedly to reverse the progression of index screens.

Once you are again viewing a single image, another press of the zoom lever to the right enlarges that image, as seen in Figure 6-2. (This function does not work if the image is being displayed in the detailed display mode, with the histogram.)

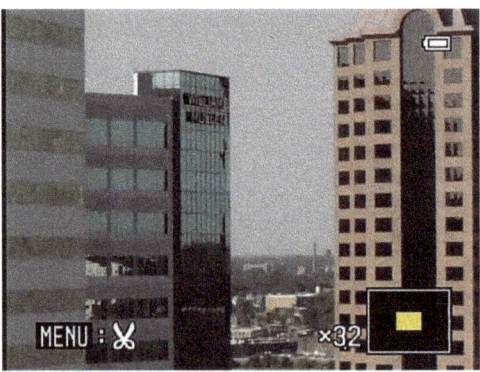

Figure 6-2: Playback - enlarged image

You will see a display in the lower right corner showing an inset yellow block that represents the portion of the image that is now filling the screen in enlarged view. (If you don't see this block, press the Display button to select the information display.) If you press the zoom lever to the right repeatedly, the image will be enlarged up to a maximum of about 10 times normal. While the image is magnified, you can scroll around within it using the four direction buttons; you will see the inset yellow block move around within the white rectangle that represents the whole image. To reduce the image size again, just press the zoom lever to the left as many times as necessary. You can also increase or decrease the zoom level by turning the command dial right or left.

While the image is displayed in an enlarged view, you will see the word MENU in the lower left corner of the screen next to a scissors icon. When you see that display, you can press the Menu button to save the visible, enlarged portion of the image as a separate file. This is actually a rather neat capability, which gives you a rough-and-ready way to edit your images in the camera. So, if you want to crop a group photo to save just the face of a single person, you can enlarge the image and scroll it around until just that face is visible, and then press the Menu button to save a separate file with that face as the only subject. This process is no match for editing with a computer, but it could come in very handy in a pinch, when no computer is available and you need a particular part of an image for a special purpose, such as a business presentation.

Calendar View

Once you have moved the zoom lever to the left repeatedly so the screen displays 72 thumbnail images, one more press of the lever to the left will put the camera into calendar view, as shown in Figure 6-3, in which the screen shows a calendar for the current month, with yellow lines under each date on which images were taken. It may take quite a while for the calendar screen to appear, if you have hundreds of images on your memory card. I just tried this with 1080 images on my memory card, and it took almost 30 seconds for the calendar screen to appear.

You can scroll through the dates using the 4 direction buttons or the multi selector dial. When you reach the date you want, press OK to begin displaying the images from that date.

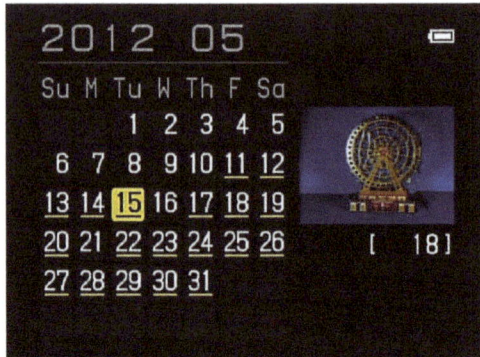

Figure 6-3: Playback calendar screen

Different Playback Screens

When you are viewing an image in playback mode, pressing the Display button repeatedly cycles through the three different screens that are available: the full image with no added information except battery status; the full image with basic information, including date and time it was taken, file name, image number, image size and quality (Figure 6-4); and a reduced-size image accompanied by detailed recording information, including aperture, shutter speed, ISO, recording mode, exposure compensation, and other data, plus a histogram (Figure 6-5).

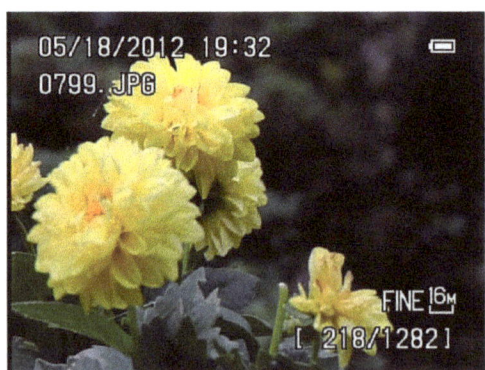

Figure 6-4: Playback - standard information screen

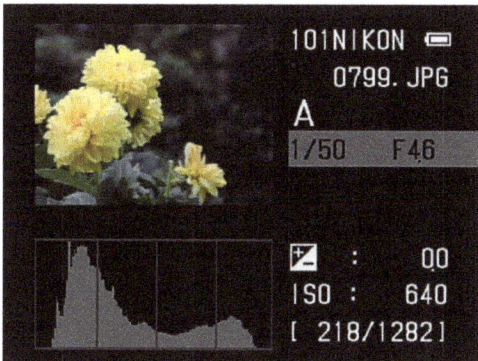

Figure 6-5: Playback - detailed information screen

(The recording mode information is rudimentary, and will display the P icon for Program even if you have used a Scene or Special Effects mode setting. If you want to see better information about what recording mode was used, you can use the ViewNX 2 software that comes with the camera.)

This more detailed display screen, as noted above, includes a histogram. The histogram is a graph, or chart, representing the distribution of dark and bright areas in the image that is being displayed on the screen. The darkest blacks are represented by vertical bars on the left, and the brightest whites by vertical bars on the right, with continuous gradations in between.

If you have a histogram in which the pattern looks like a tall ski slope coming from the left of the screen down to ground level in the middle of the screen, that means there is an excessive amount of black and dark areas (high points on the left side of the histogram), and very few bright and white areas (no high points on the right). A ski slope moving from the middle of the screen up to the top of the right side of the screen would mean just the opposite—too many bright and white areas.

A histogram that is "just right" would be one that starts low on the left, gradually rises to a medium peak in the middle of the screen, then moves gradually back down to ground level at the right. That pattern indicates a good balance of whites, blacks, and medium tones. The three illustrations included here in Figures 6-6 through 6-8 show histograms for shots of the same scene that are underexposed, overexposed, and properly exposed.

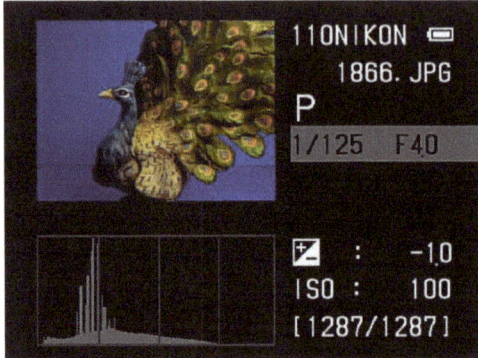

Figure 6-6: Histogram - underexposure

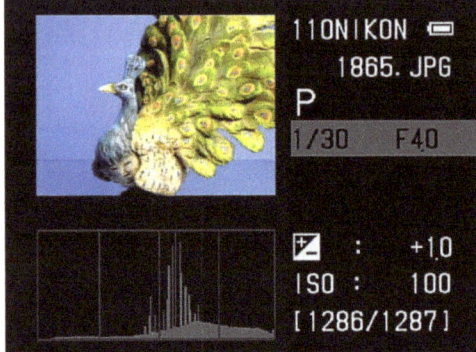

Figure 6-7: Histogram - overexposure

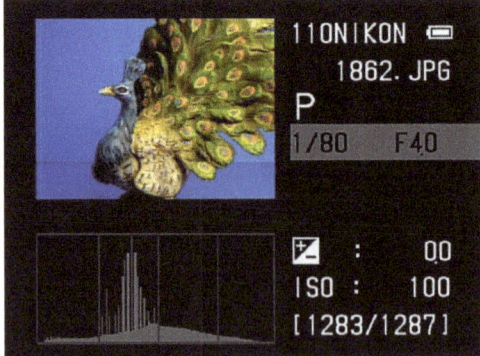

Figure 6-8: Histogram - normal exposure

The histogram is an approximation, and should not be relied on too heavily. It may be useful to give you some feedback as to how evenly exposed your image is likely to be.

Viewing Shots Taken in a Sequence

When you take photos with the Coolpix P510 in certain shooting modes or with certain functions, the images become part of what Nikon calls a "sequence." When you enter playback mode to view those images, you ordinarily will see only the "key" image of the sequence, usually the first one of the group that was taken. To see the rest of the images in the sequence, you have to take other steps. I'll discuss this process in some detail, because it can be a bit confusing at first.

Let's start with an example, which will make it easier to illustrate the way the P510 handles sequences of still photos. Suppose you have placed the camera in Program mode by turning the mode dial to P, and then selected continuous high-speed shooting by selecting Continuous H from the Continuous item on the Shooting menu. We'll say you have selected Fine for the image quality and the maximum image size, 4608 X 3456 pixels, from the Shooting menu. Now, when you aim the camera at your subject and hold down the shutter button for a second or two, you will hear the sounds of the camera operating. The LCD display (or viewfinder) will display one of the captured images for a few seconds and then revert to the view of the live image.

When the camera has settled back to the live view, you can press the Playback button to start viewing your images. If everything worked as expected, there should be five images to view, because that is the maximum number of shots the camera can take using the Continuous H setting. However, when you press the Playback button, you will see only one image from this sequence. If you press any of the direction buttons or turn the multi selector dial, you will move to an entirely different image, assuming one exists; you will not see the other 4 images from this sequence.

Where did those other images go? Well, look at the display on the screen, as shown in Figure 6-9, which has a few unusual aspects.

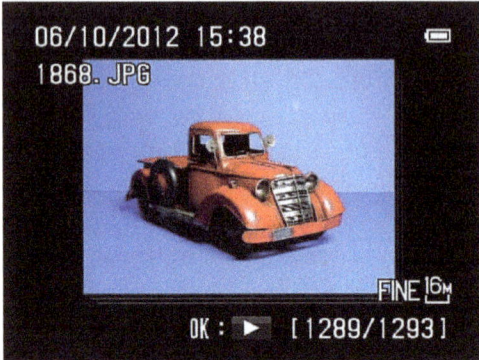

Figure 6-9: Playback display of key image

For one thing, if you press the Display button, the basic information for the image will appear or disappear, but you cannot produce the detailed display with the histogram, because you are viewing the "key" image of a sequence rather than an individual picture. For another thing, you will see the notation OK at the bottom of the screen with a triangle, indicating the Play function, to its right. What this notation means is that, in order to view the other images in this sequence, you need to press the OK button.

So, go ahead and press the OK button. You will see the same image as before, but with a different appearance, as shown in Figure 6-10. Now, pressing the Display button will cycle through the 3 possible views of the image, including the histogram view, because you are viewing this photo as an individual image, rather than as the key image.

You will no longer see the OK notation; instead, you will see a short yellow bar at the lower left, and the numbers 1/5 at the lower right. The yellow bar will progress across the bottom of the screen as you navigate through the 5 images in this sequence using the left and right (but not up and down) direction buttons or the multi selector dial, and the numbers will increase up to 5/5 as you move to the most recent images in the sequence.

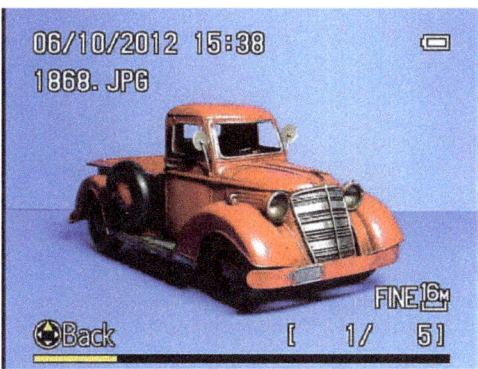

Figure 6-10: Individual image from continuous sequence

You can magnify each individual image by moving the zoom lever towards the T position, but (naturally enough) you cannot call up an index screen by pressing the zoom lever in the other direction, because only the images in the single sequence are available for viewing at this point.

Once you have "entered" the sequence by pressing OK, you will be "stuck" inside it—you can keep navigating through the images, but you will continue to navigate through the same 5 images, over and over, until you exit from the sequence and go back to viewing the key image. There is a prompt on the screen that tells you how to do this: an icon highlighting the up button, with the notation Back, meaning you have to press the up direction button to go back to the key image. That is, when you want to stop viewing these individual images and return to the key image, so you can navigate through the rest of the images on your memory card, you have to press the up button—the one marked with a lightning bolt, which controls flash functions in shooting mode.

If you would rather not have the camera display your continuous-mode shots in sequences, but would prefer to have them displayed as individual shots at all times, you can switch to that option using the Sequence Display Options item on the

Playback menu, as discussed later in this chapter. However, if you take many sequences using a feature such as Continuous H: 120 fps, which takes 60 shots at a time, you may appreciate the ability to display just the key frame from the sequence when you browse through your images in Playback mode.

The Playback Menu

Now it's time to discuss the numerous options that are available through the Playback menu.

As you recall, to get access to this menu, the camera must be in playback mode, entered by pressing the Playback button (right-facing triangle). Then press the Menu button and, if necessary, move the yellow block on the screen to the left column and navigate to the triangle icon to select the Playback menu.

Then move the yellow block back to the right to highlight the various entries in the menu, whose first screen is shown in Figure 6-11. I'll go through the options on the Playback menu one by one.

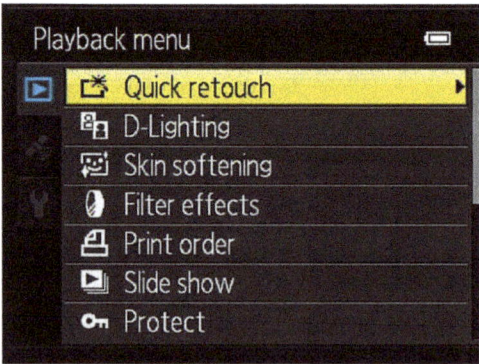

Figure 6-11: Playback menu

Quick Retouch

The Quick Retouch option gives you a way to add "punch" to your recorded images with in-camera processing. You can apply this enhancement to any individual image. If the image you want to enhance is displayed as part of a sequence, you have to use the technique described earlier (pressing the OK button) to display the individual images from the sequence. When the image you have selected is displayed, press the Menu button and choose Quick Retouch. You can then use the up and down direction buttons or the multi selector dial to choose the desired amount of alteration—Low, Normal, or High, as shown in Figure 6-12.

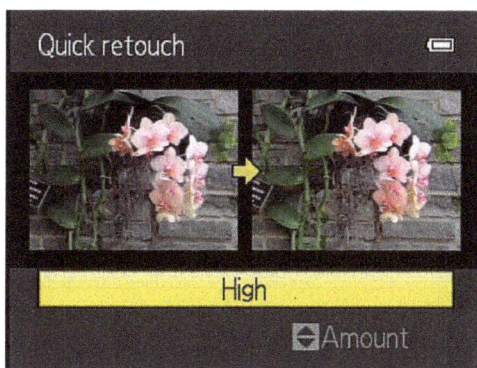

Figure 6-12: Quick Retouch menu option

As you change the amount, you will see a preview of the finished product in a thumbnail on the right of the screen, and the original on the left, for comparison. When you have selected the amount of change, press the OK button to confirm, and a new image will be saved with the retouched appearance and a new file number. It will have the Quick Retouch icon at the lower left of the image.

You cannot make any choices other than the level of the retouching. When it applies this processing, the camera increases the image's contrast (amount of difference between light and dark areas) and saturation (intensity of the colors).

This is one of those features that I don't find too much use for myself, because I prefer to do my processing with computer software. But there could be situations in which you take images at a party and want to display them on a TV set during the party. You could use this function to brighten up some muddy images and make them livelier for the audience.

D-Lighting

The D-Lighting option works in exactly the same way as the Quick Retouch feature. Select an image that is being displayed individually (not as the key frame of a sequence), press the Menu button, select D-Lighting, press the OK button or the right button to get to the next screen, and then choose Low, Normal, or High for the degree of enhancement, as shown in Figure 6-13.

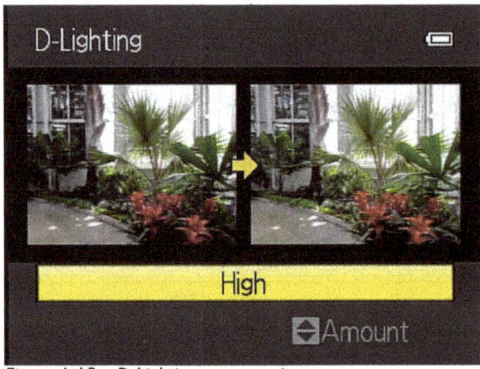

Figure 6-13: D-Lighting menu option

In this case, the camera will attempt to add details in both the shadow and highlight areas, as it does when you use the Active D-Lighting option in shooting mode. (That option was discussed in Chapter 4.)

Skin Softening

This next entry on the Playback menu presents you with another opportunity to modify your already-recorded images. In this case, you can add a softening effect to the areas in an image that the camera considers to be human faces. As with the previous two menu options, you select the image, press the Menu button, and then select how strong the effect should be. One difference with this feature from the other ones is that the camera will decide whether or not there are any faces in the image you have selected. If it does not detect any, it will display an error message that the image cannot be modified, and return you to the menu without carrying out any processing. If it does detect a face, it will take you to another screen with a larger view for a preview of the effect; you can then press OK to save the processed image, or press Menu to go back and revise your setting.

Filter Effects

The Filter Effects menu selection has five sub-options, shown in Figure 6-14, giving you a considerable variety of additional operations the camera can perform to create copies of your images with altered aspects. Some of these are similar to the settings available in the Special Effects shooting mode.

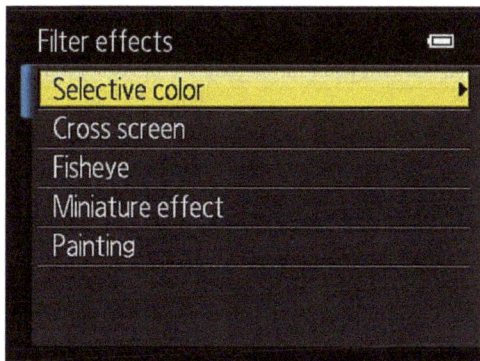

Figure 6-14: Filter Effects menu option

First on the list is the Selective Color effect, similar to the Special Effects mode setting of that name, discussed in Chapter 3. As you can see in Figure 6-15, when you display an image on the screen, the camera places a vertical spectrum of colors to the left of the image, with a pointer that you can move up and down the scale using the multi selector dial or the up and down buttons. As you move the pointer next to a color on the scale, the image changes to preserve only the portions that are approximately that color. If no parts of the image are that color, the image turns completely black-and-white. If you use this effect carefully, you can take an image with one area of bright color, remove all other colors using this effect, and end up with a photo that dramatically highlights the single colored object or area that remains, surrounded by a monochrome environment.

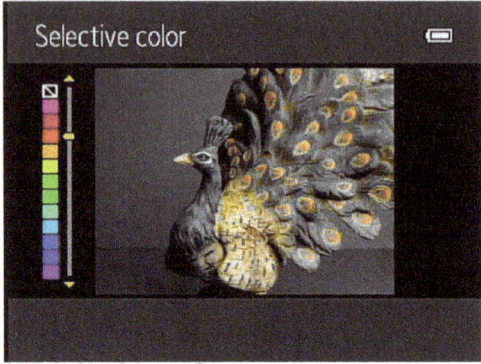

Figure 6-15: Selective Color menu option

The second choice on this menu is Cross Screen, illustrated in Figure 6-16. With this option, there are no adjustments to make; you either save a copy of the image using this processing feature, or you cancel out of the selection. If you choose to go ahead, the camera makes a copy of your selected image that has streaks of light radiating outward from bright objects such as lights. If there are no bright objects of that nature in the image, this option will not produce any changes at all, though the camera will still produce the new image. The image here shows the final product, after the camera saved a new copy.

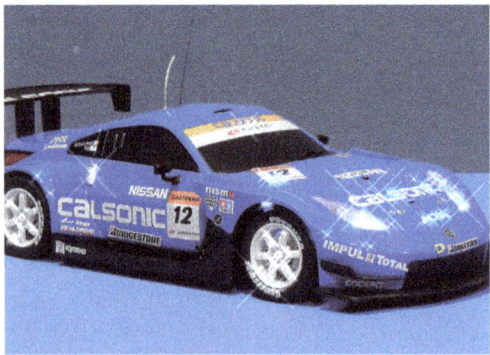

Figure 6-16: Cross Screen example

Next down on the list of Filter Effects is the Fisheye effect. You have probably seen photographs taken with a fisheye lens, a super wide-angle lens that greatly distorts the image, making it look spherical as if seen through a fishbowl. With this option, the camera applies processing that simulates this effect. Figure 6-17 is an example of this effect, again showing the final product after the camera produced its new image.

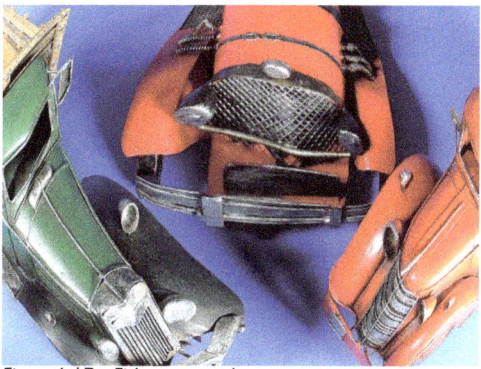

Figure 6-17: Fisheye example

The result of using this effect will not look attractive unless you choose your subject wisely. It can be appealing or entertaining to distort a person's face or a building, perhaps; it generally works best with a single, clearly identifiable subject. If you use the Fisheye effect on a busy or cluttered scene, it may be difficult to make out the subject at all, because of the distortion.

The next menu option is called Miniature Effect. When you apply this effect to an image, the camera adds blurring at the sides, to simulate the appearance of a photograph of a tabletop model or miniature. Such images often appear blurred at the edges, either because of the shallow depth of field of these close-up photos, or because of the use of a tilt-and-shift lens, which causes blurring at the edges. This is a rather odd and specialized effect, but I have seen it show up on television commercials and elsewhere, so it evidently is becoming increasingly popular. Here, again, you need to choose an appropriate subject. I have found that you are best off selecting something like a street scene or a house, which might actually be reproduced in a tabletop model. For example, if you are able to get a high vantage point above a road intersection, you may be able to get a very effective photo of the traffic at the intersection, and then apply this processing to make it look as if you had photographed a high-quality mock-up of an intersection with model cars. This was the approach I took for Figure 6-18.

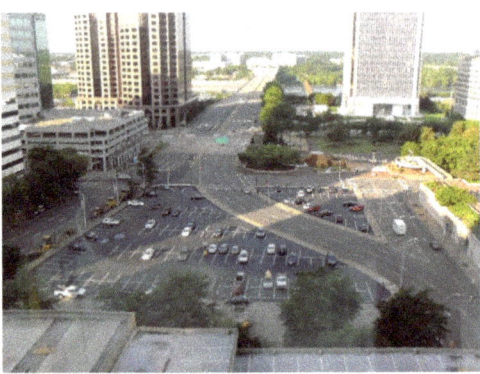

Figure 6-18: Miniature Effect example

The final option on the Filter Effects menu, Painting, is similar to the item of the same name in the Special Effects shooting mode, as discussed and illustrated in Chapter 3. It produces an image that is usually altered quite dramatically using the posterization process.

Print Order

If you want to select multiple photographs before sending them to the printer, use the DPOF (Digital Print Order Format) function, which is built into the camera. The DPOF system lets you mark various images on your memory card to be added to a print list, which can then be sent to your own printer. Or, you can take the memory card to a commercial printer to print out the selected images.

To add images to the DPOF print list, select the Print Order option from the Playback menu, then choose the Select Images option from the next screen, and the camera will display thumbnail versions of your images in groups of 12 per screen.

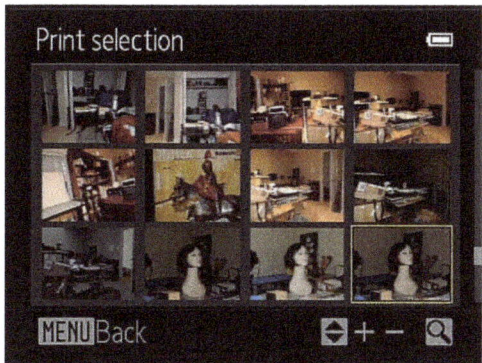

Figure 6-19: Print Selection menu screen

Use the multi selector dial or the left and right direction buttons to move through the images. When an image you want to have printed is highlighted with a yellow frame, press the up direction button to mark it for printing; press it repeatedly to increase the number of copies up to nine. Press the down button to decrease the number of copies or to unmark the image. You can then keep browsing through your images and adding (or subtracting) them from the print list. If you want to see larger thumbnails, press the zoom lever towards the T position to produce a larger view of each image.

When you have finished selecting images to be printed, press the OK button to confirm your choices and exit from the selection screen. On the next screen, you can navigate to boxes for Date and Info to specify whether the printed images will include the date and shooting information. Then highlight the Done message on that screen and press the OK button. You can take the memory card to a service that prints photos using the DPOF system, or you can connect the camera to a PictBridge compatible printer to print the selected images.

Slide Show

Like most modern digital cameras, the Coolpix P510 has a capability for displaying the images on your memory card (or in the camera's internal memory) in a slide show that plays back on the camera's display or on a connected TV or HDTV. The P510 does not offer elaborate options such as music or a variety of transitions; your pictures are played back with straight cuts between them, and in silence. The only choices you can make from the Slide Show menu option, shown in Figure 6-20, are the length of time between images and whether the show should repeat in a loop. (The loop is not endless; the show will repeat for a maximum of 30 minutes.)

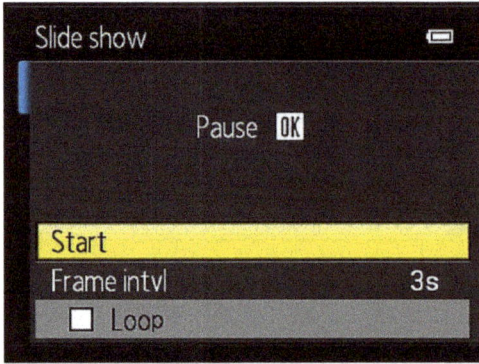

Figure 6-20: Slide Show menu option

To start a slide show, go to the Playback menu and choose Slide Show. You can then navigate to the option for Frame Intvl and select 2, 3, 5, or 10 seconds for the time between images; next, press the left direction button to go back to the previous screen, and press the OK button while the Loop option is highlighted, if you want the show to repeat. After selecting these options, highlight the Start option and press OK to start the show. To pause the show while it is running, press OK again. To restart the show, highlight the playback triangle that appears on the screen and press the OK button. To stop the show, highlight the square "stop" icon and press the OK button. You also can stop the show at any time by pressing the Playback button. To skip forward or backward to the next image, you can press the left or right direction button at any time; hold either of those buttons down to move more rapidly through the images.

Note that there is no way to select the images that will be played; all images on the memory card (or in the internal memory) will be played. For movies, only the first frame will be played.

Protect

With the Protect feature, you can "lock" selected images so they cannot be erased with the normal erase functions using the Trash button. However, if you format the memory card using the Format command, all data will be erased, including protected images.

To protect images, after selecting this menu option, navigate through your images and use the up and down direction buttons to mark or unmark any image that you want to protect.

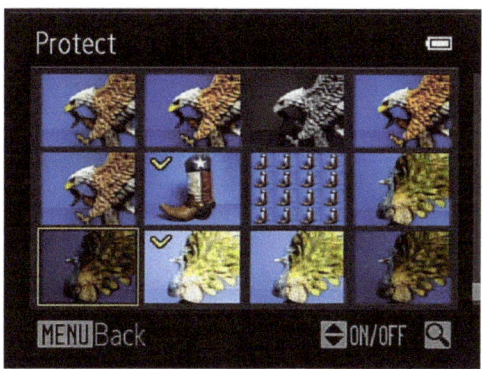

Figure 6-21: Protect selection screen

Press the up button to mark an image or the down button to unmark it. As with the Print Order function, you can use the zoom lever to enlarge an image before deciding whether to apply protection to it. When you have marked all images as you want them, press the OK button to apply the protection. An image that is protected will have a key icon in the upper right corner below the battery icon, as shown in Figure 6-22.

That icon will be visible when the image is viewed with the basic information screen; the icon will not appear in the image-only view or in the detailed view with the histogram.

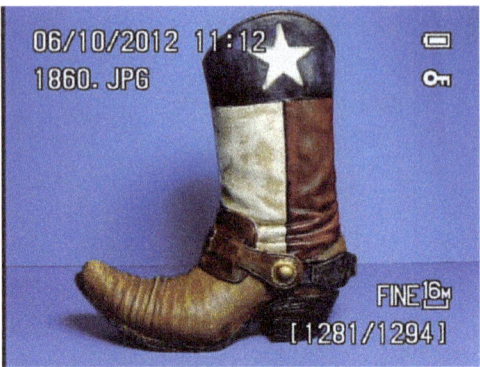

Figure 6-22: Protected image with key icon in upper right

Rotate Image

Using this option, as shown in Figure 6-23, you can rotate your still photos 90 degrees clockwise or counter-clockwise. You cannot rotate the key image of a sequence when it is displayed in sequence mode; you have to display the pictures from the sequence individually in order to rotate them.

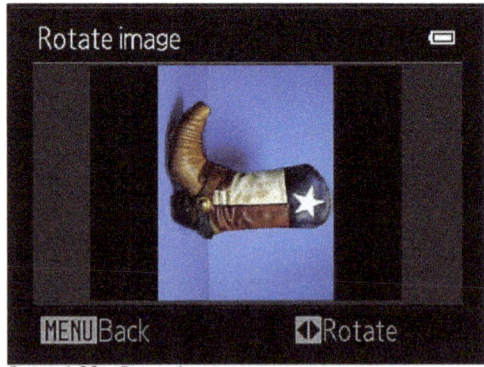

Figure 6-23: Rotate Image menu option

After you select the Rotate Image option from the Playback menu, the camera displays the Select Image screen. Navigate with the multi selector dial or the left and right direction buttons until you have highlighted with a yellow frame the image

CHAPTER 6: PLAYBACK

you want to rotate, then press the OK button to select it.

On the resulting screen, you will be prompted to use the left or right button to rotate the image counter-clockwise or clockwise. (You can also do the rotation using the multi selector dial.) Press OK when it is rotated to the orientation you wish, then press the Menu button to exit from the Rotate screen.

Small Picture

This option provides you with another way to do a rudimentary form of in-camera editing. This feature can be quite useful. It allows you to take any of your saved images and create a new version in a small file size that is suitable for sending by e-mail or posting on the internet. This function could come in handy if you need to take a quick photo and then e-mail it to a friend or colleague. If you don't have software available on your computer to edit the image down to a smaller size, you can let the camera take over this task. Of course, you could take the image in the small size to begin with, but you might want to have a higher-resolution version available for later editing or printing, and be able to create a small version for e-mailing after you have already recorded the original version.

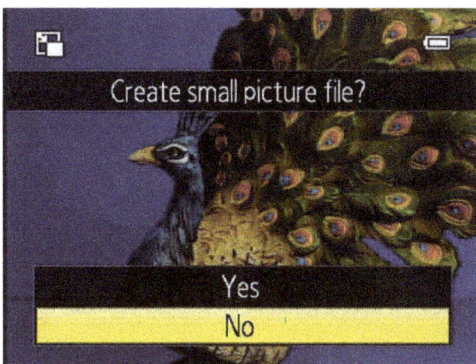

Figure 6-24: Small Picture menu option

To use this feature, you first have to navigate to the image you want to alter. Once it is displayed, in either full-frame or thumbnail view, press the Menu button, then select the Small

207

Picture option as shown in Figure 6-24. On the next screen, you can choose from 3 options: 640 X 480 pixels, 320 X 240 pixels, or 160 X 120 pixels. Each of these sizes represents a low-resolution image, well under 1 megapixel in size. If you confirm the operation, the camera will make a copy of the selected image at your chosen size, and copy it to the end of the images on the memory card (or in internal memory). The image will be displayed in the camera with a large, black border area around the image itself, to signify that this is a "Small Picture" copy. This border does not become part of the actual image; it displays only in the camera.

Voice Memo

This option gives you the ability to record a memo of up to 20 seconds with any picture that is stored on your memory card; the image must have been taken with the Coolpix P510, not with another camera. When the image is displayed on the screen, press the Menu button, select the Voice Memo option, and press the OK button or the right direction button to get to the voice memo recording screen, shown in Figure 6-25.

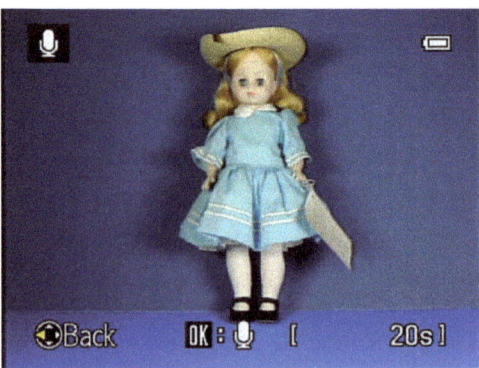

Figure 6-25: Voice Memo recording screen

You will see a microphone icon in the upper left corner and another one in the bottom center of the screen, with the word OK next to it. When you're ready to record, press and hold the OK button and talk into the microphone, which is on top of the viewfinder housing. The recording will stop when you release the button, or after 20 seconds, whichever comes first. Make sure you actually hold the button down; if you just press and release it, nothing will be recorded.

To play back a voice memo, display an image that has a voice file attached; the image will have a musical note icon in the upper left, to the right of the file name. When the image is displayed, press the Menu button and select the Voice Memo option. Press OK or the right button, and then press OK on the next screen to play the audio file. You can adjust the volume using the zoom lever on top of the camera.

To delete a voice memo, from the Voice Memo playback screen, press the Trash button, then press OK to confirm when prompted by the camera. You also can delete the voice memo by deleting the image that has the memo attached.

Copy

The Copy option lets you copy your images from the camera's internal memory to the currently installed memory card, or from the memory card to the internal memory. When you choose this menu option, shown in Figure 6-26, the camera first displays a screen with these two choices, Camera to Card and Card to Camera.

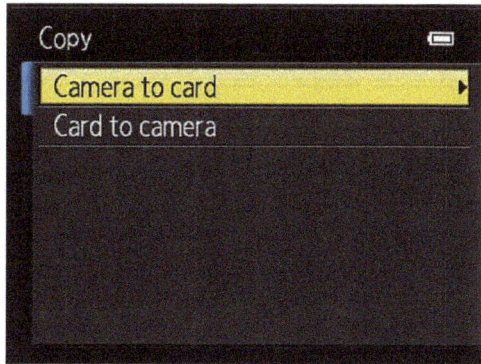
Figure 6-26: Copy menu option

If there are no images available to be copied in one or the other of these locations, that option will be grayed out and unavailable for selection. For example, if no images are currently stored in the camera's internal memory, the Camera to Card option will be grayed out.

Highlight one of those options and press OK or the right button to move to the next screen. The camera will then give you the choice of copying all your images or just selected ones. If you choose the latter, the camera will take you to the familiar image selection screen. There, you can mark (or unmark) each image to be copied using the up (or down) direction button. Then press OK, and the camera will ask you once more to confirm the operation. If you choose to copy all images or a large volume of images from a memory card to the internal memory, they will not all fit, and the operation will terminate with an error message.

If you regularly copy your images to a computer, you probably won't have much need for this option, but, like many of the options on the Playback menu, it can serve as a backup procedure when a computer is not available. Also, if you have taken a few images with the internal memory, it can be quite convenient to copy them to a memory card so you can save them, and then format the internal memory for future use.

Copying from an SD card to the internal memory is not likely to be a function you need often, but it could be useful if you're at an event with another photographer who got some great shots with another camera (even if it's not a P510) that you need copies of. You could copy several shots from his or her SD card to your internal memory to take home with you.

Black Border

This menu item provides yet another way the Coolpix P510 lets you perform some degree of editing of your images inside the camera. In this case, the menu option lets you create a new copy of an image with a black border around it. To use this feature, you first have to select the image you want to copy and display it, either in full-screen or thumbnail mode. Then select this menu option, and, when prompted, choose from a thin, medium, or broad border, as shown in Figure 6-27.

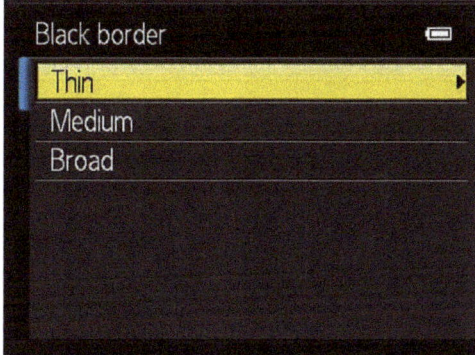

Figure 6-27: Black Border menu option

The camera will ask you to confirm your decision, and then it will create a new image with the chosen width of border.

The border will overlap and cut off some parts of the original image. Also, when you view the new image on the camera's screen, it will appear as if you had created a white border, not a black one, because the camera displays the bordered image on a light background, so you can see the black border against that background.

For me, this is not an important option, though it could be useful if you like to have bordered images to display in a slideshow.

Sequence Display Options

This menu option lets you control how the camera displays images that were taken in one of the continuous-shooting modes such as Continuous H, Continuous L, Pre-shooting Cache, and others, which normally are displayed as "sequences." This option is a very straightforward one: You have just two choices—Individual Pictures or Key Picture Only, as shown in Figure 6-28. If you choose Key Picture Only, then, as you navigate through your images, when you come to a sequence, only the key image will display; it will be displayed in a frame that appears like a stack of images, indicating that it is the key frame of a sequence, and there will be a prompt to press the OK button to enter into the sequence.

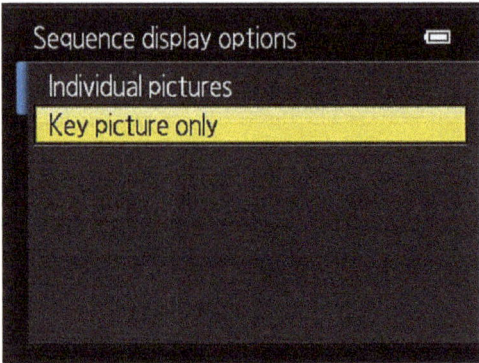

Figure 6-28: Sequence Display Options menu item

You cannot call up the detailed information display of that key image with the Display button or use any of the Playback menu options to manipulate the image; you first have to press the OK button to "enter" the sequence and display the individual images. If you choose the Individual Pictures option, all sequences will automatically be opened up, so the images from the sequence all display as you scroll through your saved images; you will not see any key images or have to "enter" into the sequences.

Choose Key Picture

This final option on the Playback menu is provided for a very specific purpose—to change the key picture that displays when you select a sequence. Ordinarily, the first image in a sequence is used as the key picture. If you have a sequence in which you would prefer to display one of the other images when the shots are being displayed in sequence mode, you can use this feature. First, you have to make sure the previous menu option, Sequence Display Options, is set to Key Picture Only. Then display the sequence whose key picture you want to change. Select this menu option, shown in Figure 6-29, and press the OK button or the right button to activate it.

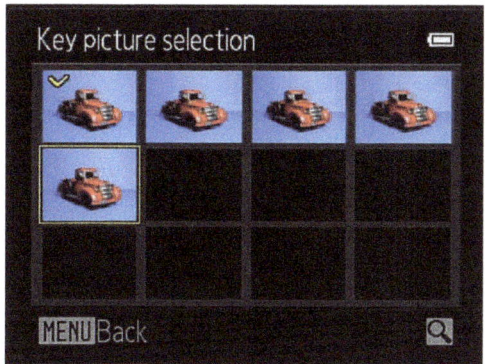

Figure 6-29: Key Picture Selection screen

The camera will display all of the images from the sequence; navigate through those images using the multi selector dial or the left and right direction buttons. Press the OK button when the picture you want to choose is highlighted.

Because of the nature of continuous shooting, which captures a stream of images rapidly, in most cases the images will be quite similar. However, there may be occasions when one image stands out above the others in quality and you will want to have it display as the representative of its sequence, so it will show up in slide shows, for example.

Printing Images

There is a great deal of variation among photographers with respect to how often they print their photographs on a printer. Some people are content to view their images on the camera's screen; many save them to a computer and share them on sites such as Flickr and Facebook; others send them to friends by e-mail. Still others print enlargements on fine photo paper.

If you want to produce copies of digital photographs on paper, there are various approaches to getting that done. You can import the photographs into a program such as Adobe Photoshop or Photoshop Elements, or use the software supplied by Nikon with the Coolpix P510, or any of many other programs that are available for photo editing. Once you have edited the images to your satisfaction, you can print the finished products from that software.

However, in some cases you may not be willing or able to spend the time to manipulate the pictures in software before printing them out. You may have access to a printer that will connect directly to the camera, and you may need or want to print out copies on photo paper without going through the time-consuming process of transferring the images to a computer first. Or, you may want to try a service that will take your memory card and produce high-quality prints directly from that card. The following discussion will cover the high points of these procedures.

Printing Directly from the Camera

The Coolpix P510 uses the PictBridge printing protocol, which lets it communicate directly with a wide variety of printers. The basic procedure is quite simple: Just plug the black USB cable that came with the camera into the mini-USB port inside the door on the left side of the camera. (This is the upper of the two ports in that location.)

Then plug the other end of the cable into the USB port of a PictBridge-compatible printer. (This USB port is different from the one for the cable that connects the printer to a computer; this one is rectangular; the port for the cable to the computer has more of a square shape.) The printer does not have to be made by any particular company; I plugged the camera directly into my HP Photosmart C6180 printer, and the two devices communicated with no problems.

Once the connection is made and the printer is turned on, the camera should turn on automatically and display a special screen that appears only when it's connected to a PictBridge printer, as shown in Figure 6-30.

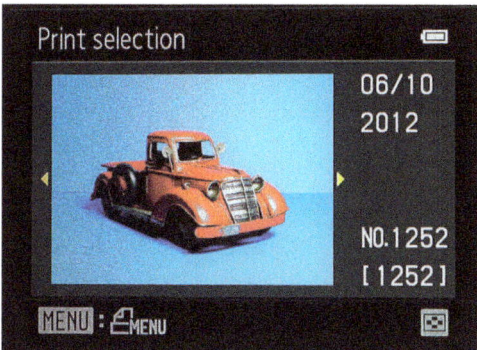

Figure 6-30: PictBridge print selection screen

To print an individual image, navigate to the one you want to print and press the OK button; the camera will prompt you for the number of prints and the paper size. To print multiple images, when the print display screen initially displays, press the Menu button to bring up the Print menu, shown in Figure 6-31, from which you can select images to print, print all images, or use the DPOF selection of images, as discussed earlier in this chapter.

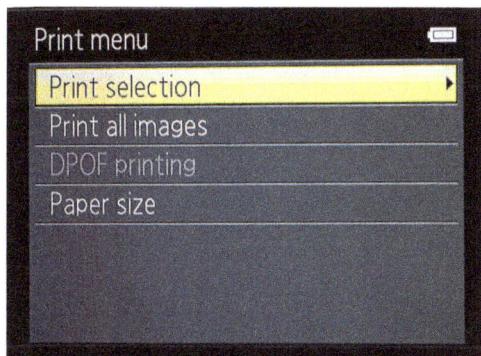

Figure 6-31: Print menu

Once you have all of the settings as you want them, press the OK button on the camera to print out the photograph or photographs. For further details about these procedures, see the Nikon P510 Reference Manual at pages 26-30.

Chapter 7: Setup and GPS Menus

Now I have discussed the options available to you in the Shooting menu and Playback menu systems. The next menu systems to discuss are the Setup menu and the GPS Options menu. (I'll discuss the Movie menu along with the various options for Movie mode in Chapter 8.)

The Setup Menu

The Setup menu gives you various choices for housekeeping matters such as screen brightness and operational sounds, but it also includes some important settings that affect how you take your images, including Vibration Reduction, Motion Detection, and Digital Zoom. In addition, this menu is where you perform the crucial operation of formatting a memory card or the internal memory.

As a reminder, you enter the menu system by pressing the Menu button. The available menus change depending on whether the camera is set to shooting mode or playback mode, and, in shooting mode, which exposure mode is selected (Program or Scene, for example). However, no matter what mode the camera is set to, you can always enter into the Setup menu. After you first press the Menu button, use the left direction button to move the selection to the far left column and highlight the wrench icon, indicating the Setup menu. Once that icon is highlighted, use the right button to move the yellow selection block back into the list of menu items, and then use the multi selector dial or the up and down direction buttons to navigate through the various options on the menu. The first screen of the Setup menu is shown in Figure 7-1.

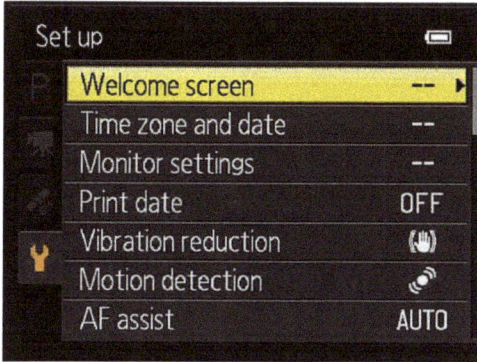

Figure 7-1: Setup menu

I'll discuss all choices on the menu in the order in which they appear.

Welcome Screen

When the camera comes from the factory, it does not display any start-up image when you turn on the power. This menu option gives you a way to have it display a standard Nikon start-up logo or one of your own images. Choose this item on the Setup menu, then use the right button or the OK button to move to the next screen, where you can select from None, Coolpix, or Select an Image, as shown in Figure 7-2.

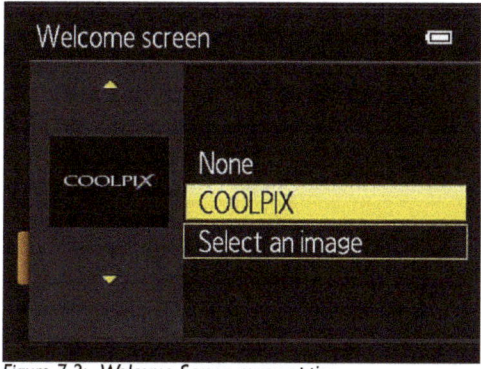

Figure 7-2: Welcome Screen menu option

217

If you want the standard Nikon image, select Coolpix, and the next time the camera is powered on it will display the Coolpix logo in a nice-looking graphic on the screen for a few seconds, as shown here.

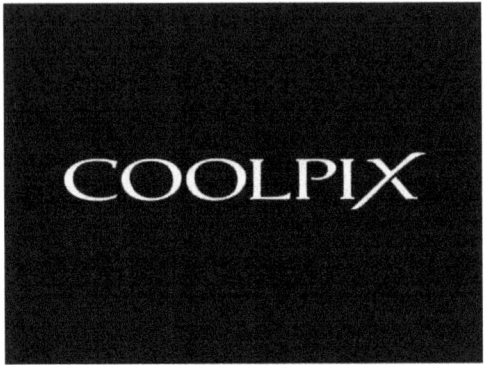

Figure 7-3: Coolpix logo for welcome screen

If you want to select one of your own images, the image must be stored in the camera's internal memory or on the memory card that is in the camera. Choose the Select an Image option from the Welcome screen menu, and then navigate through your images. When you find the image you want, press the OK button to select it. That image will then appear for a couple of seconds every time you start up the camera, unless you change it again using the same process. There are certain limits on the size of image you can select. For full details, see the Nikon P510 Reference Manual at page 74 of the reference section.

Time Zone and Date

Chances are you set the date, time and time zone when you first set up the camera. If you haven't done so or need to change them, use this menu option and navigate through the various selections using the left and right direction buttons or the multi selector dial; change the values using the multi selector dial or the up and down buttons, as shown in Figure 7-4.

When you get to the time zone option, you have two choices—the home time zone and the travel destination. Set the home zone to the location where you spend most of your time, and set the travel zone for an area you are most likely to travel to, as shown in Figure 7-5.

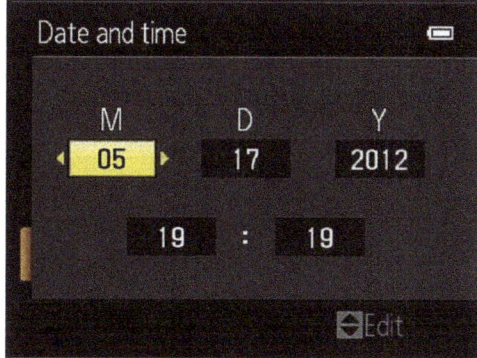
Figure 7-4: Setting Date and Time

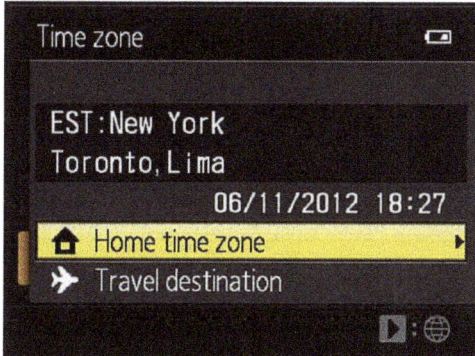
Figure 7-5: Home and travel time zone selection

Then, whenever you travel, just select the travel time zone from this menu option, and the camera's time and date will change as required, so your images will have the correct dates and times when you take pictures in your destination time zone.

Monitor Settings

With this menu item, you are able to control several aspects of the way your camera's monitor (LCD screen or viewfinder) displays images, as shown in Figure 7-6.

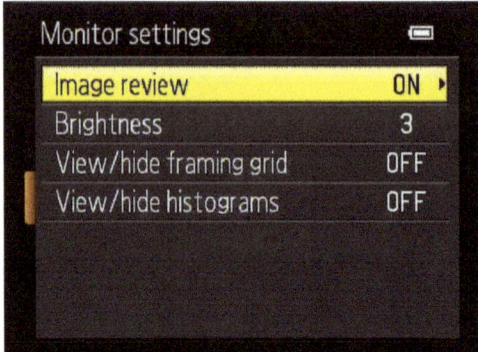

Figure 7-6: Monitor Settings menu option

First, you can turn the Image Review feature on or off. If it is turned on, a new image shows up on the screen for about a second when you first take the picture. If it is turned off, the display immediately goes back to the shooting screen when you take a picture. There is no way to control the length of time the image displays; this feature is either on or off. If you want to view a new image for a longer period of time, just press the Playback button and use the normal playback procedures.

The next option, Brightness, lets you select from 5 levels of brightness for the LCD monitor on the back of the camera. Just choose this option and navigate to the setting you prefer. Note that this setting has no effect on the brightness of the display in the viewfinder window or on a TV set; if you have activated the viewfinder using the Monitor button to the left of the viewfinder or have the camera connected to a TV set, the Brightness option will be unavailable for selection.

Next, the View/Hide Framing Grid option lets you turn on or off a grid of vertical and horizontal lines that divide the screen into nine blocks. You may appreciate having this grid available to help you compose your images according to the Rule of Thirds, which calls for placing your most important subject close to the intersections of these lines, to increase visual interest in the photo. The grid also may help you keep a subject properly horizontal or vertical by lining it up against one of the lines on the screen. The grid displays whenever the camera is in shooting mode, regardless of what display mode has been selected with the Display button. If you don't find the grid useful, just leave it turned off.

The final option under Monitor Settings, View/Hide Histograms, gives you a way to control whether or not the histogram is displayed when the camera is in shooting mode. If you turn this option on, the histogram appears in the upper quarter of the screen when the camera is set to shooting mode. However, unlike the situation with the framing grid, the histogram displays only when the more detailed information display is selected with the Display button.

Also, even when this option is turned on and the detailed information screen is activated, the histogram does not display under certain conditions, including when you are recording a movie, when Subject Tracking AF is active, or when certain other screens are displayed.

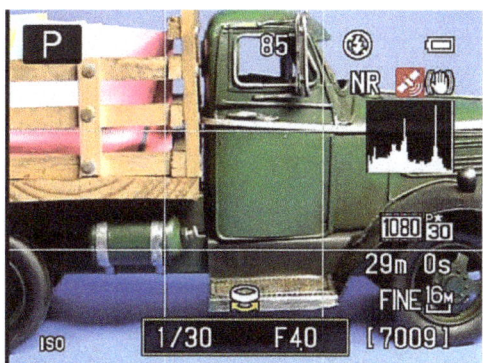
Figure 7-7: Framing grid and histogram in use

Note that, if this option is turned off, you can still display the histogram in shooting mode by pressing the exposure compensation button (right direction button) to adjust the exposure. The histogram will turn on in that situation to help you gauge how much exposure compensation to apply.

You should also note that the histogram will always display

for still images in playback mode when you have selected the histogram display screen by pressing the Display button, as discussed in Chapter 6. In Figure 7-7, both the histogram and the framing grid are in use.

Print Date

With this option, you can control whether the camera places the current date, or date and time, on the image when the image is recorded, as shown in Figure 7-8.

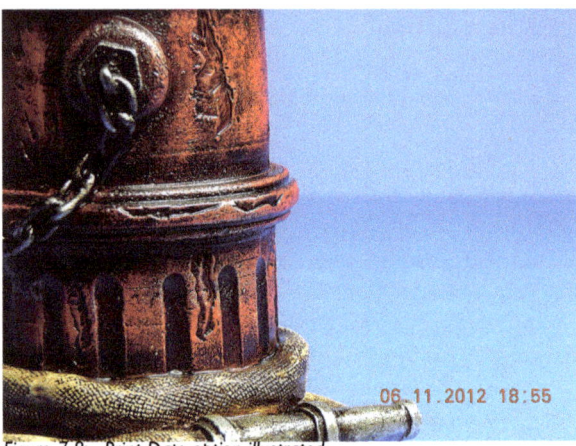

Figure 7-8: Print Date option illustrated

Note that this option places this information permanently on the image, and the information cannot be deleted (unless you use Photoshop or similar software to edit it out). You might want to use this feature if you are taking images as part of a scientific experiment in which you need to record this information as part of your data, but you ordinarily would not want to use it for general picture-taking, because the date (or date and time) information will mar the image. For ordinary images, you can always use editing software to retrieve the date and time information, which is recorded invisibly with the images (assuming the camera is set to the correct date and time). To use this feature, go to the Print Date option on the menu, then select either Date, Date and Time, or turn the option off altogether.

Vibration Reduction

This is one of the more important settings for the camera, particularly because of the extreme telephoto capability of the P510's lens. When you activate Vibration Reduction (VR), the camera uses its lens-shift system to stabilize the image. When you are hand-holding the camera, there is bound to be a slight amount of camera motion or shake. At slow shutter speeds, this motion can cause blurring of your images. Any such blurring is magnified at higher telephoto levels, as you can see if you look through the lens at a zoomed-in level. The slightest motion can make the image appear to jiggle uncontrollably.

There are just two available settings for the VR system: Off or On. When you have the camera placed on a tripod, you should make sure the VR setting is Off, because the camera's circuitry can get confused and attempt to correct for camera shake when there is none, thereby degrading the image. When this feature is turned on, the camera places a hand icon on the screen, as shown in Figure 7-9. (That image also shows the icon for Motion Detection, discussed next.)

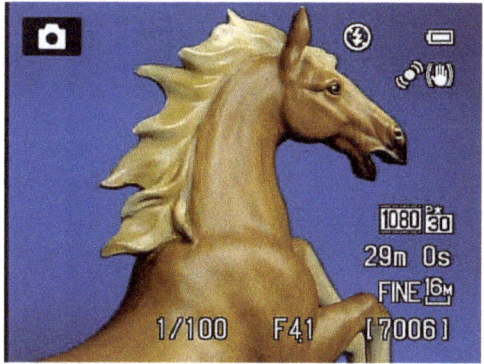

Figure 7-9: Motion Detection and Vibration Reduction in use

For most shooting, you can probably do best with the default setting of On. With this setting, when the camera detects motion, it causes the lens to shift slightly in a direction to compensate for that motion, so that the optical image that is captured by the sensor is, ideally, free of motion blur. In addition, if you are panning the camera (moving it steadily in a horizontal direction for a panoramic view) or tilting it (moving it vertically in a steady way), the camera will detect that motion, and not attempt to compensate for it; it will only try to negate any movement that is not part of the panning or tilting motion.

I recommend that you use the On setting whenever you're using the camera without a tripod, particularly when zooming in with the P510's super-telephoto lens.

Motion Detection

The Motion Detection option on the Setup menu is a rather interesting feature. It is related to Vibration Reduction, but operates quite differently.

Just as with the VR system, the camera detects motion of the camera that could cause blur and takes action to counteract the possibility of image blur. However, instead of shifting the position of the lens, the camera makes adjustments to its shooting settings for capturing the image. That is, when motion is detected, the camera automatically raises the ISO sensitivity level and sets a faster shutter speed in an attempt to use an exposure that is brief enough to avoid blur.

For example, if the camera would normally take a picture at 1/15 second at f/3.4, if the Coolpix P510 detects motion, the camera may increase the ISO level so that the sensor's sensitivity to light is increased and less light is needed to expose the image. In that way, the camera may be able to take the picture at 1/50 second rather than 1/15 second, resulting in an exposure that is short enough in duration to prevent any camera motion from blurring the image.

There is one somewhat unusual aspect to this setting: It is not available in any of the more advanced shooting modes—Program, Aperture Priority, Shutter Priority, or Manual exposure. It is available only in Auto mode and some (but not all) of the

Scene modes.

When this setting is in effect, an icon that looks like a ball with curves emanating from it displays in the upper right corner of the screen, as shown in Figure 7-9. When the motion detection system actually causes the camera to change its settings, the icon turns green to let you know.

In my opinion, this is a useful setting, because it can possibly rescue a shot that would be unusable because of motion blur. Given that it is only available when you are using the more automatic shooting modes, I recommend turning it on. If you want to exercise more control over the camera's settings, you can shoot in Program or one of the other advanced shooting modes and use the Vibration Reduction feature instead of Motion Detection. When you are using the Auto or Scene modes, the Motion Detection setting can be of considerable benefit if you are shooting in dim light where the use of a slow shutter speed may result in motion blur.

AF Assist

This menu option lets you turn on or off the reddish light beam that emanates from the Autofocus Assist lamp on the front of the camera. This beam comes on when the camera is trying to focus in a dark area; the light helps the autofocus mechanism find the patterns and shapes it needs to evaluate in order to achieve proper focus. You should usually leave this setting turned on, but you may want to turn it off when you're taking pictures in a place where the beam could be distracting or annoying to others, or where it might alert the subjects of your candid photography. The choices for this setting are Auto or Off. With the Auto setting, the lamp will fire when needed, except with some focus settings and some Scene modes in which it is disabled and cannot activate.

Note that this lamp will still light up when the self-timer is used; there is no way to disable the self-timer lamp, though you can cover it with black tape if you need to suppress it.

Digital Zoom

This feature lets you zoom in on a scene electronically, beyond the magnifying power of the camera's optical zoom capability. Because it is an electronic zoom and not an optical one, it does not really increase the information received by the camera; instead, it just enlarges the image digitally, which can result in a blocky, pixellated look. That's not to say that digital zoom is completely useless. It can help you to compose a scene the way you want to, or to measure the exposure on a small part of the scene before you zoom back out to take the picture without the digital zoom effect, for example. And, in some cases, the use of digital zoom does not actually degrade the quality of the image; it just uses a smaller portion of the image sensor's surface, resulting in a lower-resolution image, but without the pixellation of an artificially magnified image.

Here is how to use this feature. There are two settings available on the Setup menu for this item: On and Off. If you choose Off, the camera will be limited to using its optical zoom, which is really not too much of a limitation, since the P510's lens has the impressive range of 24mm to 1000mm.

If you choose On, the lens will "zoom" electronically beyond the optical limit of 1000mm, up to a maximum of an amazing (though somewhat illusory) 2000mm. With this unrestrained digital zoom setting, beyond a certain level of magnification the camera will use its electronic circuitry to "interpolate" pixels—that is, it will use an educated guess to create new pixels in between those that are actually produced by the image sensor, in order to be able to expand the image to a greater magnification. When the camera is using interpolation, the image naturally deteriorates to some extent because the camera is showing you pixels that are not part of the original image.

If you use an Image Size setting smaller than the maximum, then you can use Digital Zoom to a certain extent without image deterioration. This is because the camera needs a smaller number of pixels in order to create the desired image. There-

CHAPTER 7: SETUP AND GPS MENUS

fore, instead of interpolating new pixels among the existing ones, the camera crops out the actual pixels that appear on a portion of the image sensor, and enlarges that area to fill the entire area of the sensor. In this way, the camera uses only the actual pixels captured through the lens to the image sensor; it does not have to interpolate any new pixels.

Whenever you operate the zoom lever, a small camera-shaped icon appears underneath the zoom scale. As shown in Figure 7-10, when the optical zoom is in use, the zoom scale is white, and the bar stays to the left of that small icon.

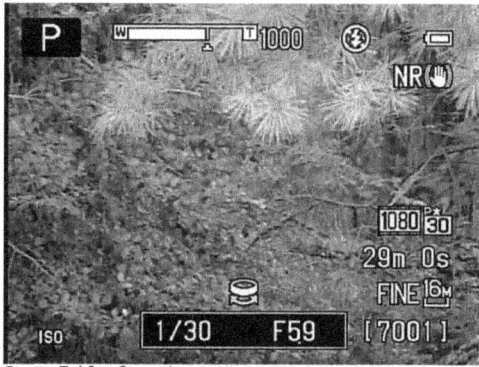
Figure 7-10: Optical zoom in use

That icon appears toward the right side of the scale; its position indicates the point where image deterioration will occur if you proceed further, using the digital zoom. (If the digital zoom is not turned on, then you will not be able to zoom past that camera icon.) If you proceed to zoom so the zoom scale moves past the camera icon, the zoom scale will turn yellow, as shown in Figure 7-11, indicating that digital zoom is being used, and that picture deterioration will occur because interpolation of pixels is taking place.

The camera icon will appear further to the right as you set the image size to smaller levels, because there is more capacity for the camera to enlarge the image and still preserve that image size. The scale will stay white in color as long as the zoom level stays to left of the camera icon. An example of this effect is

227

shown in Figure 7-12, in which Digital Zoom was used with the Image Size set to one of the smallest sizes, 1920 X 1080.

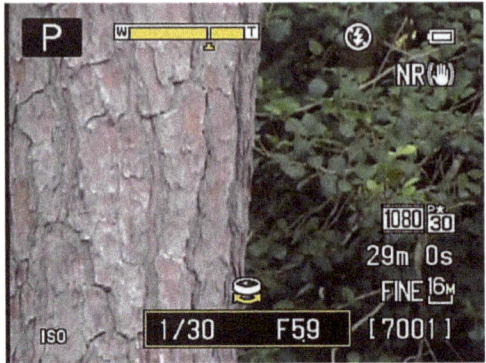

Figure 7-11: Digital zoom in use

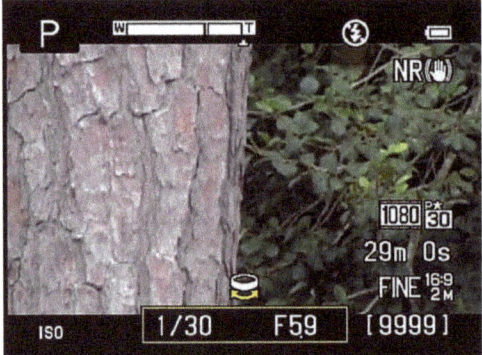

Figure 7-12: Digital zoom in use for small-sized image

How should you use the Digital Zoom setting? Well, the optical zoom range of the P510's lens is so phenomenal (1000mm) that there really should not be much need to zoom beyond that. It becomes very difficult to maintain a completely steady image, even with a tripod, at magnifications greater than that. However, if you are trying to capture an elusive bird or other creature with your lens, or have some other special photographic need, I recommend you use the Digital Zoom option if it will help you, bearing in mind that you may want to use some of the smaller image sizes in order to preserve image quality. I suggest you normally avoid the full digital zoom, with its yellow zoom scale. There is usually no great advantage to be gained from pushing the camera to this limit.

Note that Digital Zoom is not always available, depending on other settings that are in use. Specifically, it cannot be used along with any of the following settings: manual focus, Smile Timer, Multi-shot 16, with Zoom Memory turned on, or with AF Area Mode set to Subject Tracking.

Assign Side Zoom Control

I mentioned this option briefly in Chapter 5, in discussing the Side Zoom Control. This switch, on the left side of the lens, ordinarily serves as an alternate zoom control. When you leave it set to that function, you may find that you can hold the camera more steady by using the side control rather than the zoom lever on top of the camera. (Personally, I don't notice much difference; when using the regular zoom lever I can hold the camera quite steady.)

If you want to use the Side Zoom Control for one of its two other possible purposes, use this menu option to choose either manual focus or snap-back zoom, as shown in Figure 7-13.

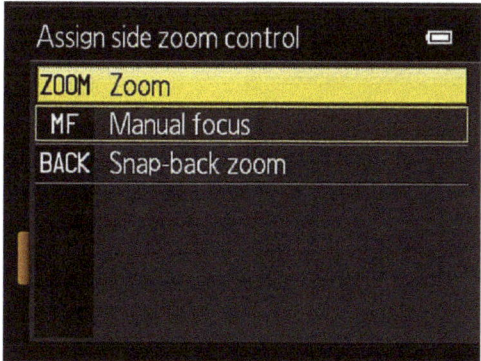

Figure 7-13: Assign Side Zoom Control menu option

If you choose manual focus, the side control can be used to adjust the focus point, but you can still use the up and down direction buttons to focus. If you choose snap-back zoom, the

Side Zoom Control can be pushed toward the W side to "snap" the zoom length back to about half of what it was each time, in several stages. Then, when you press the switch back in the T direction, the zoom reverts to its original length. In this way, you can experiment with various focal lengths, or maybe just get a broader perspective on your scene before going back to the original focal length to take the shot. Of the three possibilities for this switch, I tend to prefer snap-back zoom, because it gives the camera a capability it does not otherwise have.

Sound Settings

This next option on the Setup menu, shown in Figure 7-14, gives you a quick way to silence all of the electronic beeps and chirps that sound off when the camera performs certain actions, such as turning on, achieving focus and exposure, or having the shutter pressed to take a picture.

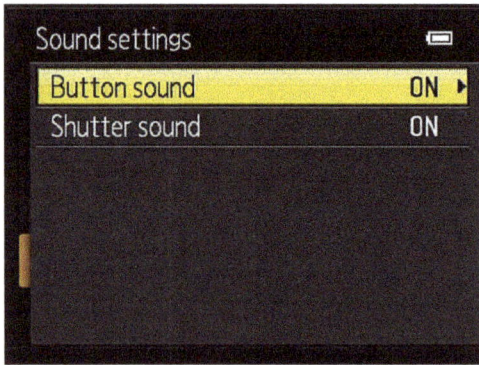
Figure 7-14: Sound Settings menu option

There are not many options here—first, you can turn the "Button sound" on or off. This option controls whether or not the camera beeps when it starts up, when settings are successfully made, when it achieves focus, and when an error occurs.

The other option for this item is whether to turn on or off the Shutter sound, which ordinarily is heard when you press the shutter release button all the way down to take a picture. This sound is automatically disabled in the Pet Portrait mode, during continuous shooting, and during movie recording.

Auto Off

This option lets you control the length of time before the camera enters standby mode to save power. By default, the camera will stay fully powered on for one minute when you are not touching the controls; after that time, it enters standby mode, in which the display goes blank and the green light around the power button blinks continuously about twice per second. After about three minutes in that mode, the camera turns completely off. During standby mode, you can bring the camera back to full-power mode by pressing the power button, the shutter release button, the Playback button, or the Movie button, or by turning the mode dial.

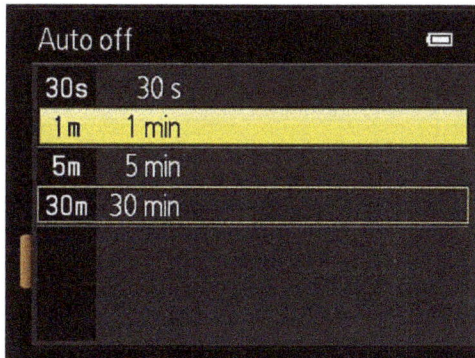

Figure 7-15: Auto Off menu option

If you would like to set a different interval before the camera enters standby mode, you can choose 30 seconds, five minutes, or 30 minutes with this menu item. Note, however, that those times apply only when the camera is in shooting mode, displaying the shooting screen. When menu screens are displayed, the camera will enter standby mode in three minutes, if a shorter setting than that is chosen for Auto Off. Also, during slide show playback, the camera will stay active for up to 30 minutes, and when the AC adapter is connected, the time before entering standby mode will always be 30 minutes.

Format Card/Format Memory

This is one of the most important menu options. Choose this process only when you want or need to completely wipe all of the data from a memory storage card or the internal memory.

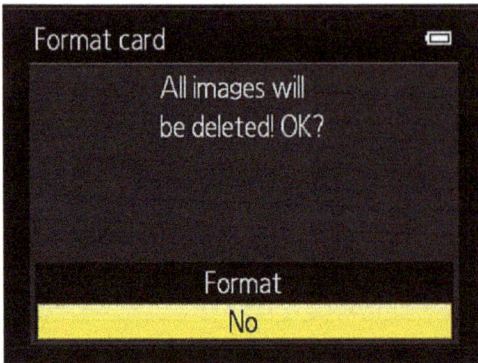
Figure 7-16: Format menu option

When you select the Format Card option, as shown in Figure 7-16, the camera will warn you that all images currently on the card will be deleted if you proceed. If you reply by highlighting Format and pressing the OK button to confirm, the camera will proceed to format the card that is in the camera, and the result will be a card that is empty of images and properly formatted to store new images from the camera.

With this procedure, the camera will erase all images, including those that have been protected from accidental erasure with the Protect function on the Playback menu. It's a good idea to periodically save your good images and videos to your computer or other storage device and then re-format your memory card, to make sure it is properly set up to start recording new images and videos. It's also a good idea to use the Format Card command on any new memory card when you first insert it in the camera. Even though it likely will work without that procedure, it's best to make sure the card is set up with Nikon's own particular method of formatting.

If you want to format the camera's internal memory instead

of a memory card, just remove the card from the camera. The name of the menu option will then change to Format Memory. When you select that command, the camera will format the internal memory. Before formatting the internal memory, you should copy any images that you want to preserve by using the Copy command on the Playback menu, as discussed in Chapter 6, or by copying them to a computer.

Language

This option gives you your choice among 29 languages for the display of commands and information on the camera's display.

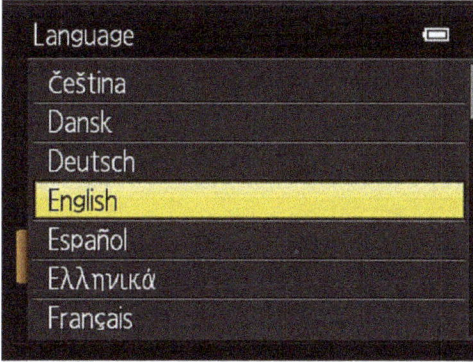

Figure 7-17: Language menu option

Once you have selected this menu item, scroll through the numerous language choices using the multi selector dial or the direction buttons and press the OK button when your chosen language is highlighted, as seen in Figure 7-17.

TV Settings

This menu item lets you choose settings for four video-related items. First, the Video Mode setting gives you the option of selecting the appropriate system for the television to which you are connecting the camera by means of the audio-video cable. There are only two options available: NTSC and PAL. NTSC is the system used in the United States, Canada, most of South America, South Korea, Japan, Taiwan, and some other countries; PAL is used in Europe and most other areas.

The second sub-option for this menu item is HDMI, which can be set to Auto, 480p, 720p, or 1080i. Ordinarily, the Auto setting will work best; the camera will set itself for the optimum display according to the resolution of the high-definition (HD) TV set it is connected to. If you experience difficulties with that connection, you may be able to improve the image on the HDTV's screen by trying one of the numerical settings for this menu option.

The third setting under this menu item, HDMI Device Control, is of use only when you have connected the camera to an HDTV set and you want to control the camera with the TV's remote control, which is possible in some situations. If you want to do that, set this option to On, follow the instructions for the TV and its remote control, and see the list of items that can be controlled at page 24 of the reference section of the Coolpix P510's Reference Manual.

The fourth and final option for TV settings, HDMI 3D output, is for use when you have the camera connected to a 3D-capable HDTV set. This setting enables the camera to send 3D information to the HDTV. This setting is turned on by default, so you should not have to bother with setting it.

Fn Button

As was discussed in Chapter 5, the Coolpix P510 comes equipped with a very convenient and powerful control in the form of the Function button, designated by the Fn label on the button itself, which is located just behind the shutter button on top of the camera. By default, this button is programmed to call up the continuous-shooting menu, but you can use this Setup menu item to change the button's function to any one of the following other choices: Image Size, Picture Control, White Balance, Metering, ISO Sensitivity, or AF Area Mode. Just highlight the desired option, as shown in Figure 7-18, and press the OK button to confirm.

CHAPTER 7: SETUP AND GPS MENUS

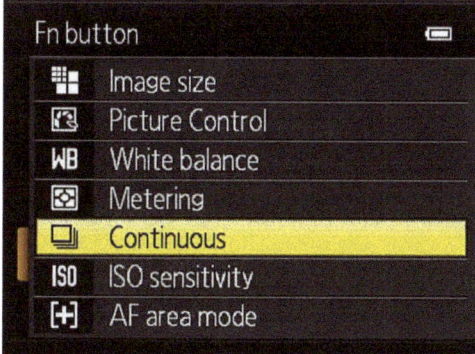

Figure 7-18: Fn Button menu option

Then, the next time you press the Fn Button, it will activate your selected function.

Charge by Computer

By default, when you connect your Coolpix P510 to a computer using the USB cable, the battery is gradually charged by power from the computer through the cable. To disable this capability, choose Off from this menu item, and the camera will not get power from the computer. You may want to turn this feature off when you are using a laptop computer and you don't want to run down the computer's battery unnecessarily. In addition, some users of the predecessor model, the P500, reported getting better battery life by turning this menu option off. So, unless you have some particular need to charge your battery by this method, I recommend going into this menu item and setting Charge by Computer to Off.

Toggle Av/Tv Selection

This menu option has just two possible settings: Off or On. If you leave it at the default setting of Off, then it has no effect. If you turn it to On, then it switches the functions of the command dial and the multi selector dial for setting aperture and shutter speed values in the Aperture Priority, Shutter Priority, and Manual shooting modes. Ordinarily, the command dial sets shutter speed and the multi selector dial sets aperture. If

235

you want to reverse those assignments, use this menu option. Using this option also affects the functions of those dials for controlling the Flexible Program option. Normally, the command dial has that function; you can re-assign that duty to the multi selector dial by turning this menu option on.

Reset File Numbering

This option resets the file numbering system back to 0001. Ordinarily, the camera assigns increasing file numbers to your images, even when they occupy many folders on the memory card.

For example, when you start out with a new camera and memory card, your first images will be stored in a folder named 100NIKON. The first image will be named 100NIKON-0001.jpg. (On your computer, there will be a prefix such as DSCN, so the name may be DSCN0001.jpg.) Once the 100NIKON folder has 200 files stored in it, the camera will automatically create a new folder called 101NIKON. If none of your files had been deleted, which would interrupt the numbering scheme, the first file in the new folder will be numbered 101NIKON-0201.jpg. That is, each folder can hold only 200 files before a new folder is created, but the individual files' numbers will keep increasing, even over multiple folders, until the individual file numbers reach 9999. Thus, after roughly 50 folders are filled with files, the individual numbers start over again at 0001.

If you don't like the idea of your folder and file numbers continuously increasing, you can use this menu option at any time to reset the file numbering back to the beginning. That is, if the file numbers have increased to a number such as 0476.jpg, and you don't want to wait until the numbers reach 9999 before they start over, you can invoke this procedure, select Yes when prompted by the menu, and the camera will start numbering your next image back at 0001.jpg. The folder numbers will continue to increase, however. Whenever the newest folder contains 200 files, a new folder will be created.

Blink Warning

This feature gives you an automatic alert if the camera detects that a person blinked his or her eyes in a picture that has just been captured. If you turn this option on, then it will operate in certain conditions—that is, when you are using Face Priority for the AF Area Mode, including when you are shooting in the Night Portrait, Scene Auto selector, or Portrait mode.

If this option is turned on, the camera will display the message "Did someone blink?" on a special screen if it detects what appear to be closed eyes in the newly captured image. On this screen, the camera will place a yellow frame around the culprit's face. You can then zoom in on that face using the zoom lever and take whatever other action you wish, including deleting the image or re-shooting the picture.

Filmstrip

Filmstrip is a special option for viewing your images in playback mode. If you turn this option on, then, when you are viewing your images in playback mode, if you rotate the multi selector dial rapidly, the images will form a stream of small thumbnail images at the bottom of the screen, giving a flowing view of multiple images, as shown in Figure 7-19.

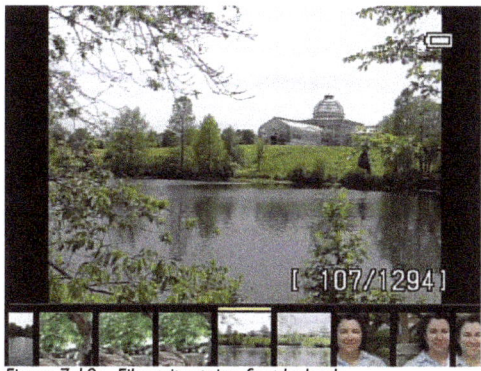

Figure 7-19: Filmstrip option for playback

Once the filmstrip appears, you can stop moving the multi selector dial; the filmstrip will stay on the screen. You can then scroll through the images in the filmstrip slowly if you want, until you find one you are searching for. The larger versions of the images will continue to scroll by on the upper part of the screen, though not so quickly. This function in effect gives you a peek at the "past" and "future" of your stream of images, so you can see when the one you want will be coming into view. You can cancel the filmstrip view by pressing the OK button.

Eye-Fi Upload

As discussed in Chapter 1, an Eye-Fi card can be a very useful storage device for your Coolpix P510 because it wirelessly uploads your images to your computer (or other device) over a wireless network. In order for those uploads to work, this menu option, shown in Figure 7-20, must be turned on. (It is turned off by default.)

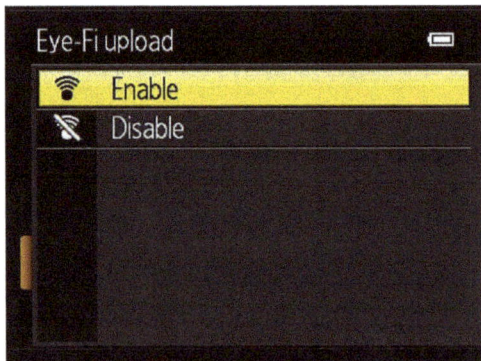

Figure 7-20: Eye-Fi Upload menu option

If you are on an airplane or in some other area where such devices are not allowed to be turned on, you can disable this option using this menu item. You also may save some battery power by disabling it when it is not needed. Of course, if you are using an Eye-Fi card and the images are not uploading properly, you should check this menu option to make sure it is turned on.

Reverse Indicators

This menu item has a single, very specific purpose—to reverse the plus and minus sides of the exposure scale that appears when the camera is set to Manual exposure mode. By default, the plus side (indicating brighter exposure) is on the left and the minus side (indicating darker exposure) is on the right. You can change this setting here, as shown in Figure 7-21.

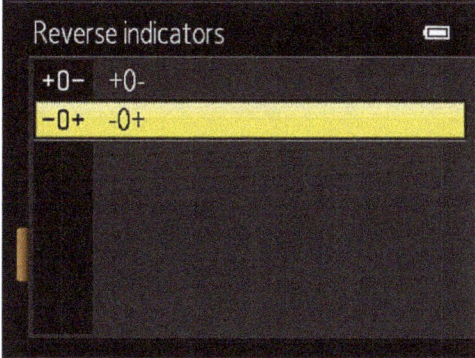

Figure 7-21: Reverse Indicators menu option

I must admit, it seems more natural to me to have the positive value on the right, so I do like to use this menu option. The good news is, I only have to use it once, and the scale is changed according to my preference.

Reset All

Choose this menu option when you want to reset all of the camera's settings back to their original (default) values. This action can be useful if you have been experimenting with different settings and you find that something is not working as expected. It will give you a fresh start with known values for all of the major settings on the menus and for shooting. There are a few settings that will not be reset, including items such as date and time, time zone, language, and video system. The complete lists of the items that will or will not be reset are at Pages 94-97 of the reference section of the Coolpix P510 Reference Manual.

Firmware Version

The final entry on the Setup menu gives you a way to find out the current version of the firmware that is installed in your camera. The Coolpix P510, like other digital cameras, is programmed at the factory with firmware, which is a semi-permanent set of computer instructions that are electronically implanted in the camera. These instructions control all aspects of the camera's operation, including the menu system, functioning of the controls, and in-camera processing of your images. The reason you might want to check to see what version is installed is that, in many cases, the manufacturer will release an updated version of the firmware that may fix problems or bugs in the system, provide minor enhancements, or, in some cases, even provide major improvements, such as including new shooting modes or menu options.

To determine what firmware version is currently installed in your camera, highlight this menu option, then press the OK button or the right direction button, and the camera will display the version number, as shown in Figure 7-22.

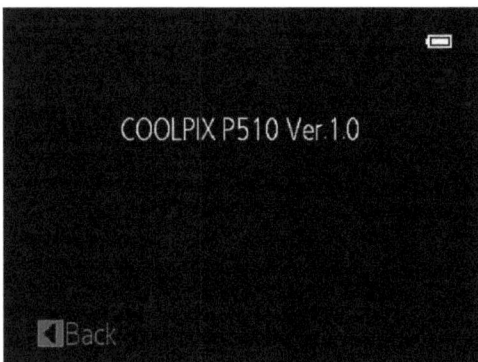

Figure 7-22: Firmware version screen

To determine whether any firmware upgrades have been released, I recommend that you visit Nikon's support web site; for United States customers, the address is http://support.nikonusa.com; for Europe, the site can be found by starting at http://www.europe-nikon.com. Find the Download Center, and look for the link to current firmware versions. The site will provide detailed instructions for downloading and installing the new firmware.

GPS Options Menu

The other menu system to be discussed in this chapter is the GPS Options menu, shown in Figure 7-23.

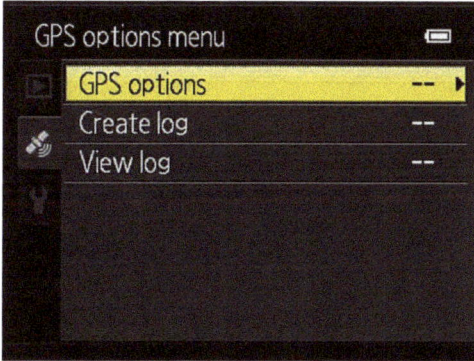

Figure 7-23: GPS Options menu

This menu is represented by a satellite icon in the column to the left of the menu screens, between the Movie (or Playback, in playback mode) and Setup menu icons. The Coolpix P510 has a solid set of GPS capabilities, and you need to use the options on this menu to take advantage of them.

I have to say that I do not rely heavily on GPS because I do not travel much, and when I do go on a trip to take photos, I return home fairly quickly and put the photos into a folder on my computer that I name for the location where the images were taken. For other photographers, though, especially those who go on extended trips, it can be very useful if not indispensable to have the camera record your locations automatically.

Once you have the GPS data recorded, various computer programs can use the data to map out the locations where the images were taken. For example, I recently took a trip to a park by the James River to take some photos for this book. I had enabled the GPS recording function, as discussed below, so the camera recorded the location of each shot. Then, when I loaded the images into Nikon's ViewNX 2 software and clicked on the GeoTag option at the top of the screen, the program produced the map shown in Figure 7-24, with a blue push-pin icon marking each of the images that were shown in the thumbnails at the bottom of the ViewNX 2 browser.

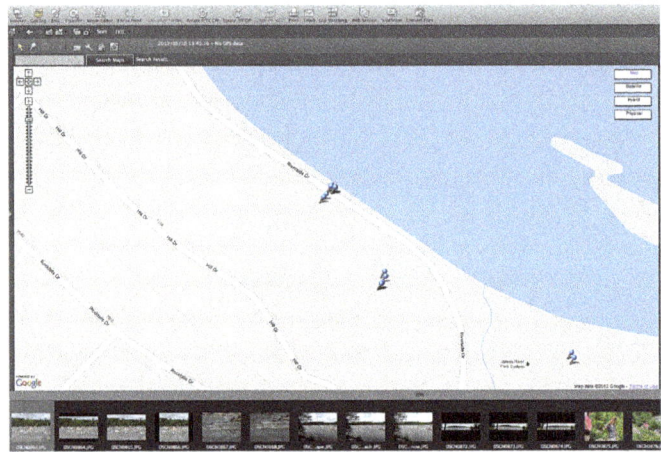

Figure 7-24: GPS locations mapped in Nikon software

With that introduction, it's time to examine how to use the P510's GPS capabilities.

GPS Options

The first line on the GPS settings menu, GPS options, leads to another screen with three sub-options: Record GPS Data, Synchronize, and Update A-GPS File, as shown in Figure 7-25. I will discuss these in turn.

Record GPS Data

This setting in effect turns the camera's GPS capability on or off. By default, the GPS settings are turned off, and the camera does not actively receive any data from the 24 GPS satellites that constantly orbit the earth and transmit location data. You need to turn this option on if you want the camera to record the locations where images are taken.

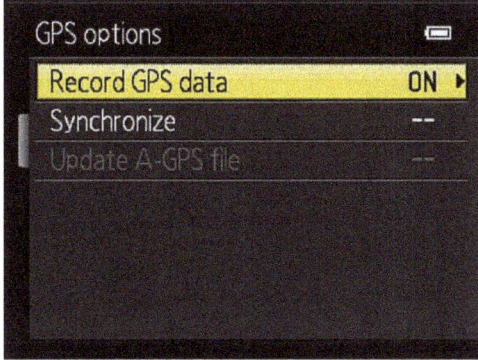

Figure 7-25: GPS Options menu items

You should turn this option off when you are in a location where devices of this sort are not permitted to be used. (Some countries do not permit the use of GPS to record location information.) You also should turn it off if you don't need the location information to be recorded, because you can save battery power by turning the GPS functioning off. Also, you should turn it off if you will be sharing your photos with others and don't want location information revealed.

Synchronize

This menu option is available for selection only if the previous option, Record GPS Data, is turned on. If it is, then, if you select this item, the camera will display a message asking if you wish to use the GPS to set the camera's clock. If you highlight Yes and press OK, the camera will attempt to synchronize its clock using data from the GPS satellites. If you have the camera indoors or in a location where it cannot receive the GPS data, the camera will display an error message saying it could not carry out the operation. This option could be useful if you are out away from civilization and don't have a reliable timepiece with you; the camera can act as a highly accurate clock, using information from the GPS satellites.

Update A-GPS File

This third option on the GPS Options sub-menu is available for those users who are quite serious about having the most up-to-date data. To use this option, you have to go to a special web site, http://nikonimglib.com/agps2/index.html.en, and download the latest version of a computer file that contains the updated data. Then you have to copy that file to an SD card that has been used in your camera; you have to copy it into the folder on that card called NCFL. Then, place the SD card back into the camera, turn the camera on, and go to this menu option. When you select this option, the camera will ask if you want to update the file. If you say yes, it will display a message saying not to remove the card during the updating process, which will take about two minutes or so.

When you have finished, you will have the latest data, which should speed up the GPS location function of the camera. I have not found this operation to be necessary, but it may be useful to those who rely heavily on GPS and need the greatest accuracy and speed in fixing locations.

Create Log

The second major option on the GPS Options menu, Create Log, is available only if you have turned on the Record GPS Data option, discussed above. This function enables the camera's GPS capability to record your locations and movements over a period of time, at set intervals. The default settings are to record for 6 hours at 15-second intervals.

View Log

Once the log has been recorded and saved to your memory card, you can use the View Log menu option to view it. When you select this option, the camera will display a chart that shows the route that was taken during the time the log was being recorded. For more details on creating and viewing GPS logs, see pages 71-73 of the reference section of the Coolpix P510 Reference Manual.

Viewing GPS Location Screen

Finally, there is one more GPS option to discuss, even though it does not appear on the GPS menu. This option lets you view a special screen with the GPS data (latitude and longitude) that was recorded for an image, as shown in Figure 7-26. If you activated the Synchronize function, the date from the GPS system appears above the location data; if you created a log of your route, the diagram in the upper part of the screen shows the route taken while the log was being recorded. The image included here shows all of these items.

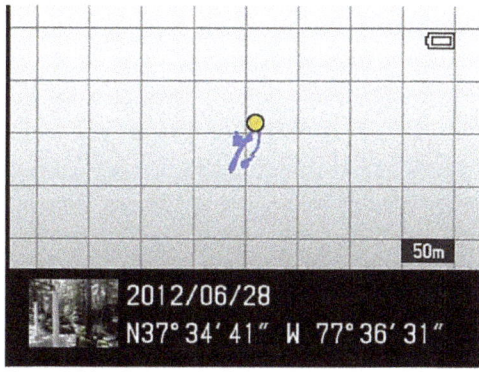

Figure 7-26: Pressing the Fn button produces a GPS screen

To view this screen, press the Function button while an image is displayed in playback mode. To dismiss it, press the button once more. The grid above the navigation coordinates will display a series of connected lines indicating your route, if you have activated the function to create a GPS log through the Create Log menu item, discussed above.

Chapter 8: Motion Pictures

Nowadays it seems that it's a necessity for any DSLR or advanced compact digital camera to include movie-making capabilities. Most recently, it's become standard practice for camera manufacturers to incorporate high-definition (HD) video recording into their premium cameras, and the Coolpix P510 is one example of that trend. And, along with HD video, the P510 offers some extra benefits such as high-speed video recording, which results in slow-motion footage when you view it. I will explain the various options for movie-making in this chapter. Before I get into the specific settings you can make for your movies, I'll begin with a brief overview of the process.

Movie-making Overview

In one sense, the fundamentals of making videos with the Coolpix P510 can be reduced to four words: "Push the red button." Having a dedicated motion picture recording button makes things easy for the user of this camera, because anytime you see a reason to take some video footage, you can just press that easily accessible button while aiming at your subject, and you will get results that are very likely to be usable. So, if you're more of a still photographer and not particularly interested in movie-making, you don't need to read any further. Be aware that the red button exists, and if flying saucers start to land in your neighbor's back yard, the red button will be there for you.

But for those P510 users who would like to delve further into their camera's motion picture capabilities, there is considerably more information to discuss. Even though you can just press the red button at any time to start recording a video sequence, there are several settings that can have a significant impact on your footage. The shooting mode the camera is set to for still images, and the menu and control-button settings you make, all have some effect on your movie recordings. So, it is helpful to be aware of the current settings, even if you just want to capture a brief clip of a scene during your vacation.

Quick Guide to Recording a Movie Clip

I will discuss the details of movie-related settings later in this chapter. For now, here are some suggested guidelines for quick settings when you just want to record the action and you don't care about fine-tuning the menu options and other settings. I'll discuss these steps with a bit of extra detail, in case you have turned to this section before reading about the camera's various controls and menus.

1. Turn the mode dial on top of the camera, to the right of the viewfinder, so the green camera icon is at the white indicator mark, putting the camera into the Auto shooting mode, as shown in Figure 8-1.

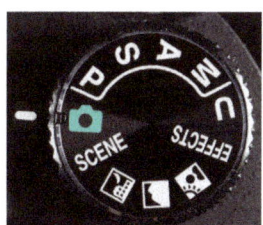

Figure 8-1: Auto mode

2. Remove the lens cap and turn on the camera with the power button.

3. Press the Menu button at the bottom left of the control area on the right side of the camera's back, and then press the left direction button (left edge of the ridged dial that surrounds

the OK button), which will move the yellow selection block to the far-left column of menu icons.

4. Press the down direction button to move the yellow selection block down so it highlights the movie camera icon.

5. Press the right direction button to move the yellow selection block into the list of menu options. Using the direction buttons or the multi selector dial (the ridged dial that surrounds the OK button), highlight the top line of the menu, Movie options.

6. Press the right direction button to get to the next menu screen, and make sure the top line is highlighted. It should say HD 1080p, with a star, and (1920 x 1080). Press the OK button to select this option, as shown in Figure 8-2.

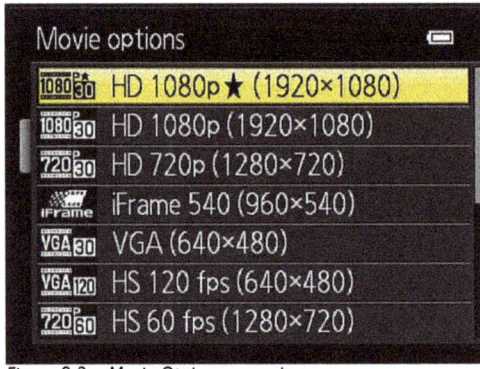

Figure 8-2: Movie Options menu item

7. Press the Menu button to go back to shooting mode.

8. Aim at your subject and use the zoom lever on top of the camera to frame the scene as you want, zooming in or out as needed. Press the shutter button halfway down until you hear a beep, to have the camera evaluate the exposure and focus. When the action starts or you're ready to begin, press the red Movie button to start the recording. Then take your finger off the button and hold the camera as steady as possible.

8. Continue to hold the camera steady, and pan (move the

camera from side to side in one direction) slowly and smoothly if appropriate to take in the scene before you. When the scene has ended, press the red Movie button again to end the recording.

Other Settings for Movies

The above steps will get you started recording video with the Coolpix P510 using the highest quality recording format and standard settings for white balance, autofocus, and other options. Once you have become familiar with the basic steps for movie-making, though, you may want to experiment with some of the other available settings. There are quite a few items that can be adjusted for recording videos with this camera.

Still Photo Settings Available for Movies

When you are recording movies with the Coolpix P510, several of the settings that you make for still photos, either through use of the controls or through the Shooting menu, carry over to your movies, provided that the camera remains set to a shooting mode in which that setting remains in effect. For example, if, as discussed above, the camera is set to the Auto shooting mode, the Auto mode settings will be in effect, including autofocus and Auto White Balance. If, on the other hand, the camera is set to the Program mode, the settings for focus and white balance will be whatever you have set through the Shooting menu. In Program mode you can select manual focus, any white balance setting you want, and several other options, although not all items on the Shooting menu will carry over to affect your video recordings. I will discuss below the settings you can make that will work for movies.

Focus Mode

The first setting that carries over to video shooting is the focus mode, set by pressing the down direction button, as shown in Figure 8-3. You can adjust this setting to some extent in Auto mode and you can adjust it more fully in the advanced shooting modes (Program, Aperture Priority, Shutter Priority, and

Manual exposure.) You cannot adjust it in any of the Scene modes. Whatever setting you make will remain in effect for video shooting, as long as the camera stays set in the mode in which you made the setting.

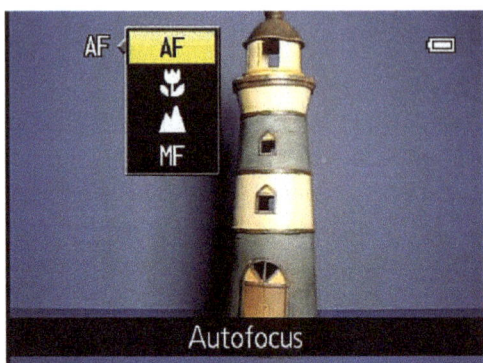

Figure 8-3: Focus mode selection

So, for example, you can use macro focus if you are taking close-up footage. Also, in the P, A, S, or M shooting mode, you can select manual focus. In that case, you can adjust the focus manually while recording the movie, by pressing the up and down direction buttons or using the Side Zoom Control, if you assigned it to adjust manual focus using the Setup menu. Later in this chapter I will discuss other focus settings you can make for movie recording.

Exposure Compensation and Exposure Lock

The next adjustment you can make that stays in effect during video recording is exposure compensation, which is available in all shooting modes except Manual exposure. Whatever adjustment you make before pressing the red Movie button, to either brighten or darken the image, will stay in effect during video recording, and you will see the effects on the screen in the brightness level of the image. You cannot make any changes to this setting during the video recording. However, you can press the right direction button to lock the exposure at any point while recording a movie. You will see a prompt at the bottom of the screen stating that you can press that button for

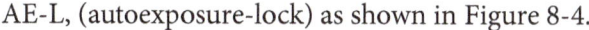

AE-L, (autoexposure-lock) as shown in Figure 8-4.

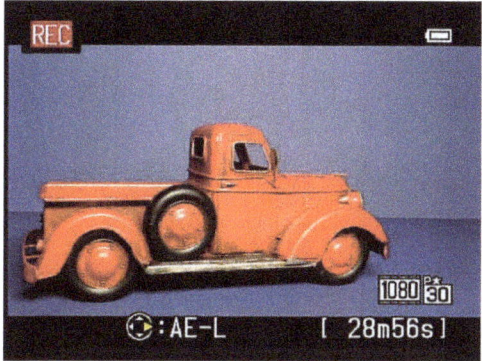

Figure 8-4: Movie recording screen

Once you press the right button to lock the exposure, that message will change to indicate that you can turn AE-L off by pressing the same button again.

Note that you cannot change the overall exposure mode used by the camera for recording movies; it will use automatic exposure adjustment, as if it were in Auto or Program mode, no matter what mode is set on the mode dial. For example, even if you select Manual exposure on the mode dial and dial in fairly extreme settings for shutter speed and aperture, such as 1/500 second and f/8.3, the P510 will use its autoexposure programming to expose the footage as normally as possible, subject only to whatever exposure compensation and exposure lock functions you employ.

Self-timer

The self-timer also will function for movie recording. Just set it as you normally do, by using the left direction button and selecting either 2 seconds or 10 seconds for the delay. Then, when you press the red Movie button, the camera will delay the designated length of time before starting to record.

Picture Control

Turning to menu options, the first item on the Shooting menu that works for movie recording as well as stills is the Picture Control feature, as shown in Figure 8-5.

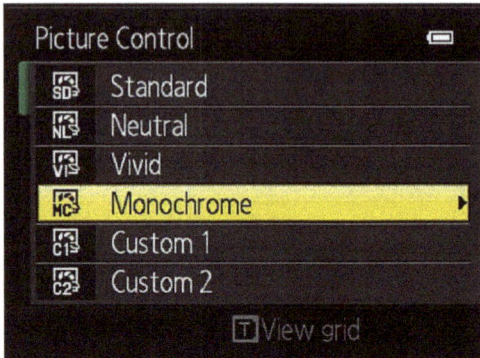

Figure 8-5: Picture Control is available for movies

The availability of this selection for movies can be quite useful, because it lets you add a distinctive style to your video footage. You can shoot in black-and-white, for example, or you can use the Vivid setting to enhance colors. In most cases, though, you are likely to be satisfied with the Standard setting.

Of course, you can only use this option for movie recording if you set it while the camera is in the P, A, S, or M mode, and if the camera remains in that mode during the video recording.

White Balance

The next Shooting menu option that carries over to video shooting is White Balance. Generally, Auto White Balance is adequate, so you can usually use the Auto shooting mode with no problem in this respect. However, if you happen to be shooting your movie indoors, perhaps with non-standard artificial lighting, you may want to turn to the P, A, S, or M mode and use one of the specific preset White Balance settings or even the Preset Manual option. Also, being able to set white balance however you want it gives you the option of purposely setting a "wrong" white balance in order to achieve an unusual color cast. For example, if you set manual white balance using a blue surface as the standard rather than a gray or white one, your footage will take on an eerie reddish appearance, suitable for some science fiction or horror scenes, perhaps.

Metering

You can set the Metering option however you want it for movies, if you set it while the camera is in one of the advanced shooting modes (P, A, S, or M). Here, as with White Balance, the standard setting (Matrix) is likely to be quite satisfactory for most of your shooting. However, having the option to use Center-weighted or Spot metering may be of use in some specific lighting situations. You need to be careful, though, because using Spot metering can result in a dramatic, and potentially unwelcome, shift in the lighting of a scene if the center spot of the frame is pointed at a particularly bright or dark object. Also, note that the camera does not display any small circle or other indicator showing the area that the Spot metering uses, so you will not have any reminder that Spot metering is in effect until you see a sudden change in the scene's exposure.

Vibration Reduction

The Vibration Reduction setting on the Setup menu carries over for your movie recording. I recommend that you always have this setting enabled when shooting movies, unless you have the camera on a tripod. When you are hand-holding the camera, this setting can reduce the shakiness that may result from an unsteady hand. You don't need to worry when you are purposely moving the camera in a panning motion, because the camera will detect that motion and ignore it for purposes of vibration reduction; it will attempt to counteract only the vertical shakiness that may be caused by your hand motions.

Zoom

The optical and digital zoom both will function during video recording. However, to use digital zoom, you have to stop at the limit of optical zoom, release the zoom control, and then start zooming again to cause the digital zoom to start working. I have to say that I don't have much of a problem with this limitation of the P510. My own preference is to zoom in, if necessary, before starting the recording. I try to avoid zooming while shooting a video if at all possible, because I find that the zooming motion can be unsettling to the viewer. Also, as Nikon points out in its reference manual, the noise of the zoom mechanism is likely to be audible on your recording. So, unless you're following action that requires you to adjust your zoom range, you're probably better off adjusting it before you start recording. (Of course, if you don't mind using editing software, you can later edit out any parts of the movie where you adjust the zoom range.)

Shutter Release Button: Does Not Operate

When you are shooting movies with the Coolpix P510, the shutter button has no effect. Although the P500 has the capability to take still pictures during video recording, the P510 does not. If you press the shutter button while a movie is being recorded, you are likely to add some unwanted sounds from that operation to the movie's sound track, but no still image will be taken. If you want to produce a still image from your video footage, you can extract a frame using the procedure discussed later in this chapter.

Fn Button: Does Not Operate

Several of the settings that you can program into the Function button are not applicable for movie recording, such as Image Size, continuous shooting, ISO, and AF Area Mode. However, there are a few settings that you can assign to this button that do affect video recording: Picture Control, White Balance, and Metering. The Function button does not operate while a movie is being recorded. However, you can, of course, press this button before pressing the red Movie button, to activate whatever setting is programmed into the Function button.

Settings That Are Not Adjustable for Video Recording

Although, as discussed above, several settings for still photography are available for use during video recording, several others are not. You cannot adjust the ISO, aperture, shutter speed, Autofocus Area Mode, or Active D-Lighting. Several other settings from the Shooting menu do not apply for shooting movies, either because there are specific settings for movies (Image Quality, Image Size, and Autofocus Mode) or because, by their very nature, they apply only to still photography (exposure bracketing, flash exposure compensation, and long exposure noise reduction).

The Movie Menu

Whenever the camera is in shooting mode, you can get access to the Movie menu, which is represented by the movie camera icon. To reach this menu, press the Menu button, then use the left direction button to move the yellow selection block to the left column on the screen and use the up or down direction button or the command dial to navigate to that icon. Then use the right button to move the yellow block back into the list of menu options on the main part of the screen. There are only two main options on this screen, though there are numerous sub-options.

Movie Options

The first choice on the Movie menu, shown in Figure 8-6, lets you choose the size, aspect ratio, quality, and speed of your video footage from 8 possibilities. Before I discuss the specifics of these options, I should point out a limitation of the Coolpix P510 with respect to the length of its video sequences. Like many modern digital cameras that are not primarily video cameras, the P510 is limited to recording only about 29 minutes or 4 GB of video, whichever comes first, in any single sequence. You can store quite a lot of video on a large SD card (for example, you can fit 140 minutes of the highest-quality HD video on a 16GB card), but you can only record 29 minutes at a time; you have to then stop and re-start your recording. And, as noted, any one sequence cannot exceed 4 GB in size, which means there is an effective limit of 25 minutes for recording a sequence at the highest quality. So, choosing a video format that lets you store a great deal of video may not mean as much as it would if you could store a very long single sequence.

With that introduction, here are the details about your various movie format options.

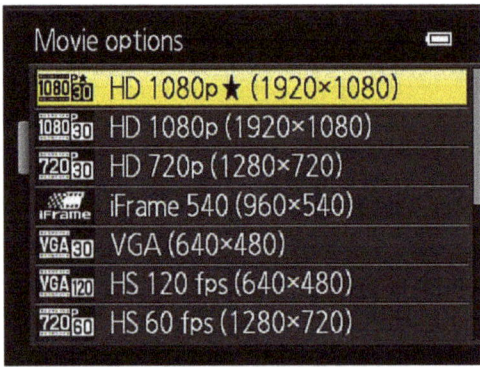

Figure 8-6: Movie Options menu item

The top two selections look very similar on the menu; they both are designated as HD 1080p, which means they provide high-definition video with 1080 vertical pixels and 1920 horizontal pixels, the same amount on the highest-quality HDTV sets. This standard is sometimes called "Full HD" to distinguish it from the lesser-quality HD that provides only 720 vertical pixels and 1280 horizontal pixels. The letter "p" following the number 1080 stands for "progressive," which provides higher quality than 1080i, where the "i" stands for "interlaced." The only difference between the two 1080p settings is indicated by the presence of a star on the top one. The top setting is of a higher quality because it provides a higher "bit rate" than the second setting. The bit rate represents the volume of data recorded per second: 18.8 megabits per second for the top option versus 12.6 megabits per second for the second one.

To reduce all of this technical information to its essence, both of the first two choices display your video in the standard 16:9 "widescreen" aspect ratio common to HDTV sets, and both provide excellent results. Choose the top option, which is the default choice, when you want the highest-possible quality for your HD videos. For example, if you plan to show them on a high-quality HDTV set, you have ample storage space on your memory card and computer, and you have a fast SD card (Class 6 or faster) to record to, choose the top option. If you need to conserve storage space but still want a very high level of quality, choose the second one.

The third option on the Movie menu screen, HD 720p, produces footage with 720 vertical and 1280 horizontal pixels, which still provides high-definition video in the 16:9 aspect ratio, but with fewer pixels and somewhat reduced quality. Choose this option if you want HD, but with less-taxing storage and speed requirements for your memory card and computer.

Next, you can chose the iFrame standard, which records your footage with 960 horizontal pixels and 540 vertical ones. This choice still provides the HD quality and the 16:9 widescreen aspect ratio of the standards discussed above. This format was developed by Apple Computer, Inc.; its purpose is to provide increased ease of editing your footage in Apple's iMovie software. So, if you plan to edit your video on a Macintosh using iMovie, you may want to try using the iFrame format. Otherwise, there probably is no advantage to using it.

The next option on the list, VGA, is the last option available for normal-speed movies, and it is the only non-HD format offered for non-high-speed video recording with the Coolpix P510. The VGA format is named after the standard resolution of an old-fashioned (video graphics array) computer monitor, which has a display of 640 horizontal pixels and 480 vertical ones, resulting in an aspect ratio of 4:3, like that of the camera's LCD display. This format has the advantage of using virtually all of the area of the camera's display, but, of course, it does not provide the quality of high-definition video. Its appearance will be noticeably coarse and rough in comparison to that of HD footage. You may want to choose this option if you don't need high quality and just need to record information, such as doing a video inventory of your household goods. Or, you may choose this option if your memory card is running out of space or does not provide the speed that is required for recording HD formats. Also, if you plan to send the footage by e-mail, this format will be easier to deal with than the HD ones.

HS Movie Options

The next choice on the Movie Options menu, HS 120 fps, is the first one for recording HS (high-speed) movies with the Coolpix P510. I have not discussed the HS capabilities of the camera before now, so I will take this opportunity to explain the use of this very interesting feature.

First, the use of the abbreviation HS, for high-speed, is something of a misnomer. Actually, the HS choices include both high-speed and low-speed options. It would be more accurate to use a term such as "non-standard-speed," but that would be rather awkward. HS is a convenient shorthand, but bear in mind that it is not precisely accurate.

With that introduction, here is a brief explanation of how the HS feature works. The standard rate for recording and playing back video (in the United States) is 30 frames per second. That is, the camera takes 30 individual images each second and then plays them back at that same rate. When your eyes see those images, the pictures follow each other so rapidly that it seems as if the motion in the scene is continuous, rather than 30 separate still photos, which is the actual situation.

If you have seen old silent movies, they sometimes seem unnaturally fast and jerky. That happens because those movies were recorded at a slower speed than movies of today, but sometimes are played back on modern projectors at a faster rate. So, if a movie were recorded at, say, 15 frames per second, and then played back at 30 frames per second, the action in the movie would appear to be twice as fast as normal, resulting in a jumpy, jerky, speeded-up appearance.

Similarly, if you were to set a camera to record at 60 frames per second, and then play back the footage at 30 frames per second, the action would appear to be slowed down to one-half its normal rate.

The Coolpix P510 gives you the ability to either increase or decrease the frame rate at which it records video footage. It's important to note that the video will always play back in the camera at the standard 30 frames per second; the only factor you can change is the speed at which the video is recorded.

With that background, I will discuss each of the HS options on the Movie Options menu screen.

The first choice, HS 120 fps, sets the camera to record video at 120 frames per second, which, of course, is 4 times faster than the normal 30 fps. When this footage is played back in the camera, any movement will appear to be at one-fourth normal speed. This setting provides a capability for slow-motion video, which you can use to analyze a golf swing, slow down the beating of a hummingbird's wings, or for any of a myriad of sports and nature applications. Or, you might just like slow-motion for its dreamlike, underwater-style appearance.

One major caveat with this setting is that, not surprisingly, the use of this setting requires a sharp trade-off of speed against quality. When you set the camera to record 120 frames per second, it automatically reduces the quality to VGA, which provides noticeably lower quality than HD. The aspect ratio is 4:3. There also is another limitation: The camera can only record for 7 minutes and 15 seconds at this rate, which results in a playback time of 29 minutes, the limit for video playback. However, for many applications, that amount of time should be sufficient.

The next setting, HS 60 fps, gives you half as much slow-motion capability as the first one, at greater quality. In this case, your footage will play back at one-half normal speed, and at 720p HD quality. You can record at this speed for 14 minutes and 30 seconds, again resulting in the full 29 minutes of playback time.

Finally, we come to the last option on the list, which turns the whole exercise in a different direction. This option, HS 15 fps, is the only one in which the camera records video at a slower than normal speed. In this case, when played back at the normal 30 frames per second, the footage will appear to be speeded up to twice the normal speed. And, as a bonus, because the camera is actually doing less work in terms of speed, it can provide higher-quality video: full HD, at 1920 by 1080 pixels, recording for 29 minutes, with a playback time of 14 minutes and 30 seconds.

What would you use this option for? Well, one possibility is if you would like to create a movie with the speeded-up look of old silent films, maybe to inject a light touch into a business presentation, or just for some fun with footage of the family at the beach. You also could use this mode for some situations in which you need a video record, but you don't need (or want) to have a real-time recording. For example, if you would like to record the patterns of automobile traffic at an intersection near your home or office, you could set up the camera on a tripod, turn it on in HS 15 fps mode, and you would then have a video that would reveal the pattern at twice the normal speed, which actually might be easier to interpret than a real-time movie.

Of course, shooting half-speed movies (to show them at double speed) is a mild form of time-lapse photography. If you really want to do time-lapse photography for applications such as showing a flower opening up or recording the progress of a construction project, you would be much better off using the interval timer function of the Continuous shooting item on the Shooting menu, as discussed in Chapter 4.

Autofocus Mode

This second and final choice on the Movie menu controls how the camera focuses when recording videos.

Your focus options for movie-making are a bit tricky, so I'll go through them again here. First, it's important to remember that the shooting mode you select has an impact on video recording in this area. That is, if you choose the Auto shooting mode, the camera will use autofocus for video shooting. However, if you choose the Program, Aperture Priority, Shutter Priority, or Manual exposure mode, you have the option of choosing manual focus, and that choice will carry over to video shooting.

So, if you want to use the Autofocus Mode option while shooting a movie, you have to make sure that you have the camera set for autofocus, not manual focus. If the camera is set for manual focus, you will still be able to set the Autofocus Mode option on the Movie menu, but it will have no effect. When you press the red Movie button to start recording, you will see the MF indication on the screen, indicating that manual focus is in effect. At that point, you cannot switch the camera into autofocus mode; you will have to focus manually using the up and down direction buttons or the Side Zoom Control, if you have programmed that control to handle manual focus.

Assuming that you have activated autofocus, you have the choice of two options for Autofocus Mode on the Movie menu, as shown in Figure 8-7: AF-S for Single AF, or AF-F for Full-time AF. These labels are self-explanatory. If you select AF-F, the camera will continually adjust its focus as the scene changes. The camera will focus on any object in the center of the frame. The advantage of this mode is that the focus will remain sharp (with some fuzziness during focus adjustments) throughout the scene; the disadvantage is that the camera likely will pick up the sounds of the autofocus mechanism. So, if you are planning to use the sound track as recorded by the camera, you might want to avoid using the AF-F setting.

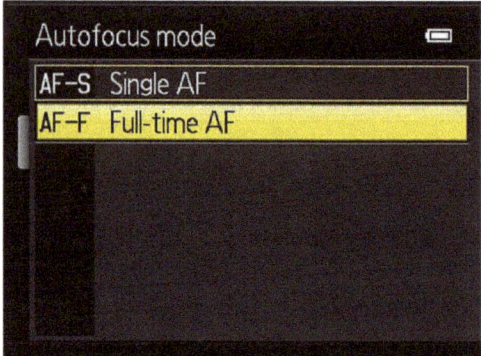

Figure 8-7: Autofocus mode for movies

If you select the AF-S setting, the camera will initially focus just once, when you start recording. However, while the recording is in progress, you can force the camera to re-focus at any time by pressing the left direction button. You will see a prompt at the bottom the screen, with an icon that highlights that button in yellow, as shown in Figure 8-8.

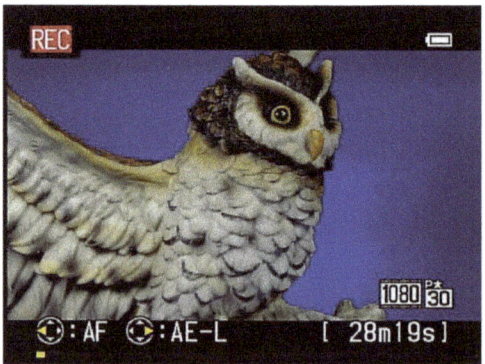

Figure 8-8: Movie recording screen showing AF prompt

So, you don't need to worry that the scene will get out of focus if the distance to the subject changes; just press the left button and the lens will focus again. Here, again, there is a good chance of recording the sounds made by the autofocus mechanism, but at least you can control when that action takes place.

I recommend that you choose your autofocus setting according to the situation. For example, if you are filming in an environment where the focus distance is likely to keep changing and there is a good deal of ambient sound in any event, or the sound does not matter much (say, at a carnival or fair), I recommend using the AF-F setting so the camera continues to adjust its focus as needed. However, if you are recording a school play or concert, where the focus sounds may detract from the sounds of the performance and the focus distance should not change that dramatically, you may be better off using the AF-S setting, with the knowledge that you can adjust the focus by pressing the left direction button if necessary.

Movie Playback and Editing

In Chapter 2, I discussed the fundamentals of movie playback. Now it's time to go into more detail about that topic and to discuss how to edit your video footage in the camera.

Playback

When the camera is in full-screen playback mode, you can recognize a movie by the movie format icon in the lower right corner of the display, as shown in Figure 8-9

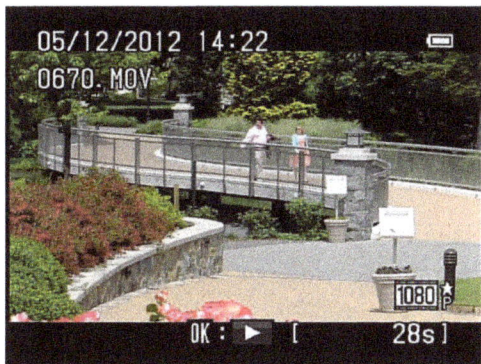

Figure 8-9: Movie ready for playback

When the camera is showing thumbnail images in screens of 4 or 16, you can recognize a movie by the sets of small gray blocks that look like movie film sprockets on the sides of the images, as in Figure 8-10. (With screens of 72 thumbnails, there is no way to distinguish movies from stills; you need to move the zoom lever to the right to get to a screen with larger thumbnails to tell which ones represent movies.)

With a movie's frame on the display, press OK to start it playing. You will see a line of VCR-like icons at the top left, as seen in Figure 8-11. Use the left and right direction buttons to move to any of those icons, then press OK to choose that function. The controls are, from left, rewind, play/pause, stop, and fast-forward. You can also turn the command dial or multi selector dial to the left or right to rewind or fast-forward the movie.

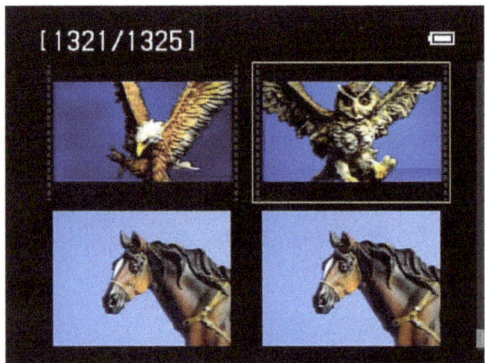

Figure 8-10: Index screen showing two movies at top

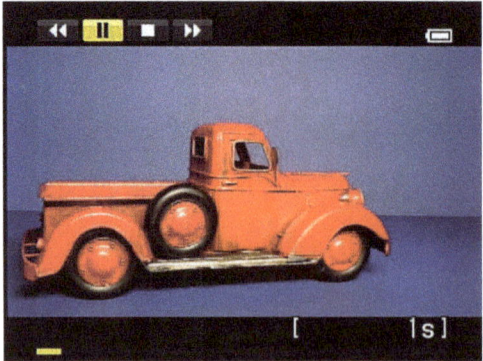

Figure 8-11: Movie playback screen with playback controls

Shortly after the movie starts playing, the icons will disappear. You can then press the OK button again to pause the playback and bring the icons back on the display. At that point, while the movie is paused, there will be a somewhat different group of icons, as shown in Figure 8-12.

From the left, those icons represent single-frame back, play, stop, single-frame forward, edit, and extract and save a single frame. If you hold down the OK button while highlighting the single-frame forward or back icon, the frames will advance continuously, one at a time, at a slow rate. You can also use the command dial or the multi selector dial to advance and rewind the frames at that rate.

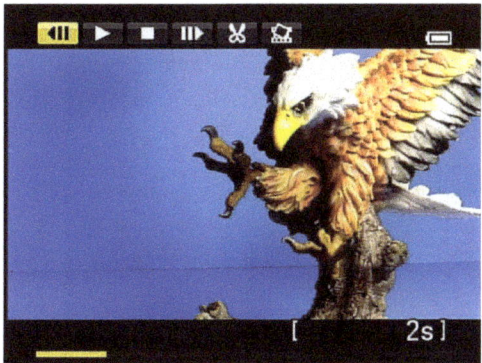

Figure 8-12: Movie playback showing full controls

Editing

Of course, you cannot do anything like full-blown video editing in the camera; if you want to get really involved in editing, you need to import your video footage into a computer program that has serious editing capabilities, like Adobe's Premiere or Premiere Elements, or Apple's Final Cut or Final Cut Express. If you don't want to purchase a dedicated editing program, if you're a PC user you may already have Windows Movie Maker; Mac users often have iMovie available. Finally, if you purchased your Coolpix new, you have Nikon's software suite, which includes Nikon Movie Editor software.

However, if you're out on a camping trip away from your computer or you need to put together a quick video show to play on a hotel's TV screen, you have the ability to perform some rudimentary trimming of your P510 video files in the camera. (You cannot perform any in-camera editing with videos recorded in the iFrame format.) Here is what you can do.

First, you can save a portion of an original video to a new file by trimming away footage at the beginning and/or end of a clip. To do this, start by playing the video to the approximate location where you want the new, shorter clip to start. Then pause the clip by pressing the OK button, and quickly (while the icons stay on the screen), use the right direction button to highlight the scissors icon and press OK to select that icon.

You will now see a vertical menu of icons, representing, from top to bottom: Choose Start Point; Choose End Point; Preview; Save; and Back, as shown in Figure 8-13.

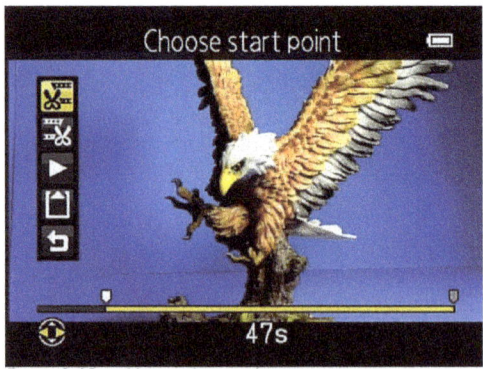

Figure 8-13: Movie editing - choosing start point

There will be a yellow bar at the bottom of the screen, with a white pointer at the left end and a gray pointer at the right end.

The top icon, Choose Start Point, will be highlighted. You can now use the left and right direction buttons to adjust the position of the white pointer, indicating the starting point for the new clip. If you prefer, you can use the command dial or the multi selector dial to move the pointer. If you have to move the start point more than a few seconds, it may take you quite a while to do so, because each press of the direction buttons moves the pointer only a small fraction of a second in the clip.

When you have finished moving the left (start) point, press the down direction button to highlight the second icon down in the menu, for Choose End Point. Repeat the previous procedure, but move the right (end) point in towards the center of the yellow bar.

When both the start and end points are set as you want them, highlight the third icon, which looks like a Play button; this control lets you preview the adjusted clip. If the preview looks okay, press the OK button to stop it if necessary, and move down to the next icon, a rectangle with a small triangle at its top. When that icon is highlighted, press the OK button, and the camera will ask if you want to save the clip in its new length, as shown in Figure 8-14.

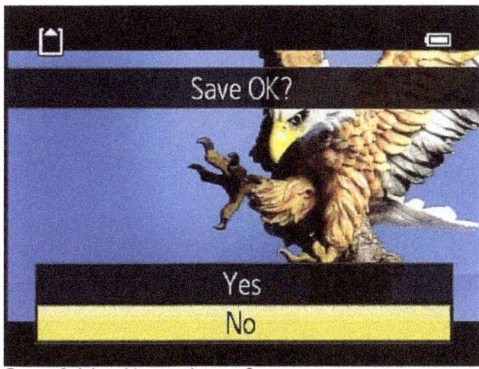

Figure 8-14: Movie editing - Save prompt

If you want to save the clip, highlight the Yes bar and press the OK button. The camera may take quite a while to save the new, shorter version of the clip; the original will remain untouched.

Finally, you can save a single frame from any video clip taken with the P510, except for clips made in the iFrame format. To do this, start playing the movie to the approximate point where you want to extract a frame, then press the OK button to pause the movie. You will then (briefly) see the icons for playing, advancing or reversing by single frames, as well as editing and saving a single frame. (If the icons disappear before you can use them, press the OK button to bring them back on the screen.)

Use the advance and reverse controls to move to the exact frame that you want to save. Then, if necessary, press the OK button to bring the icons back onto the screen, highlight the one at the far right that looks like a frame next to some movie footage, and press the OK button. When the camera displays a message asking if you want to copy that frame as a still image, as shown in Figure 8-15, highlight the Yes bar and press the OK button to confirm.

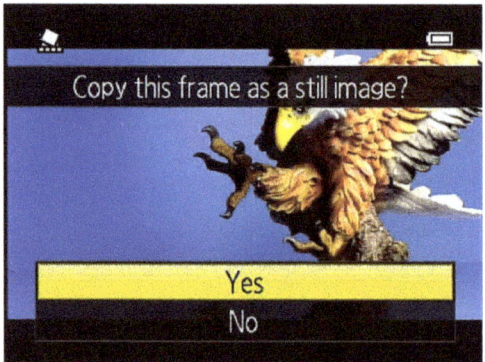

Figure 8-15: Movie editing - copy frame

The camera will then display your new still image with a .jpg file name. The still picture is saved in the Normal quality, with the same image size as that of the format of the movie it was extracted from.

Chapter 9: Other Topics

Using the Superzoom Lens

The first special topic to discuss for the Coolpix P510 is, naturally enough, its lens, which is remarkable for its range at both ends—wide-angle and telephoto. To put it in non-technical terms, the focal length of a lens is a measure of how wide is its view of a scene and of how powerfully it enlarges the view. The standard for stating focal lengths for digital cameras such as the P510 is called "35mm equivalent," meaning the focal length is stated as if the camera were a SLR or rangefinder camera that uses 35mm film.

With those cameras, a "normal" lens—one that is used for everyday shooting of family scenes, portraits, and the like—is often considered to be a 50mm lens. Using that system, a "wide-angle" lens would be in the range of 35mm or lower, and a "telephoto" lens would be one with a focal length of 100mm or greater. The P510, of course, has a "variable focal length" lens, more commonly known as a "zoom" lens. The 35mm equivalent focal lengths of this lens range from a very wide 24mm to an astounding 1000mm at the telephoto end, for an overall range of about 42 times optical zoom. (None of this discussion will involve digital zoom, which is not a "real" zoom capability, as discussed in Chapter 4.)

Of course, as with many things in life, there are trade-offs for having this tremendous zoom range. It is not possible to provide the same quality in a zoom lens of this type as in lenses used by professional photographers at professional sporting events, for example. A good Nikon zoom lens for a DSLR can easily cost more than $1,000, and a top-quality Nikon telephoto (non-zoom) lens can cost more than $10,000. However, for everyday photography, the P510 provides you with the ability to capture scenes with an array of focal lengths that is practically unmatched in the world of consumer cameras.

At the wide-angle end, the P510's lens gives you several millimeters more than most cameras in its class. A wide-angle range starting at 28mm is often considered quite adequate, and only a few compact digital cameras offer a zoom range starting as low as 24mm. The 24mm focal length of the P510 is very useful when you need to photograph a large group of people without standing back a great distance. Also, if you need to photograph the interiors of rooms, this focal length is a great bonus, because you will likely be able to capture an excellent view of the entire room by standing in one corner.

But it is the telephoto range of the P510's lens that is the most dramatic feature of the camera, so I will concentrate on discussing its use.

First, and maybe most obvious, the extreme telephoto range of the P510's zoom lens is so powerful that it can capture details that you cannot even begin to see with the naked eye. For example, the image in Figure 9-1 was taken with the P510's lens zoomed all the way out to its 24mm wide-angle setting. This shot shows the conservatory building at a botanical garden. Although you can see the building and its surroundings, you cannot make out any details about the building or its entrance.

Now, look at Figure 9-2. This shot was taken at the same time and place as the other shot, with the camera on the tripod as for the wide-angle shot. This time, though, the lens was zoomed in to the full 1000mm extent of the optical zoom. You can see close-up details about the entrance that are not in any way visible in the first view.

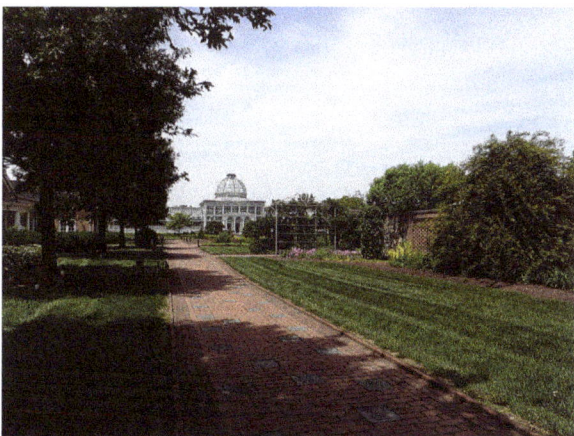

Figure 9-1: Wide-angle view of conservatory

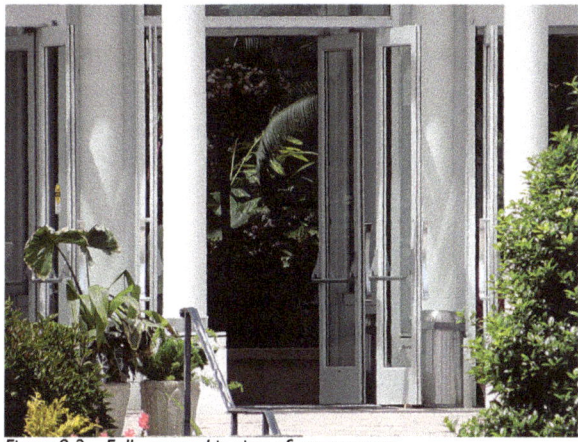

Figure 9-2: Fully zoomed-in view of conservatory

Because the superzoom capability of the P510 is one of its hallmark features, I am going to include one more example of the way in which this camera can reveal things you could not see without the zoom lens. When I took my trip to the park by the James River, as I noted in the discussion of GPS features in Chapter 7, I took quite a few shots of the river from the shore. In Figure 9-3, you see an image taken at the 24mm wide-angle setting.

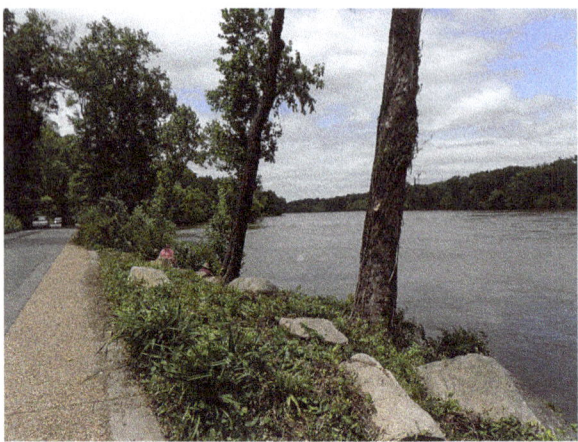

Figure 9-3: Wide-angle view of river

In this view, at the size the picture will appear in this book, you won't be able to see anything at all in the spot that the zoomed-in image focuses on. That spot is between the two trees in the center of the image, just about in the exact center of the scene. Figure 9-4, taken at the 1000mm maximum optical zoom range, reveals the group of turtles basking in the sun.

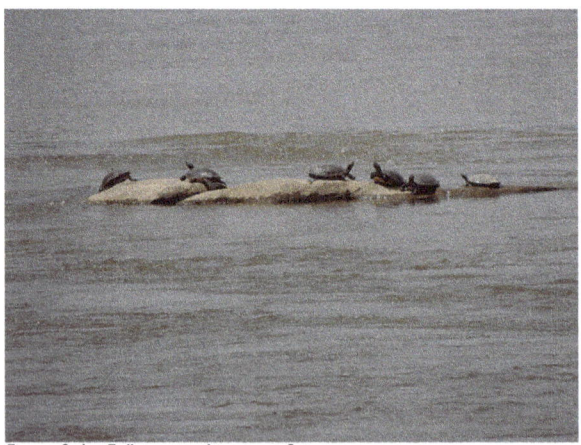

Figure 9-4: Fully zoomed-in view of river

When you use the Coolpix P510's powerful zoom lens at its highest power, you will encounter some issues. For one thing, as you may be able to tell from the shot of the turtles, images shot at this power suffer somewhat from the compression of the atmosphere; in other words, you're shooting through a lot of air, which can add a hazy aura to the image.

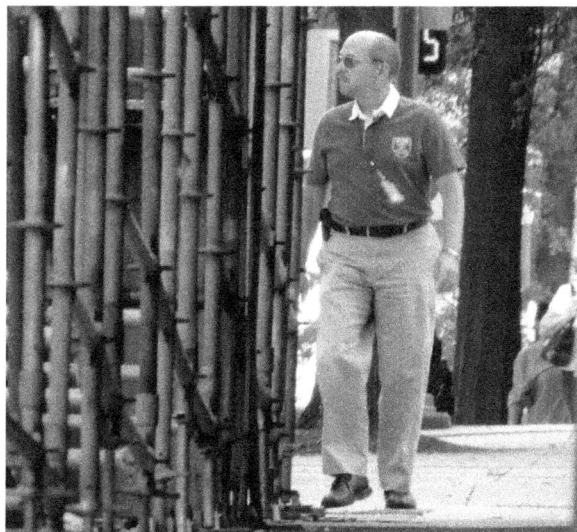

Figure 9-5: Compression effect from maximum zoom

Figure 9-5, also taken at the full optical zoom range of 1000mm, illustrates the haze effect as well as another phenomenon— flattening or compression of the objects you are photographing. In this case, I was using the P510 for street photography at some distance. The result of using such a powerful zoom in this case is that everything appears flattened up into a single plane, even though the subjects actually are separated by some distance. So, if you take photographs that show people or objects at various distances from the camera, don't be surprised if they are flattened out with this two-dimensional effect.

However, you very well may find creative uses for this flattening effect, which can give a distinctive look to your photos.

Another positive side of the super-long zoom range is its ability to isolate a single subject. If you use the zoom to focus on a particular person in a crowd or on a particular animal in a pack, you can fill the frame with that single subject, thereby emphasizing its importance.

Perhaps the greatest overall benefit of the superzoom lens on the Coolpix P510 is that it gives you the equivalent of a whole range of focal lengths without the need to carry around a bag crammed full of lenses. In practical terms, with the P510 you have at your fingertips every focal length that a photographer could reasonably want or need for everyday photography, ranging from the wide-angle 24mm with a strong macro capability to the super 1000mm telephoto.

Here is one more use for the superzoom lens—astrophotography. Of course, the Coolpix P510 is not a camera that a dedicated sky photographer would likely choose; a more likely choice would be a DSLR with a telescope adapter, or a specialized astrophotography camera. However, because of its very long zoom range, the P510 actually can achieve some pleasing results for subjects that are easy to track, such as the moon. The shot seen in Figure 9-6 was taken with the P510 at the full 1000mm zoom range, at f/6.6 with a shutter speed of 1/160 second and an ISO setting of 400. As you may expect, I used a tripod.

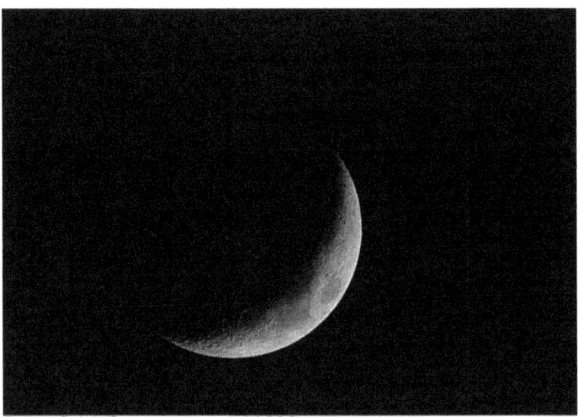

Figure 9-6: Crescent moon at 1000mm zoom range

If you were to work for National Geographic or a professional photography firm, you would not use a P510 to capture your images. But, if you have a chance to go on a safari or a cruise around the world and you want to be able to bring back a complete photographic record of your trip using one lightweight, easy-to-use camera, the P510 fills the bill very nicely.

Now, let's discuss how to avoid some of the problems that come along with a superzoom capability.

First, and probably foremost, is the problem of camera movement. When the lens is zoomed in to its full 1000mm focal length or anywhere close to that range, any slight motion of the camera is multiplied because of the magnification of the image. You will notice how jittery the image looks on the display, and you will find it hard to keep the picture steady.

There are several steps you can take to reduce the effects of camera movement. First, if possible, use a tripod. It can be inconvenient to do, but using a solid tripod is one of the best ways to ensure high-quality images. If you can't manage a full-blown tripod, use a monopod, a lightweight travel tripod, or any support available, such as a fence post, or just sit on a bench and hold the camera steady on your lap, folding the LCD display up toward your face to view your image.

Suppose, though, that you are walking through a field in search of wildlife shots and there is no physical support available. There are several things you can do to minimize the effects of camera shake. First, you should make sure that the Vibration Reduction feature is turned on through the Setup menu. This system counteracts camera movement quite effectively, up to a point. Also, you may find you can hold the camera steadier if you activate the electronic viewfinder (using the Monitor button to the left of the viewfinder), so you can hold the camera against your forehead and look into the viewfinder, rather than using the LCD display at some distance from your face.

Next, use the fastest shutter speed you can. If the shutter is open for only a very brief instant, there will not be time for camera motion to register on the image. According to one rule of thumb, when hand-holding a zoom lens you should use a shutter speed no slower than the fraction of a second with the focal length of the lens as the denominator. So, if the lens of the P510 is zoomed all the way in to 1000mm, you would use a shutter speed of 1/1000 second or faster. In the case of the P510, the choices would be 1/1000, 1/1250, 1/1600, 1/2000, 1/2500, 1/3200, and 1/4000, though not all of these speeds are available at all times, as discussed earlier in connection with the discussion of shooting modes.

Of course, if you want to control the shutter speed, you should use Shutter Priority as your shooting mode, as discussed in Chapter 3. You also could use Manual mode, if you are willing to accept the added task of setting the aperture correctly. Or, if you would like to use Program mode, you can let the camera set the shutter speed and aperture initially, and then use the Flexible Program feature, which lets you turn the command dial to select new combinations of shutter speed and aperture that are equivalent to what the camera selected.

However, you are quite likely to run into a problem if you use the camera's standard settings and try to set a fast shutter speed. One of the unfortunate characteristics of the super-zoom lens on the P510 is that, as was discussed in Chapter 3, its maximum aperture when zoomed in is quite narrow. When the lens is zoomed all the way out to wide-angle, the maximum (widest open) aperture is f/3.0, which is not exceptionally wide to start with, though it is wide enough for most purposes. But, when the lens is zoomed in, it rapidly loses the ability to use a wide aperture.

When the lens is zoomed all the way in, the maximum aperture is f/5.9. In order to use a shutter speed of 1/1000 second or faster at that rather narrow aperture, there will have to be a good deal of light, unless you change some other settings. If the light is not sufficiently bright to expose your images well at a fast shutter speed, you still have some options available.

In this case, your best option probably is to increase the ISO sensitivity of the camera, which will mean that the camera's image sensor will require less light to expose the picture, at the risk of increased visual noise in the image. Using the ISO Sensitivity setting in the Shooting menu, you may want to try setting ISO to Auto, in which case the camera will set it as high as 1600 if conditions warrant. If you want to be sure a high ISO is set, you should use a specific level, such as ISO 800, ISO 1600, or even ISO 3200.

If you prefer not to boost the ISO, which will introduce grainy noise into the image, one strategy you can employ is to zoom back out somewhat until the camera can use a wider aperture, such as, say, f/5.1 or f/4.6. Later on, when editing your photos with software, you can crop them to achieve the same field of view you originally saw with the zoomed-in lens, though with some loss of quality because of the cropping.

Another possible strategy for getting good, clear images with the superzoom lens is to take advantage of the P510's excellent array of continuous-shooting options. With several of these options, the camera will take multiple shots in rapid succession, increasing the likelihood that one or more shots will be usable. You also will experience a decline in image size and quality with some of these settings, though, so you need to consider the balancing factors.

One more excellent feature of the Coolpix P510, also found on the list of continuous-shooting options, is the Best Shot Selector (BSS), the 7th choice down on the menu of those choices. When you select BSS, the camera takes a series of 10 consecutive shots and preserves only the single shot that includes the most sharp detail. The downside to this feature is that you can't second-guess the camera; you will never see the nine shots it discarded. However, using BSS is a great way to increase your chances at getting a good, clear shot. Also, it is available in the more advanced shooting modes, so you can, for example, use

Shutter Priority mode and select a fast shutter speed while using BSS to cast a wide net for a super-sharp shot.

If you are not comfortable making so many settings through the menu system and otherwise, all is not lost. You can set the camera to the Auto shooting mode by turning the mode dial to the icon of the green camera, and then make just one setting: Go into the Setup menu and set the Motion Detection item to Auto. Then, if the camera senses motion, it will automatically raise the ISO level and use a faster shutter speed in order to counteract the effects of camera motion.

One more note: Don't forget that the Coolpix P510 offers the very useful U slot on the mode dial, for User Setting. If you use the lens zoomed in frequently, you may want to save your preferred settings for those occasions, so you can quickly call them up just by turning the mode dial to the U setting. For example, you may want to set up the camera in Shutter Priority mode, with a shutter speed of 1/1000 second, with an ISO setting of 1600 and with BSS enabled.

Finally, I recommend that you take advantage of the Side Zoom Control on the P510—the switch on the left side of the camera, below the flash pop-up button. As discussed in Chapter 5, this switch can be of use in two ways in connection with your use of the zoom lens. First, with its default function as an alternative to the zoom lever around the shutter button, this switch can let you hold the camera more firmly in both hands. If you zoom with the left-side switch, you can use your right hand to keep a tight grip on the right side of the camera without having to reach up to the zoom lever.

Second, if you use the Setup menu to assign the snap-back zoom function to this control, you gain a different benefit. In that case, you can use this switch to quickly pull back from a zoomed-in view, so you can get your bearings and see exactly where your subject is in relation to its surroundings, before quickly zooming back in to take the picture. It can be very difficult to locate your subject when the lens is zoomed all the way in to its 1000mm maximum; use the snap-back zoom to get the wider view quickly when you need it for orientation.

Macro (Close-up) Shooting

Macro photography is the art or science of taking photographs when the subject is shown at actual size (1:1 ratio between size of subject and size of image) or slightly magnified (greater than 1:1 ratio). So if you photograph a flower using macro techniques, the image of the flower will be about the same size as the actual flower. You can get wonderful detail in your images using macro photography, and you may discover things about the subject that you had not noticed before taking the photograph.

The Coolpix P510 is quite capable of shooting macro photographs, like the one in Figure 9-7 showing a small toy soldier.

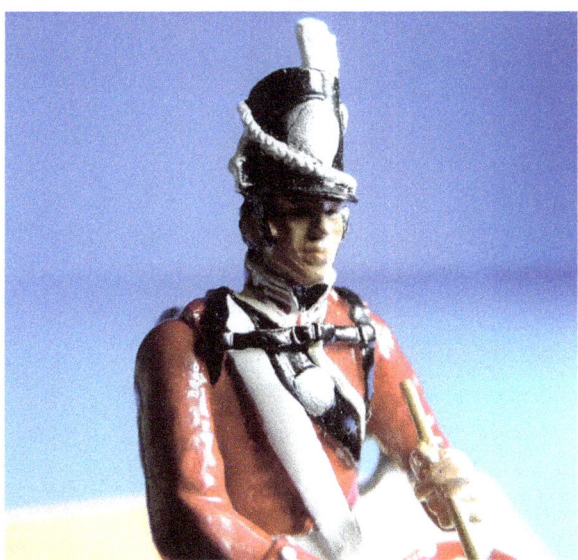

Figure 9-7: Macro shot taken 1 inch (2.5 cm) from lens

This figure is only about 2.5 inches (6.35 cm) tall, but in this view, taken at a distance of about 1 inch (2.5 cm), it looks like a considerably larger model.

As was discussed in Chapter 5, you activate macro focus as follows: Press the bottom direction button on the multi selector to bring up the focus menu, then press the up and down buttons or use the command dial or multi selector dial to move to the flower icon, indicating macro autofocus mode, as shown in Figure 9-8.

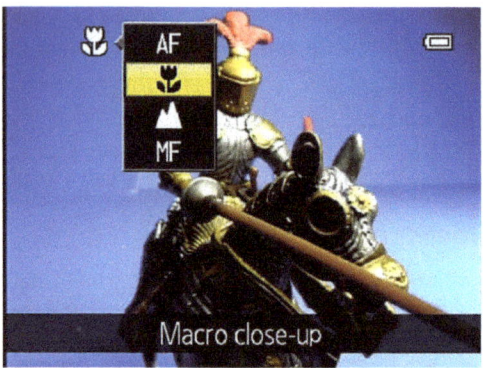

Figure 9-8: Macro focus selection on focus menu

You can choose macro autofocus in Auto mode or in the Program, Aperture Priority, Shutter Priority, or Manual exposure mode, as well as the following Scene modes: Beach, Snow, Museum, Black and White Copy, Pet Portrait, and 3D Photography. In the Close-up and Food modes, macro focus is selected automatically. Macro focus is available for selection with all settings of the Special Effects shooting mode.

On the Coolpix P510, with the autofocus mode set to macro the camera is able to focus as close as four inches (10 centimeters) when the lens is in the near-wide-angle range. This range is indicated on the display by the flower icon and the zoom bar, both of which turn green when the camera's lens is in the range for macro shooting as close as this. So, just watch the flower icon and the bar; as long they both stay green, you can focus as close as four inches. The image in Figure 9-9 shows the zoom scale at this range.

CHAPTER 9: OTHER TOPICS

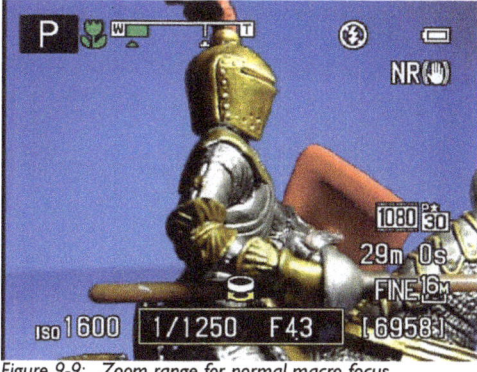

Figure 9-9: Zoom range for normal macro focus

That is not the closest macro range available with the P510, however. At its optimum zoom range, as shown in Figure 9-10, the camera can focus on objects as close as about 0.4 inch (one centimeter). This capability exists from the full wide-angle setting of 24mm up to a point when the lens is zoomed in slightly, to a focal length of about 32mm. The camera doesn't provide a readout of the focal length, so you won't see any numbers to let you know when the lens is zoomed to the 32mm mark, and that focal length is not one that is available with the Zoom Memory feature.

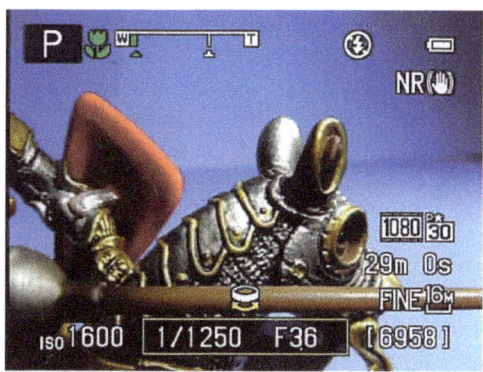

Figure 9-10: Zoom range for closest macro focus

However, you can tell when you have reached this focal length by looking carefully at the zoom bar that the P510 places at the top of the screen when you are zooming. When the lens

281

is zoomed to the upper limit of the optimum focal length for macro shooting, the bar extends out just to the position of a small green triangle that is right below the bar, as shown in Figure 9-10. Throughout this narrow range, you should be getting the closest possible macro focusing.

With normal autofocus, the camera can focus only to about 1 foot 8 inches (50 cm) at the wide-angle position, and only to about 5 feet (1.5 meters) at the full telephoto position.

If you don't want to have to fine-tune the zoom position to set macro focusing as close as possible, there are two easier methods. First, you can use the Close-up setting in Scene mode. The camera will adjust for the closest possible macro shooting, setting the focus and the zoom position. It also turns on continuous autofocus and sets the AF Area Mode to Manual, so you can adjust the position of the focus frame on the screen. To move the frame, press the OK button and then use the direction buttons to adjust the frame's position. Press OK to anchor it in place.

Another possibility for close-up focusing is to select the Food setting within Scene mode. This setting is similar to Close-up, except that it adds an adjustment slider so you can fine-tune the hues of the foods (or other items) you are photographing.

You don't have to use either the macro autofocus setting or one of the Scene settings to take macro shots; if you set the camera to manual focus by pressing the down direction button and then selecting MF from the on-screen menu, you can also focus on objects very close to the lens. You do, however, lose the benefit of automatic focus, and it can be tricky finding the correct focus manually. However, the camera does enlarge the view on the screen when manual focus is in use, and I have had good success using manual focus for macro shots.

When shooting extreme close-ups, you should use a tripod or other solid stand, because the depth of field is very shallow and you need to keep the camera steady to take a usable photograph. It's also a good idea to take advantage of the self-timer. If you take the picture using the self-timer, you will not be touching the camera when the shutter is activated, so the chance of camera shake is minimized. You should also leave the built-in flash retracted so it can't fire. Flash from the built-in unit at such a close range would be of no use.

Using Flash

As I discussed earlier, pressing the up direction button on the multi selector, the one marked with a lightning bolt, gives you access to the various settings for the built-in flash unit on the Coolpix P510, as shown in Figure 9-11.

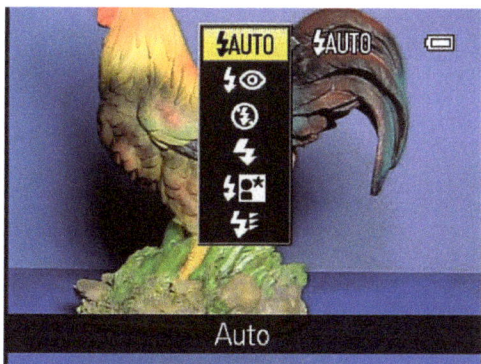

Figure 9-11: Flash mode menu

Before I discuss the details of those settings, it's important to recall one basic fact about this camera: The flash cannot fire unless you first pop it up by pressing the flash pop-up button marked by a lightning bolt on the left side of the flash housing, near the top of the camera. If you think there's any chance the flash may be used, go ahead and press that button to have the flash ready. (If you're shooting movies, though, you should make sure the flash is down out of the way, because it can't be used and might interfere with your shooting.)

The next point to note about the built-in flash on the P510 is that a lot depends on the shooting mode you have set on the mode dial. If that dial is set to Auto, Program, Shutter priority,

Aperture priority, or Manual exposure, you will generally have access to all six settings for the flash. However, other shooting modes place limits on your flash choices. For example, in Night Portrait mode, the flash is set to Auto with Red-eye Reduction—in other words, the flash will fire if necessary, and the camera will use its built-in processing to counteract the red tinge that may result from the red-eye effect of shooting straight into human eyes.

In Night Landscape mode, the flash will be forced off and cannot fire. In Backlighting mode, if you turn on the HDR option through the menu, the flash will be forced off; if you turn off HDR, the flash will be forced on. In various other modes available when the mode dial is set to SCENE, the behavior of the flash varies according to the particular characteristics of the mode. For example, the Museum setting forces the flash off, on the theory that museums generally do not permit flash.

Apart from the shooting mode, there are other factors that affect how the P510 uses flash. So, even if you have the camera set to Program mode, in which you normally would have all six flash modes available, there are some conditions that will disable the flash. For example, you cannot use the flash if you have set the focus to infinity, turned on exposure bracketing, or activated any of the continuous-shooting options other than interval shooting. If you believe the flash should fire but you are unable to turn it on using the flash mode button, check to see if one of the settings mentioned above has been set.

Once you have set the camera to a mode that allows choice of any of the six possible flash settings, such as Program mode, you have to decide whether to choose Auto, Auto with Red-eye Reduction, Off, Fill Flash, Slow Sync, or Rear-curtain sync.

Auto is a mode you are already familiar with—the camera's automatic exposure system will fire the flash if it's needed to achieve a good exposure.

Auto with Red-eye Reduction is a special mode that adds a

technique to prevent or minimize the effects of "red-eye," the unpleasant reddish glow that can appear in people's eyes when the light from the on-camera flash bounces off their retinas and picks up the red from blood vessels. In order to correct for this effect, the P510 performs in-camera processing to remove the red tint from eyes as the image is being saved. In some cases, this processing could affect other areas of the image in unexpected ways, so you should use this setting with care. I personally prefer not to use it; if red-eye appears in an image, it can be corrected with Photoshop or similar software.

Let's consider the other possibilities. Why would you use the Off setting? Wouldn't it be easier to just push the flash unit back down so it won't fire? Well, yes, it might. But you may be a photographer who likes to experiment with various settings. Maybe you are taking portraits outdoors in the shade, and you want to see how they look with and without flash. If you are using Program mode and have the flash set to Auto, it may or may not fire. If you set it to Off, it definitely will not fire, and you can adjust other settings, such as exposure compensation, ISO, Active D-Lighting, and others, to achieve the effect you want without the possibly harsh appearance of flash.

On the other hand, what about the Fill Flash setting? Why would you want to force the flash to fire, when you could set it to Auto and let the camera decide whether it's needed? One case is when there is enough backlighting that the camera's exposure controls could be fooled into thinking the flash isn't needed. If, in your judgment, the subject will be too dark for that reason, you may want to force the flash to fire. Another such situation could be an outdoor portrait for which you need fill-in flash to highlight your subject's face adequately.

How about the Slow Sync setting? Normally, when the P510's built-in flash fires, the camera uses a fast shutter speed because the flash provides enough light to expose the image quickly. If you use the Slow Sync setting, the camera will attempt to take the picture with a considerably slower shutter speed so that the ambient (natural) lighting will have time to register on the image. In other words, if you're in a fairly dark environment and fire the flash normally, it will likely light up the subject (say a person), but because the exposure time is short, the surrounding scene and background may be black. (In Shutter Priority mode, the camera will use whatever shutter speed you set, even with Slow Sync in effect.)

If you use the Slow Sync setting, the slower shutter speed allows the surrounding scene to be visible also. For example, the two photographs in Figures 9-12 and 9-13 were taken at the same time and in the same conditions.

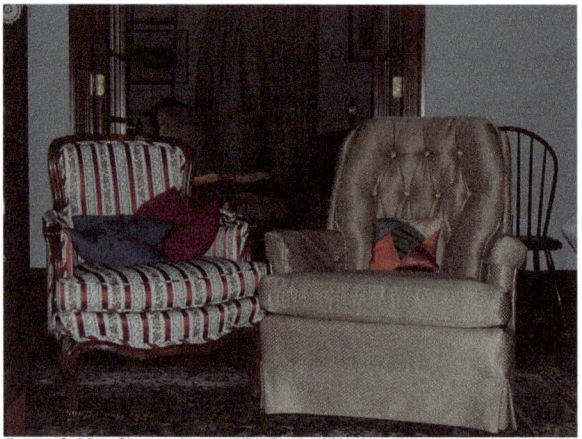

Figure 9-12: Shutter Priority, Fill Flash, 1/160 second

The only difference is that the photo in Figure 9-12 was taken with the shutter speed set at 1/160 second, in Fill Flash mode, while Figure 9-13 was taken in Slow Sync flash mode with a shutter speed of 0.4 second, which allowed the ambient lighting from the farther room to light up that room and make its furniture visible in the picture.

CHAPTER 9: OTHER TOPICS

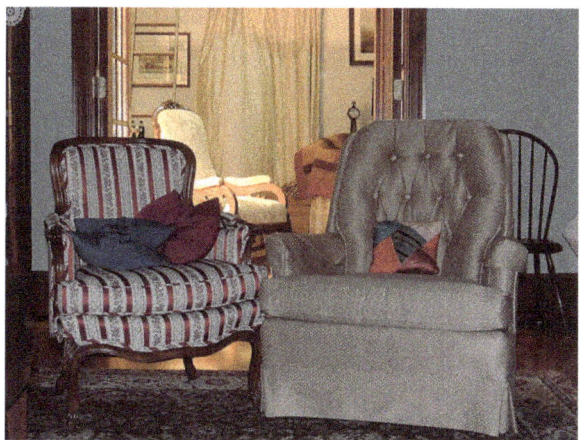

Figure 9-13: Program, Slow Sync, 0.4 second

The last setting on the flash mode menu is Rear-curtain sync. This option is one you may not have a lot of use for unless you encounter the particular situation it is designed for. If you don't activate this setting, the camera uses the unnamed default setting, which could be called Front-curtain sync. In that mode, the flash fires very soon after the shutter opens to expose the image. If you choose the Rear-curtain setting instead, the flash fires later, just before the shutter closes.

The reason for using Rear-curtain sync is to help you avoid a strange-looking result in some situations. This issue arises, for example, with a relatively long exposure, say one-half second, of a subject with lights, such as a car or motorcycle at night, moving across your field of view. With normal (Front-curtain) sync, the flash will fire early in the process, freezing the vehicle in a clear image. However, as the shutter remains open while the vehicle keeps going, the camera will capture the moving lights in a stream extending in front of the vehicle. If, instead, you use Rear-curtain sync, the initial part of the exposure will capture the lights in a trail that appears behind the vehicle, while the vehicle itself is not frozen by the flash until later in the exposure. With Rear-curtain sync in this particular situation, if the lights in question are taillights that look more natu-

287

ral behind the vehicle, the final image is likely to look more natural than with the Front-curtain (default) setting.

Figures 9-14 and 9-15 illustrate this concept using a remote-controlled model truck with no lights, but shot with fairly strong ambient light, so that "ghost" images of the truck appeared during the parts of the exposure before or after the flash fired. Both pictures were shot with the P510's built-in flash, using an exposure of one-half second in Shutter Priority mode. In Figure 9-14, using the normal Front-curtain setting, the flash fired quickly, and the truck continued on during the long exposure to make the "ghost" streaks of red in front of the truck. In Figure 9-15, using Rear-curtain sync, the flash did not fire until the truck had traveled to the right, overtaking the place where the truck had traced a smear of red streaks.

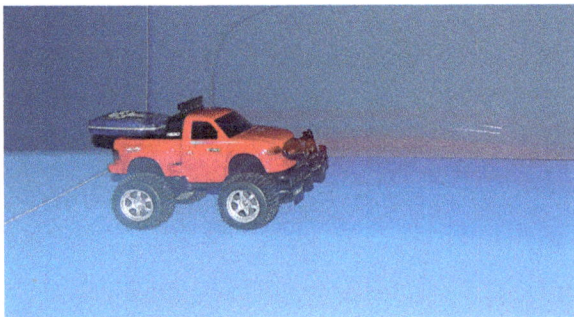

Figure 9-14: Front-curtain sync

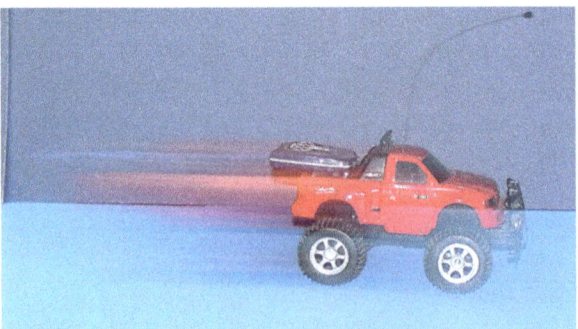

Figure 9-15: Rear-curtain sync

To sum up the situation with the Rear-curtain sync setting, a good general rule is not to use it unless you are sure you have a definite need for it. Using the Rear-curtain setting makes it harder to compose and set up the shot, because you have to anticipate where the main subject will be when the flash finally fires late in the exposure process.

One other setting you should keep in mind is flash exposure compensation, which is available through the Shooting menu when the camera is set to the more advanced shooting modes.

This setting allows you to reduce the intensity of the flash, even when the camera is automatically setting the exposure. Just as with normal exposure compensation, when using flash you can adjust this setting if your test shots appear too bright or too dark. Just go into this menu item and set the value to a positive number to brighten the image or to a negative number to darken it, as shown in Figure 9-16. Just remember to set it back to zero when you no longer need the adjustment, so it does not affect other shots when you don't need it.

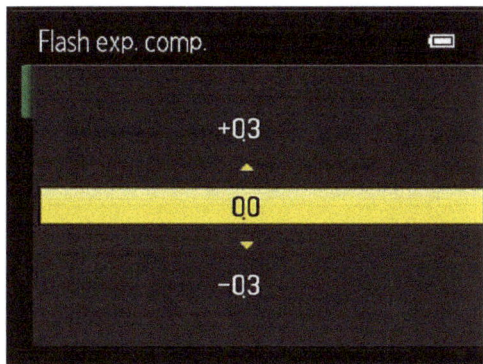

Figure 9-16: Flash exposure compensation

Infrared Photography

In a nutshell, infrared photography involves finding a way for the camera to record images that are illuminated by infrared light, which is invisible to the human eye because it occupies a place on the spectrum of light waves that is beyond our ability to see. In some circumstances, cameras, unlike our eyes, can record images using this type of light. The resulting photographs can be quite spectacular, producing scenes in which green foliage appears white and blue skies appear eerily dark.

Shooting infrared in the times before digital photography involved selecting a particular infrared film and the appropriate filter to place on the lens. With the rise of digital imaging, you need to find a camera that is capable of "seeing" infrared light. Many cameras nowadays include internal filters that block infrared light. However, some cameras do not, or block it only to a relatively small extent. (You can do a quick test of any digital camera by aiming it at the light-emitting end of an infrared remote control and taking a photograph while pressing a button on the remote; if the remote's light shows up as bright white, the camera can "see" infrared light at least to some extent.)

The Coolpix P510 can take good infrared photographs. In order to unleash this capability, you need to take a few steps. The most important is to get a filter that blocks most visible light, but lets infrared light reach the camera's light sensor. (If you don't, the infrared light will be overwhelmed by the visible light, and you'll get an ordinary picture based on visible light.)

As with most experimental efforts, there are many ways to accomplish this. For example, if you search on the internet, you will find discussions of how to improvise an infrared filter out of unexposed but developed (*i.e.*, black) photographic film.

A more reliable way to make infrared photographs with the P510 is to get an infrared filter along with an adapter that lets you attach the filter to the camera. There is an adapter available from a company called Kiwi Foto, which I found on eBay.

This adapter is not ideal, because it extends fairly far out from the lens to avoid letting the filter hit the lens as it extends outward. Because of its length, the adapter causes considerable vignetting—that is, when the camera's lens is at the wide-angle end of its zoom range, your pictures will be shown in a circle, with much of the surrounding image cut off. However, you can work around this problem by zooming the lens in partway, or by cropping away the darkened corners of the image. (I discuss this adapter in more detail in Appendix A.)

The infrared filter I have seen most often recommended is the Hoya R72, and that is what I use. It is a very dark red and blocks most visible light, letting in mainly infrared light rays in the part of the spectrum that produces interesting images.

The next question is to figure out the exposure. Photographers have different approaches, and time spent looking on the internet for discussions of those approaches will be rewarding. For the image shown in Figure 9-17, I set a custom white balance, using brightly sunlit green foliage as the base. That is, I used the camera's White Balance menu setting on the Shooting menu, and, in the screen for setting a Preset Manual white balance, I aimed the camera at the bright green foliage and pressed the OK button. The results were essentially what I expected from infrared photography; scenes with tree leaves and grass that look white, and other unusual, but pleasing effects.

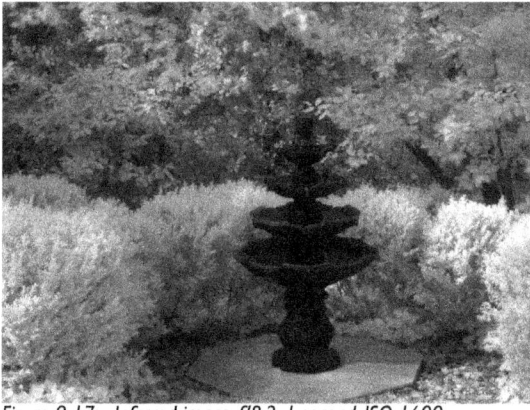

Figure 9-17: Infrared image, f/8.2, 1 second, ISO 1600

For exposure, I set the camera to shoot in Aperture Priority mode and let it select the necessary long shutter speed. (Necessary because of the dark filter.) I set the camera on a tripod and disabled Vibration Reduction, because it is not needed when the camera is stabilized by a tripod. The P510 did the rest, exposing the image for 1 second at f/8.2, with an ISO setting of 1600. You can often get interesting results if you include a good amount of green grass and trees in the image, as well as blue sky and clouds.

Street Photography

The Coolpix P510 is not the first camera that would come to mind for what I normally think of as street photography—that is, shooting candid pictures in public settings, often without the subject's knowledge. In my opinion, cameras that are well-suited for this type of work are small, lightweight, and unobtrusive in appearance, so they can easily be held casually or hidden in the photographer's hand. The P510, of course, is somewhat bulky and not that easily concealed from view. However, it does have its good points for this type of photography. Its 24mm equivalent wide-angle lens is excellent for taking in a broad field of view, for times when you shoot from the hip without framing the image carefully on the screen.

In addition, I have come to appreciate the P510's movable LCD screen for street photography, because, if you fold it out so it is parallel to the ground, you can look down at the screen to frame your shots without drawing a lot of attention to yourself. With this system, I have found that I can even zoom in on a subject across the street and keep the framing accurate while looking down at the screen. Also, the camera shoots quickly and performs well at high ISO settings, so you can use a relatively fast shutter speed to avoid motion blur. The numerous options for continuous shooting, including the Best Shot Selector setting, give you a good chance to get a sharp image under difficult circumstances. And, you can make the camera completely silent by turning off the beeps and shutter sounds through the Setup menu.

What are the best settings for street shooting with the Coolpix P510? If you ask that question on one of the online forums, you are, naturally, likely to get many different responses. I'm going to give you some fairly broad guidelines as a starting point. The answer depends in part on your own personal style of shooting, such as whether you will talk to your subjects and get their agreement to being photographed before you start shooting, or whether you will fire away from across the street with a zoomed-in lens and accept the risk of blurry photos from camera shake at such a long focal length.

Here are a couple of approaches you can start with and modify as you see fit. Some photographers like to shoot in color at the highest quality and image size and then use post-processing software such as Photoshop or Lightroom to convert their images to black-and-white, along with any other effects they are looking for, such as extra grain to achieve a gritty look. (Of course, you don't have to produce your street photography in black-and-white, but that is the usual practice.) I recommend you shoot in Shutter Priority mode at a fairly fast shutter speed, say, 1/100 second or faster, to stop action on the street and to avoid blur from camera movement. You can set ISO to Auto, or possibly use a high ISO setting, in the range of 800 or so, if you don't mind some visual noise. You may want to set the aspect ratio to 16:9 (by selecting an image size of 4608 x 2592 pixels) in order to take in a wide field of view for street scenes. (You could shoot at the maximum image size and then crop down to this size, but then you would not have the benefit of seeing the 16:9 aspect ratio on the screen as you composed your shots.)

Another option is to set image quality and size to their highest settings and set the Picture Control feature on the Shooting menu to the Monochrome option. You may use the standard settings for Monochrome, or you may go beyond the standard screen by pressing the right direction button, and tweak the settings a bit. For example, you may want to try boosting contrast by one notch and reducing sharpening the same amount. To get the gritty "street" look, you also could try setting the camera's ISO to 1600 to include some visual grain in the image while boosting sensitivity enough to stop action with a fast shutter speed.

If you don't mind ignoring labels and trying something unconventional, you might consider turning the mode dial to the Scene setting and choosing the Black and White Copy option. Of course, that mode is designed for taking pictures of pages from a book and similar items, but it gives you another avenue for taking black-and-white photos without having to fiddle with menu settings. I suggest you at least try this option if you have an interest in street photography.

Also, consider turning on continuous shooting so you'll get several images to choose from for each shutter press. To get the best combination of quality and speed, choose Continuous H, though you are limited to five shots at a time.

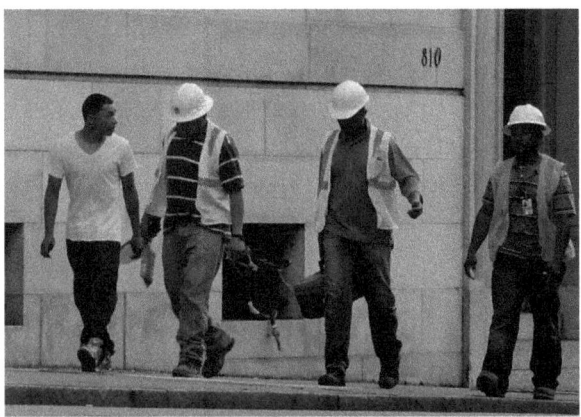

Figure 9-18: Street photograph, f/4.6, 1/200 sec, ISO 400

For the image shown in Figure 9-18, I shot at f/4.6 with a shutter speed of 1/200 second, zoomed in to 225mm, at ISO 400. I used high-speed continuous shooting to increase my chances of getting a good, clear shot.

If you don't mind letting the camera choose which shot to keep out of the 10 it takes, try the Best Shot Selector feature. For any of these options, though, you have to use one of the advanced shooting modes (P, A, S, or M)—you can't shoot in the Auto or Scene modes. Also, one drawback to using continuous shooting is that you'll have to wait for the camera to finish recording its sequence of rapid shots before you can start shooting again, so you could miss a photo opportunity while waiting.

I generally use normal autofocus for this type of shooting, though some photographers like to use manual focus, with the range set for the approximate distance where you expect your subjects to be. If I am shooting down at street level, fairly close to my subjects, I often leave the lens zoomed back to its full wide-angle position to maintain a broad depth of field and keep most of the image in focus.

With the P510, though, you may want to at least experiment with long-range street photography, taking advantage of the superzoom lens. This approach has the advantage of letting you stay at a comfortable distance from your subjects. It has the disadvantage of producing a shallow depth of field, so it is harder to keep all of the scene in focus. Also, you may find that the foreshortening effect of a powerful zoom lens is not the look you are seeking for street photographs. And, you may find it difficult to get really sharp images at a long focal length unless you use a tripod, which limits your options for candid shots. On a bright day, though, or at high ISO settings, you may be able to use a fast enough shutter speed to avoid blur from a shaky camera, even without a tripod.

Finally, although I use the term "street photography" to discuss candid photography in public places, I have found myself drifting away from city streets and taking more pictures in parks and other public areas where I find more people and where there is usually more time to find a good setting. I generally use color on these occasions, such as with Figure 9-19, when, at the local botanical garden, I spotted a circular structure that looked as if it would serve as a good framing device. I waited for some people to walk into the frame, and fired away.

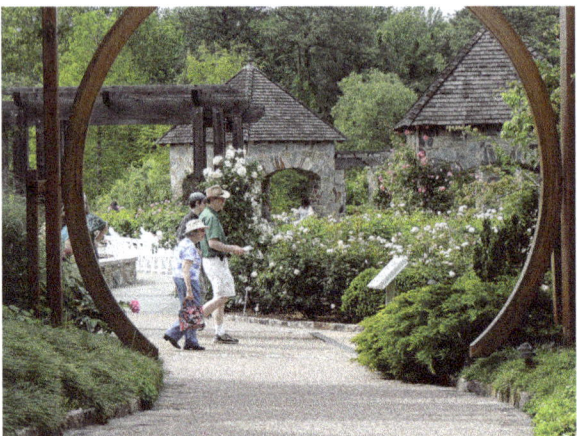

Figure 9-19:   Street photograph taken in botanical garden

I found quite a few photo opportunities in that environment, and it seemed more natural for me to be taking photos than it is on the streets, so I was able to capture a wider variety of shots of people while also getting images of the beautiful surroundings in the gardens, as in Figure 9-20.

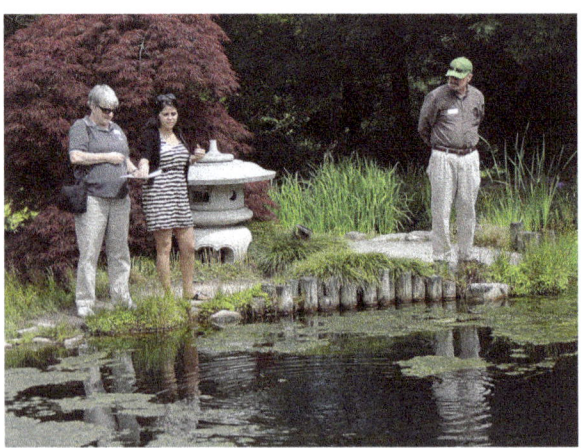

Figure 9-20:   Another candid shot in the botanical garden

Connecting to a Television Set

The Coolpix P510 is quite capable when it comes to playing back its still images and videos on an external television set. The camera comes equipped with an audio-video cable as standard equipment. The cable has a mini-USB connector at one end and three composite, or RCA, connectors at the other end. The red and white RCA plugs are for stereophonic audio, left and right; the yellow plug is for composite video.

To connect the cable to the camera, you need to open the little door on the left side of the camera (when held in shooting position) and plug the small (mini-USB) connector into the upper one of the two ports inside the door.

You then need to connect the yellow, red, and white connectors on the other ends of the cable to the composite video and audio inputs of a television set. You may need to set the TV's input selector to Video 1, AUX, or some other setting so it will display the input signal from the camera. Figure 9-21 shows the A/V cable that is supplied with the camera.

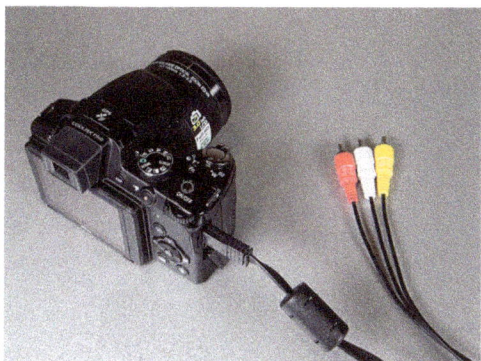

Figure 9-21: The three plugs connect to a TV set

Once the connections are set and the TV is turned on with the correct input selected, turn on the camera in Playback mode, and you can play back any images or video you have recorded. HD video will play back with no problems on a standard television set.

You can also purchase an optional HDMI cable to connect the camera to a high-definition television set. Nikon apparently does not offer such a cable, but you can use any generic HDMI cable, as long as one end has a mini-HDMI (type C) male connector, and the other end has a standard HDMI male connector, as shown in Figure 9-22.

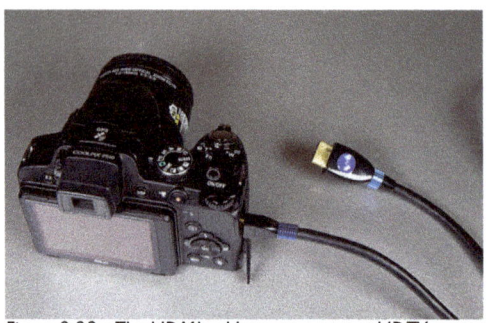

Figure 9-22: The HDMI cable connects to an HDTV set

Once you have connected the camera to a TV set, the camera operates very much the same way it does on its own. Of course, depending on the size and quality of the TV set, you will likely get a much larger image, possibly better quality (on an HD set), and certainly better sound for your movies. When the camera is connected to a TV with the standard video cable, it can not only play back recorded images; it can also record. When it is hooked up to a TV while in recording mode, you can see on the TV screen the live image being seen by the camera. So you can use the camera as a video camera of sorts, and you can use the TV screen as a large monitor to help you compose your photographs. When the camera is connected to an HDTV using an HDMI cable, though, it will only play back images and videos; it will not go into Shooting mode and cannot record.

APPENDIX A: Accessories

When people buy a new camera, especially a fairly expensive model like the Nikon Coolpix P510, they often ask what accessories they should buy to go with it. I will hit the highlights, sticking mostly with discussing items I have experience with.

Cases

There are endless types of camera cases on the market. At least for me, there is no single "perfect" case for the P510. The type of case I use with this camera depends on what activity I am involved in, and what my purpose is for carrying the camera at a given time.

The case that I purchased along with the camera, the Lowepro Rezo 110 AW, shown in Figure A-1, has turned out to be an excellent all-around choice. It accommodates the camera easily, with room to spare for extra batteries, filters, and other small items. It has a divider in its main compartment, and also has a built-in microfiber cloth, which is very handy for keeping the LCD screen clean and free of fingerprints.

When I'm going on a day trip that's specifically oriented to photography, I often put the camera into a case that can hold the camera along with some accessories and a few items such as a water bottle and notepad. One case I have used a good deal is the Kata model DW-491, shown in Figure A-2 with the P510 in the middle compartment. It can easily hold extra batteries as well as one or two water bottles and other odds and ends.

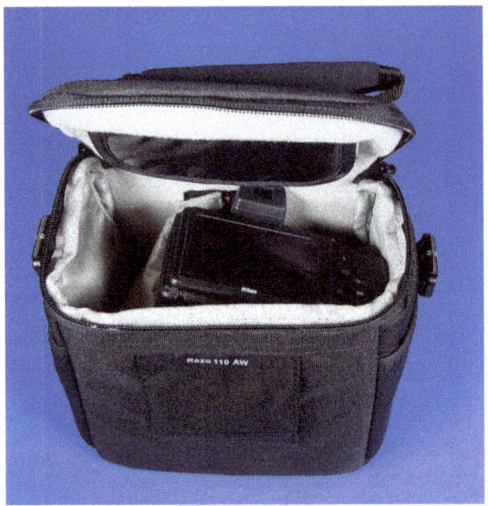

Figure A-1: Lowepro Rezo AW 110 case

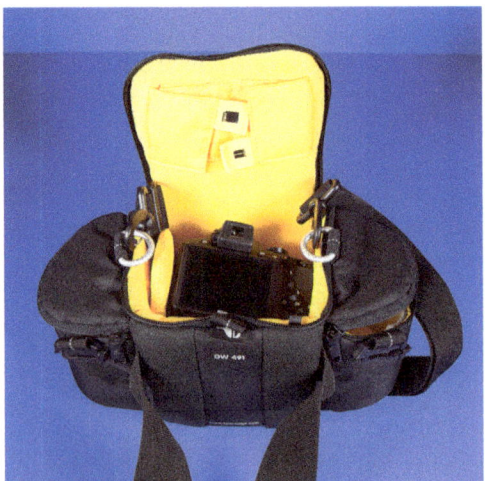

Figure A-2: Kata DW-491 case

When I need to carry more items or prefer the feel of a pack that slings over my shoulder in a more comfortable way, I often use the larger Lowepro Passport Sling bag, shown in Figure

A-3, which can hold the camera, accessories, water, and some snacks as well a guidebook for the day's hike and other items.

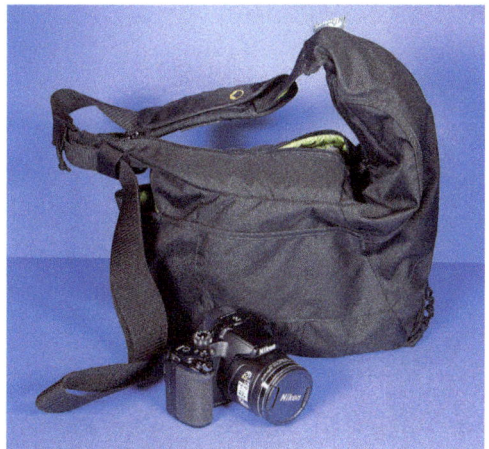

Figure A-3: Lowepro Passport Sling bag

Batteries

Here's one area where you should go shopping either when you get the camera or right afterwards. I use the camera pretty heavily, and I find it runs through batteries quickly, especially when GPS logging is activated. You can't use disposable batteries, so if you're out taking pictures and the battery dies, you're out of luck unless you have a spare battery (or an AC adapter and a place to plug it in; see discussion below). The model number of the official Nikon battery is EN-EL5. You can get a spare Nikon battery for about $21.00 as I write this. It won't do you a great deal of good by itself, though, because the battery is designed to be charged in the camera, and you can't use the camera while the battery is charging.

There is an easy solution to this problem, though. You can find generic replacement batteries, as well as chargers to charge the batteries outside the camera, very inexpensively on Amazon.com and elsewhere. I purchased a package including a generic replacement battery and a charger, with a micro-fiber cleaning cloth included, for less than $13.00 on Amazon.com, and the battery and the charger, shown in Figure A-4, work fine.

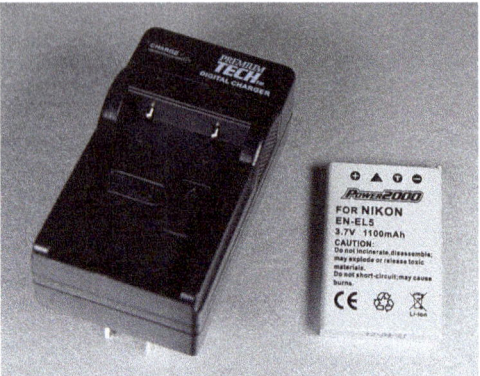

Figure A-4: Replacement battery and charger

With this setup, I can have one battery charging while another is in the camera. In this respect, the Coolpix P510 wins my vote for economy; some other cameras require the use of batteries that cost $50.00 or more.

AC Adapter

The other alternative for supplying power to the P510 is the AC adapter kit, Nikon model number EH-62A, shown in Figure A-5 connected to a Coolpix P500 camera.

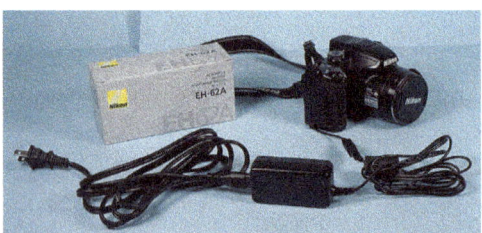

Figure A-5: AC adapter model EH-62A

There is not too much to say about this accessory. It works well for what it does, in terms of providing a constant source of power to the camera. It includes a standard-sized AC cord that you plug into a power brick and into an AC outlet. The fairly large power brick is attached to a long cable that is connected to a plastic piece the same size and shape as the camera's battery. You insert that plastic piece into the battery compartment. Before you close the battery compartment door, though, you have to pull down a small rubber flap that covers an opening where the camera's side meets the battery compartment door. You then place the cable from the AC adapter into that opening, so you can close the battery compartment door fully, as shown in Figure A-6.

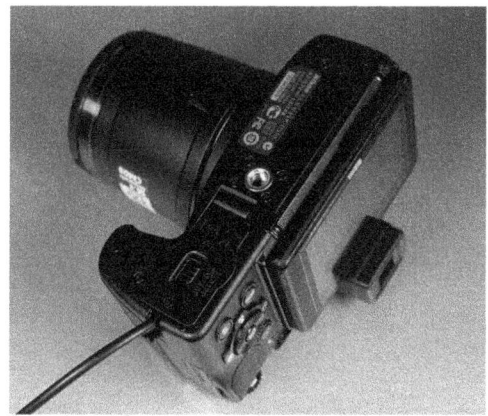

Figure A-6: AC adapter connected to P510

Providing power to the camera is all this adapter does. It is not a charger, either for batteries outside of the camera or for batteries while they are installed in the camera. It is strictly a power source for the camera. It is useful if you are using the interval timer or doing extensive work in a studio or laboratory setting, to eliminate the trouble of constantly charging and replacing batteries. It also could be useful if you are recording many images or movie scenes in a setting where you have access to AC power. However, the AC adapter's cables and power brick are quite bulky, so using the adapter can be inconvenient. If you don't have a real need for this setup, I recommend you invest in one or more extra batteries, and perhaps even an extra battery charger, so you can always have a couple of batteries ready for action. In short, the AC adapter should not be considered a high-priority purchase for most photographers.

Add-on Filters and Lenses

There is no way to attach a filter or other add-on item, such as a close-up lens, directly to the lens of the Coolpix P510, as you can with DSLRs and other larger cameras, whose lenses are threaded to accept filters and auxiliary lenses. The lens of the P510 is not set up to accept such attachments, and Nikon does not offer any adapter that accepts them.

There is at least one solution available, though it is far from ideal. To add filters or other lens accessories to the P510, you need to get a third-party adapter. The images in Figures A-7 and A-8 show one such adapter, which I found on eBay, made by a company called Kiwi Foto.

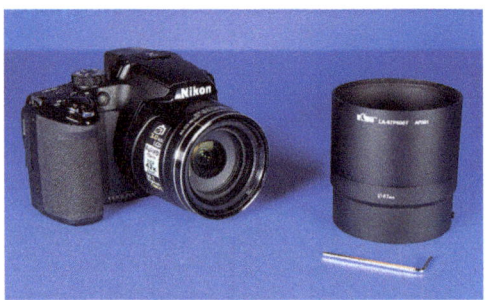

Figure A-7: Filter adapter and Allen wrench

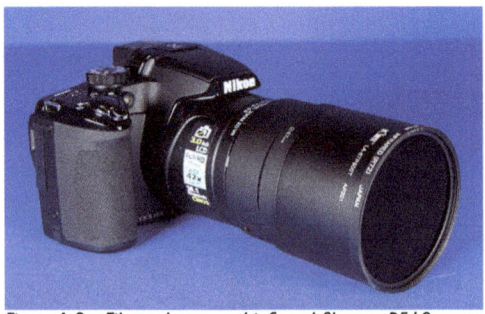

Figure A-8: Filter adapter and infrared filter on P510

The adapter consists of a sturdy metal tube that fits snugly over the end of the P510's lens housing and is secured by tightening two screws with the included Allen wrench. With this adapter tube in place, you can screw onto its end any filter or other accessory that has a 67mm diameter. For example, as shown in Figure A-8 and discussed in Chapter 9, I attached a Hoya R72 infrared filter using this system, to take infrared photos with the P510.

As you can see from the Figure A-9, the major flaw of this adapter is that it causes serious vignetting because of the distance between the camera's lens and the filter, when the lens is at a wide-angle setting. In addition, the adapter is quite bulky, and it is difficult to attach it securely to the lens.

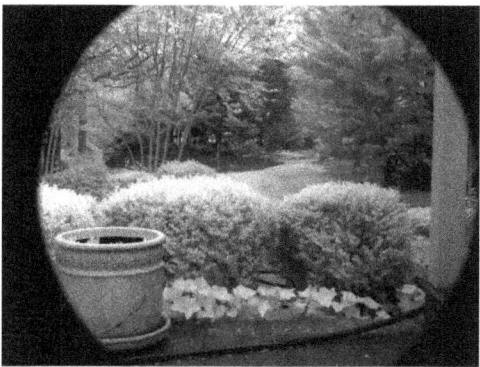

Figure A-9: Vignetting caused by using filter adapter

You can cure the vignetting by zooming in somewhat, or by cropping your photos in your editing software to remove the dark corners and edges.

Despite the drawbacks of this adapter system, just having the ability to attach filters enhances the usefulness of the camera considerably. You can use a neutral density filter when you want to force the camera to use a wide aperture to blur a background, or to use a slow shutter speed to smooth out a waterfall with a long exposure. You can use infrared filters, UV (ultraviolet) filters, polarizers, or any of a wide assortment of close-up lenses, as well.

External Flash

Clearly, Nikon did not consider the use of external flash units to be a high priority for users of the Coolpix P510, because the camera does not have an accessory flash shoe on top, as many other advanced compact cameras do. You might conclude that this camera does not need a very powerful flash, for a couple of reasons. First, it has a sensor that is capable of taking good pictures in low light, with ISO settings reaching up to 3200 (and higher, with the Hi 1 and Hi 2 settings) and features like the Best Shot Selector that help you avoid photos that are blurred from camera shake in low light.

Second, even apart from the P510's dim-light shooting abilities, for everyday shots not taken at long distances, the built-in flash should suffice. It works automatically with the camera's light-metering controls to expose the images well. It is limited by its low power, though. According to Nikon, at the wide-angle focal length, the range of the built-in flash is about 26 feet (8 m), and, at the telephoto setting, about 14 feet (4.5 m), when ISO is set to Auto. This range is not very strong.

So, if you will often use the camera to take photos of groups of people in large spaces, or otherwise need additional power from your flash, you may need to supplement the built-in unit. There are some options for this purpose, which may be worth considering depending on your type of photography.

If you will be shooting indoors in a space you can control (in a home studio, for example) you can set up an external flash unit with a separate optical slave trigger, as shown in Figures A-10 and A-11.

With that system, the external flash is attached to the hot shoe on the optical slave device, and aimed at your subject (or, as in the images included here, positioned to fire into a flash umbrella, which diffuses the flash out toward your subject).

APPENDIX A: ACCESSORIES

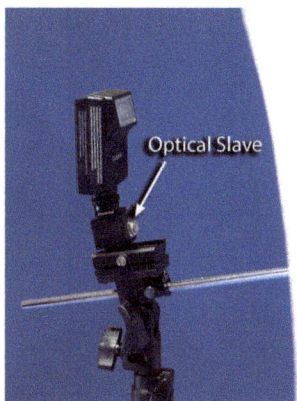

Figure A-10: External flash on optical slave unit

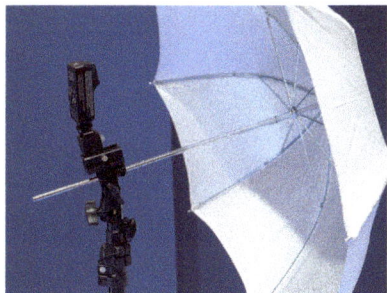

Figure A-11: External flash aimed into umbrella

When you press the shutter button on the P510, its built-in flash triggers the optical slave, which fires the external flash. With this setup, in my experience, you need to use an external flash that has a Manual setting, and leave it on that setting. You then need to set the P510 to Manual exposure mode, and experiment until you find the correct exposure.

Figures A-10 and A-11 show a setup of this type, using the SYK-3, an inexpensive optical slave unit sold by Cowboystudio, purchased from Amazon.com, attached to a Panasonic DMW-FL220 flash, which has a Manual mode. The flash umbrella is attached to an ordinary light stand using an FU SOB Umbrella Mount Bracket, sold by JJC Photography Equipment Company.

307

One advantage of using a generic optical slave unit is that you can use many different types and brands of flash unit, provided the unit is compatible with the optical slave and has a Manual mode. (Not all flash units are compatible, so you may want to check with Cowboystudio before deciding what flash to use.)

Finally, there is one other approach to using external lighting that does not involve flash, but is worth considering.

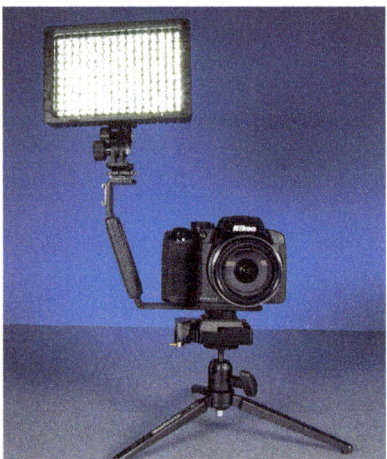

Figure A-12: 160-LED video light on P510

Figure A-12 shows the Coolpix P510 with a portable LED (Light Emitting Diode) fixture attached to it by means of a standard flash bracket. This battery-powered light has 160 LED lights, and it is continuously dimmable, so you can vary the light from very faint to quite bright. The advantage with this system is that the light stays on, so you don't have to worry about synchronization, as you do with flash, and you can see the effects of the light on your subject before you shoot. The light shown here is a model called CN-160, which at this writing is available on Amazon.com for about $38.00. I have found it to be a very reliable and useful light. You do have to purchase a compatible battery, which can add a good deal of cost; several types of batteries can be used, including some rechargeable models for Sony cameras.

APPENDIX B: Quick Tips

In this section, I'm going to list some tips and facts that might be useful as reminders, especially to those who are new to digital cameras like the Coolpix P510. My goal here is to give you small chunks of information that might help you in certain situations, or that might not be obvious to everyone. I have tried to include bits of information that might be helpful, but that you might not remember from day to day, especially if you don't use the P510 constantly.

Use continuous shooting. The P510 has great continuous-shooting capabilities, which can help you capture images that other cameras might not manage. I recommend that you consider using continuous shooting as a matter of routine, unless you are running out of memory storage or battery power, or have a particular reason not to use it. When you are using film, burst shooting is expensive and inconvenient because you have to keep changing film, and you have to pay for film and processing. With digital cameras like the P510, it just gives you more options. Even with stationary portraits, you may get the perfect fleeting expression on your subject's face with the fourth or fifth shot. So, go to the Continuous item on the Shooting menu, scroll down the list of options, and turn one of them on. (Remember that continuous shooting is not available in the Auto or Special Effects shooting modes, in most of the Scene modes, or in some other situations, such as when the flash is used.)

Take advantage of the User Setting mode. Use this feature to store your most important group of settings. For example, right now I have the U slot set up for my latest settings for street photography: Shooting mode = Program; Image Quality = Fine; Image Size = 4608 x 3456; White Balance = Daylight; Picture Control = Monochrome; ISO = 800; Continuous shooting = Continuous H; Sound Settings = Button Sound and Shutter Sound off.

Use macro shooting for subjects other than nature. Many photographers create beautiful images using the macro capabilities of the P510, shooting insects, flowers, and other natural items. But, with its focusing down to 0.4 inch (1 cm), its super wide-angle lens, and its low-light performance, the P510 can serve you in many other ways with its macro shooting. If you need a quick copy of a shopping list, memo, driving directions, sales receipt, or canceled check, it might make sense to set the P510's focus mode to macro, maybe boost the ISO to 800 or so, and snap a quick image of it. You also can use the Close-up setting or the Black and White Copy setting from Scene mode. When you get to your destination, you can display the image on the LCD and enlarge it using the zoom lever, then scroll around in the document with the direction buttons. The P510 becomes a portable copy machine, if you want it to.

Play your movies in iTunes, and on iPods, iPhones, and iPads. Because the P510 records its movies in the .mov format, which uses Apple's QuickTime software, the movies are compatible with iTunes. It's very easy to play these movies on your computer if you have downloaded Apple's free iTunes software. Just open a window on your computer to display the icon for a movie file (Windows Explorer or Macintosh Finder), open iTunes on the same computer, and drag the .mov file from the Explorer or Finder window to the panel for the Library in iTunes. You can then play the movie from iTunes. If you want to play it on an iPod, iPhone, or iPad, you will need to take one more step: Select the video in iTunes, then select Advanced from the iTunes menu, and, from that menu item, choose Create iPod or iPhone version, or iPad or AppleTV version, as appropriate. Then you can sync iTunes with your device, and the movie will play very nicely on that device.

Explore the P510's creative potential. The Coolpix P510 has several advanced features that give you the ability to explore experimental photographic techniques. Here are a few suggestions: Use Manual exposure mode with its shutter speeds as long as 8 seconds to take night-time shots with trails of lights from automobiles, storefronts, and other sources. Use the shutter speeds as fast as 1/4000 second to freeze moving motorcycles, track and field runners, skateboarders, and other speedy subjects in mid-motion. Try "camera tossing," in which you toss the camera in the air, set to a multi-second shutter speed, to capture trails of light and color as the camera spins around. (But be sure to catch it on the way down!) Try zooming in or out during a multi-second exposure. Use long exposures (on a tripod) to turn night into day.

Adjust the camera's color settings. The Coolpix P510 has several settings that let you make color-related adjustments: Picture Control, White Balance, the Special Effects shooting mode, and the Food setting in Scene mode, which lets you adjust a hue slider. Try different values for these settings until you find color and monochrome adjustments that convey what you would like to express with your images. With white balance settings, you can achieve unusual effects by purposely setting a custom white balance while aiming at a colored surface, rather than a white or gray one.

Use a neutral density (ND) filter for some shots. There are some times when you want a slow shutter speed, but, in bright light, you can't achieve it, because the aperture can only go as narrow as f/8.3. One solution is to get an adapter (discussed in Appendix A) that permits the use of filters, and use an ND filter to cut down on the light reaching the sensor, resulting in slower shutter speeds. You might want to do this to slow down the rush of a waterfall to a smooth, blended look, or to achieve a motion blur in a shot of a passing runner or walker. Note that you will have to zoom in the lens somewhat or crop the image to avoid vignetting.

Diffuse your flash or reduce its intensity. If you find the built-in flash produces light that's too harsh for close subjects or other shots, try using translucent plastic pieces from milk jugs, other food containers, or broken ping-pong balls as homemade flash diffusers. Just hold the plastic up between the flash and the subject. Another approach you can try when using fill-flash outdoors is to use the flash exposure compensation setting to reduce the intensity of the flash by about -2/3 EV.

Use the self-timer to avoid camera shake. The Coolpix P510 has an excellent self-timer capability that is easy to use; just press the left direction button and choose your setting. This feature is not just for group portraits; you can use it whenever you'll be using a slow shutter speed and you need to avoid camera shake. It can be useful when you're doing macro photography or using the superzoom lens, also, because those are both very sensitive to camera motion.

Set zone focusing. If you're doing street photography or are in any other situation in which you want to set the camera on manual focus for a specific zone or general distance, here is a quick way to do so. Set the focus mode to autofocus, then aim the camera at a subject that is approximately the distance you want to be able to focus on quickly. Once focus has been confirmed, press the down direction button and then select MF from the focus icons that appear on the screen, to select manual focus. Now you will have locked in the manual focus at your chosen distance, and you're ready to shoot any subject at that distance without the need to re-focus.

Speed up your use of the menu system. There are a couple of shortcuts that will let you zip through the menus to change your settings. First, remember that the menu screens wrap around, so that it sometimes is faster to scroll down past the last item on the menu to get to the items at the top. Also, when you are setting items with changing values, such as ISO Sensitivity, Continuous shooting, White Balance, Picture Control,

Metering, and others, you can use the command dial to change the settings without having to go to the secondary screen. Just scroll to the line for that item and turn the command dial to make the setting. You don't even have to press the OK button to confirm.

Leave good settings when you end a shooting session. There are several settings on the Coolpix P510 that are "sticky"—that is, they will remain set on their current value when the camera is powered off and then on again. These include items such as exposure compensation, ISO, and continuous shooting. It is a good idea to check the camera when you stop shooting to make sure you have not left some settings in place that could cause problems if you have to start shooting again in a hurry. For another example, you might want to leave the Special Effects mode set to the Selective Color option, with no color selected, which results in normal shots. Then, if you pick up the camera in a hurry and turn the mode dial to the EFFECTS position, you will get normal-looking shots, rather than shots with High Contrast Monochrome, Nostalgic Sepia, or some other unwanted look.

Shoot larger panoramas. When you are shooting a horizontal panorama using the Easy Panorama setting as discussed in Chapter 3, you can increase its height using a simple technique. Select your setting, such as Normal, and then hold the camera vertically, as if you were shooting a tall building, but pan it horizontally. With this approach, the dimensions of the panorama will be 1024 pixels tall by 3200 pixels wide, instead of the normal dimensions of 560 by 3200.

APPENDIX C: Resources for Further Information

Photography Books

A visit to any large general bookstore or a search on Amazon.com will reveal the vast assortment of books about digital photography that is currently available. Rather than trying to compile a long bibliography, I will list a few books that I consulted while writing this guide, which I consider to be useful resources for further exploration.

C. George, *Mastering Digital Flash Photography* (Lark Books, 2008)

J. Gulbins & R. Gulbins, *Photographic Multishot Techniques* (Rocky Nook, 2009)

C. Harnischmacher, *Closeup Shooting* (Rocky Nook, 2007)

C. Harnischmacher, *The Wild Side of Photography* (Rocky Nook, 2010)

J. Paduano, *The Art of Infrared Photography* (4th ed., Amherst Media, 1998)

D. Sandidge, *Digital Infrared Photography Photo Workshop* (Wiley, 2009)

Web Sites

Since web sites come and go and change their addresses, it's impossible to compile a list of sites that discuss the Coolpix

P510 that will be accurate far into the future. One way to find the latest sites is to use a good search engine such as Google or Bing and type in "Nikon Coolpix P510." I recently did so in Google and got more than 10 million results.

Another approach can be to go to Amazon.com, search for the P510, and read the users' reviews, though you have to be careful to weed out reviews that don't have anything to do with the camera itself. You can also visit a reputable dealer's site, such as that of B&H Photo Video, and read the users' reviews of the camera there. I will list below some sites I have found useful, though some may not be accessible by the time you read this.

Digital Photography Review

http://forums.dpreview.com/forums/forum.asp?forum=1007

This is the current web address for the "Nikon Talk" forum within the dpreview.com site. Dpreview.com is one of the most established and authoritative sites for reviews, discussion forums, technical information, and other resources concerning digital cameras.

Reviews of the Coolpix P510

The links below lead to reviews of the Coolpix P510 by dpreview.com, Photographyblog.com, CNET.com, and other sites.

http://www.dpreview.com/reviews/nikon-coolpix-p510/6

http://www.photographyblog.com/reviews/nikon_coolpix_P510_review/

http://reviews.cnet.com/digital-cameras/nikon-coolpix-p510-black/4505-6501_7-35136627.html?tag=mncol;lst;1

http://www.pcmag.com/article2/0,2817,2403846,00.asp

http://www.digitaltrends.com/digital-camera-reviews/nikon-coolpix-p510-review/

http://www.digitalversus.com/digital-camera/nikon-coolpix-p510-p12700/camera-review-nikon-coolpix-p510-n24447.html

http://www.imaging-resource.com/PRODS/nikon_p510/nikon_p510A.HTM

http://www.steves-digicams.com/camera-reviews/nikon/coolpix-p510/nikon-coolpix-p510-review.html

http://www.ephotozine.com/article/nikon-coolpix-p510-digital-compact-camera-review-18761

http://www.whatdigitalcamera.com/equipment/reviews/compactcameras/129292/1/nikon-coolpix-p510-review.html

The Official Nikon Site

The United States arm of the Nikon company provides resources on its web site, including the downloadable version of the user's manual for the Coolpix P510 and other technical information.

http://www.nikonusa.com/Nikon-Products/Product/Compact-Digital-Cameras/26329/COOLPIX-P510.html

Flickr Discussion Group

This site hosts a discussion forum about the Coolpix P510; there also are photos taken by the camera posted in other parts of the site.

http://www.flickr.com/groups/nikonp510/

Infrared Photography

This site provides some helpful information about infrared photography with digital cameras.

http://www.wrotniak.net/photo/infrared/

Index

Symbols

3D photography 94–95
 viewing images without 3D TV 96

A

AC adapter 141
 effect on standby mode 231
 Nikon EH-62A 302
Active D-Lighting 76, 155
 relationship to ISO setting 145
Adobe Photoshop Elements software 93, 154, 214
Adobe Photoshop software 73, 93, 97, 120, 154, 214, 222
Adobe Premiere Elements software 141, 265
Adobe Premiere software 265
AF Area Mode 36, 147
 Auto 148
 Center 36, 150
 Face Priority 147
 Manual 37, 85, 149
 Subject Tracking 151
 Target Finding AF 152
AF Assist menu option 225
AF Assist/Self-timer lamp 168
Anabuilder software 97
Aperture
 range of available settings 60, 64, 66
 relationship to focal length 64
 setting 63
 using to produce blurred background 62
Aperture Priority mode 59
 making settings 63
 uses for 60
Apple Final Cut software 265
Apple iMovie software 257, 265
Aspect ratio 115–117
Assign Side Zoom Control menu option 229

Astrophotography 274
Audio-video cable 183, 297
Auto Flash mode 284
Autofocus 35
Autofocus Assist lamp
  disabling 225
Autofocus Mode for movie recording 261
Autofocus Mode setting 152
Auto ISO
  in Manual exposure mode 145
Auto mode 50
  settings available in 51
  using for general picture-taking 31
Auto Off menu option 231
Auto with Red-eye Reduction flash mode 284

B

Backlighting mode 72, 75
  use of flash with 284
Battery
  charging and inserting 17
  charging by computer 20
  charging in camera 19
  inserting into camera 18
  Nikon EN-EL5 301
  replacement 301
  time for full charge 20
Battery charger
  external 301
Beach setting 81
Best Shot Selector 87, 138, 277
Black and White Copy setting 88
Black Border menu option 210
Blink Warning 237
Blurred background 62
Bokeh 62
Bracketing 146
Bridge camera
  defined 13
Brightness menu option 220

C

Calendar view 189
Camera controls
  introduction to 25–27
Cases
  Kata DW-491 299
  Lowepro Passport Sling 300
  Rezo 110 AW 299
Charge by Computer menu option 235
Choose Key Picture 212
Close-up setting 84, 89, 282
Color temperature 126
Command dial 173
  changing functions of 235
  using to set shutter speed 57
Continuous shooting 134–139, 277, 309
  60 fps option 138
  120 fps option 137
  availability in various modes 135
  Best Shot Selector option 138
  high-speed option 136
  incompatibility with self-timer 135
  Interval Timer 140
  limitations of 135
  low-speed option 136
  Multi-shot 16 139
  playback 135, 193–194, 212
  Pre-shooting Cache option 136
  uses for 134
  viewing images 47
Contrast 119, 122
Copying images to or from internal memory 210
Copying images to or from memory card 210
Copy menu option 209
Create Log menu option 244
Cross Screen (Playback menu) 200
Custom Picture Control 125
Custom white balance
  setting 129

D

Date and time
 setting 28
Date and Time menu option 218
Deleting images
 using Trash button 175
Depth of field 60
Digital zoom 163, 226–227
 degrading of image quality 226
 indications on zoom scale 227
 unavailability with some settings 229
 using with smaller image sizes 226
Diopter adjustment wheel 171
Direction buttons 178
Display
 switching between LCD and viewfinder 170
Display button 171
Display screens
 playback mode 172, 190
 shooting mode 171
D-Lighting 198
DPOF (Digital Print Order Format) 202, 215
Dusk/Dawn setting 83

E

Easy Panorama 89
EV (exposure value) 146
Exposure bracketing 146
Exposure compensation 39–40
 display of histogram with 221
 resetting to zero 41
Exposure compensation button 180
Eye-Fi card 23
 enabling function of 238
 using with iPad 24
Eye-Fi Upload menu option 238

F

File name prefix

INDEX

DSCN 236
Fill Flash mode 285
Filmstrip option for playback 237
Filter adapter 290, 304
Filter Effects adjustments for Monochrome 123
Filter Effects menu option 199
Fireworks Show setting 88
Firmware
  checking version in camera 240
Firmware Version menu option 240
Fisheye Effect (Playback menu) 201
Flash
  basic uses of 42
  diffusing 312
  disabled in certain situations 284
  external 306–307
  uses of 283
Flash button 180
Flash/charging lamp 173
  as indicator of whether flash will fire 43, 173
Flash exposure compensation 153, 289
Flash mode menu 43
Flash pop-up button 42, 166
Flattening of image by zoom lens 273
Flexible Program 51
  assigning to command dial or multi selector dial 236
Fn Button menu option 234
Focus
  off-center subject 37
Focus mode
  selecting 35
Focus mode button 180
Focus mode menu 35
Food setting 86, 282
Forced off flash mode 285
Format Card menu option 232
Format Memory menu option 233
Formatting internal memory 232
Formatting memory card 232
Full-time AF option for movies 261

Function button
  assigning a function to 234
  available settings 164
  using to view GPS data 165, 245
Function button (Fn button) 164

G

GPS data
  using to map image locations 241
  viewing with Fn button 245
GPS Options menu 111
  in general 241
GPS Options menu option 242
Grid
  displaying on screen 220

H

HDMI 3D Output menu option 234
HDMI cable 184, 298
HDMI Device Control menu option 234
HDMI menu option 234
HDMI port 184
HDR 72
  in-camera processing 73
HDR setting 76
Help screens 78, 124, 164
High-contrast Monochrome setting 100
HIgh-definition (HD) video 256
High Dynamic Range. *See* HDR
High ISO Monochrome setting 104, 145
High Key setting 100
Histogram 41
  defined and illustrated 191
  displaying in shooting mode 221
  displaying with exposure compensation screen 221
  playback mode 191
Hoya R72 filter 291
Hoya R72 infrared filter 305
HS (high-speed) movie options 258–260

INDEX

I

iFrame movie format 257
  lack of in-camera editing 266
Image numbers
  resetting sequence 236
Image Quality menu option 32, 114
Image Review menu option 47, 220
Image Size menu option 115
iMovie software 141
Index screens 163
Infrared filter 291, 305
Infrared photography 290–291
  settings for 291
Internal memory
  formatting 232
Interval Timer 140
iPad
  uploading images to 24
ISO 142–144
  Auto 143
  Fixed Range Auto 143
  in general 142
  restrictions on settings 145
  setting 143
  using to enable fast shutter speed 277
ISO 6400 144
ISO 12800 144
ISO Sensitivity menu option 142–144
  Hi 1 and Hi 2 144

L

Landscape 71
Language
  setting 30
Language menu option 233
LCD screen
  controlling brightness of 220
  swiveling capability 184
LED light 308

Lens cap
  attaching to neck strap 17
Low Key setting 101

M

Macro focus 85, 280
  range when available 281
Macro photography 279–281, 310
Manual exposure mode 64
  making settings 65
  using for creative effects 311
Manual exposure scale
  reversing indicators for 239
Manual focus
  adjusting with Side Zoom Control 229
  availability for movie recording 250
  in general 38
  locking 39
  not available in Auto mode 35
  setting and using 38
Memory card
  considerations for selecting 22
  formatting 232
  inserting into camera 24
  speed of 22
  varieties of 21–22
Memory, internal 20
Menu button 175
Menu system
  navigating 312
Metering 132
  Center-weighted 132
  Matrix 132
  setting for movie recording 253
  Spot 132
Miniature Effect (Playback menu) 201
Minimum Shutter Speed setting 144
Mode dial 162
Monitor button 33, 170
Monitor Settings menu option 47, 186, 219

Monochrome setting 121
Moon
  photgraphing 274
Motion Detection 223, 224
Movie button 45, 173
Movie formats 256
Movie menu 44, 111
  in general 255
Movie Options menu option 44, 255
Movie recording
  Autofocus Mode 45, 261
  basic procedure 44
  exposure compensation 250
  exposure control 46, 251
  exposure lock 250
  focus mode 249
  high-speed options 258–260
  limitations on duration 255
  overview of procedure 246
  Picture Control setting 252
  quick guide to recording movie clip 247
  relationship of still photo settings to movies 249
  setting metering mode 253
  settings that cannot be adjusted 255
  setting white balance 252
  sound volume 46
  still photo settings that apply 249
  use of Fn button 254
  using manual focus 250
  using self-timer 181, 251
  Vibration Reduction setting 253
  zooming 253
Movies
  editing 265–266
  in-camera editing 266
  playback 48, 263–264
  playing on computer 49
  playing with iTunes, iPods, iPads, iPhones 310
MultiMediaCard
  not compatible with Coolpix P510 22

Multi selector dial 177
  changing functions of 235
  using to set aperture 63
Multi-shot 16 139
Museum setting 87, 139

N

Neck strap 17
Neutral density filter 305, 311
  using to control shutter speed 55
Night Landscape mode 42, 69, 284
Night Portrait setting 80
  use of flash with 284
Nikon Coolpix P510 camera
  general characteristics of 13
  items included with 17
  strengths of 14
  weaknesses of 15
NIkon Movie Editor software 265
Nikon support web site 240
Noise Reduction Filter 154
Noise (visual) 143
Nostalgic Sepia setting 99
NTSC televsion standard 233

O

OK button 178
Optical slave trigger 306

P

Painting (Playback menu) 202
Painting setting 103
PAL television standard 233
Panorama Assist 91
Panorama Maker 6 software 92
Panorama setting 89–91
  shooting larger panoramas 313
Party/Indoor setting 80
Pet Portrait Auto Release 93, 183

Pet Portrait setting 93, 183
PhotoAcute software 73
Photomatix Pro software 73, 76
PictBridge printer 203, 214
Picture Control menu option 119
  adjustments 122
  availability for movie recording 252
  Monochrome 121
    adjustments 123
  Neutral 119
  Standard 119
  Vivid 120
Playback
  basic procedure 46, 186
  calendar view 189
  cropping images 189
  enlarging images 47, 163, 187, 188
  Filmstrip option 237
  index screens 163, 187
  movies 48
  reviewing images in shooting mode 47, 186, 220
  scrolling through images 47, 187
Playback button 47, 169, 187
  using to turn camera on 170
Playback menu
  in general 196
Portrait setting 79
Posterization 103
Power switch 162
Pre-shooting Cache 136
Print Date 222
Printing from the camera 214
Print menu 215
Print Order menu option 202
Program mode 51
  flash options available in 43
Protect menu option 205

Q

Quick Retouch 196

R

RAW format 24, 115
Rear-curtain Sync 287–288
Record GPS Data menu option 242
Red-eye reduction 284
Reset All menu option 113, 239
Reset File Numbering 236
Reset User Settings menu option 157
Resolution 115
Reverse Indicators menu option 66, 239
Rotate Image 206
Rule of Thirds
 displaying grid for 220

S

Saturation 119, 122
Save User Settings menu option 157
Scene Auto Selector setting 67, 77
Scene menu 78, 110
SCENE position on mode dial 67, 68, 77
Scene settings
 in general 66
 limitations of 68
 listing of 67
SD card 21
SDHC card 22
SDXC card 22
Selective Color (Playback menu) 199
Selective Color setting 101
Self-timer
 incompatibility with continuous shooting 135, 181
 using for movie recording 251
 using to avoid camera shake 312
 using to take high-angle shots 185
Self-timer button 180
Self-timer lamp 225
Sequence Display Options 195, 211
Setup menu 111
 in general 216

INDEX

navigating 216
Sharpening 119, 122
Shooting menu 34
  in Auto mode 109
  incompatible settings 113
  in general 109
  in Scene modes 109
  navigating 111
  unavailable items 113
  using command dial to adjust settings 112
Shooting modes 34
  in general 50
Shutter Priority mode 53
  making settings 57
  uses for 53
Shutter release button 162
  using during movie recording 254
Shutter speed
  availability of 8-second setting 66
  range of available settings 53, 66
  relationship to ISO 66
  setting 58
  table of fractional speeds 59
Side Zoom Control 167, 278
  assigning function to 229
  using to adjust manual focus 229
Silhoutte setting 105
Single AF option for movies 261
Skin Softening 198
Slide Show 203
  options 204
Slow Sync flash mode 285
Small Picture menu option 207
Smile Timer 182
Snap-back zoom 167, 229, 278
Snow setting 82
Soft setting 99
Sound Settings menu option 230
Special Effects mode 97, 110
Sports setting 79

Standby mode 162, 163, 170, 231
Startup Zoom Position 160, 163
Stereo Photo Maker software 96
Street photography 292–295
  settings for 293
  using swiveling LCD screen for 185
Sunset setting 83
Synchronize menu option 243

T

Televsion set
  connecting to 297
Time-lapse photography 140
Time zone
  selecting 219
Toggle Av/Tv Selection 235
Toning adjustment for Monochrome 124
Trash button 175
TV Settings menu option 233

U

Update A-GPS File menu option 244
USB port 183
User Setting mode 106–107, 278, 309

V

VGA video format 257
Vibration Reduction 223, 224
  using with movie recording 253
Video bit rate 256
View/Hide Framing Grid 220
View/Hide Histogram 221
View Log menu option 244
ViewNX 2 software 242
Vignetting
  caused by filter adapter 305
Voice Memo 208
  deleting 176, 209
  playing 209

W

Welcome screen
   selecting your own image for 218
Welcome Screen 217
White Balance 126–130, 127
   chart of sample images 131
   further adjustments 128
   Preset Manual setting 129
      using for creative effects 130
   setting for movie recording 252
White Balance settings list 127
Widescreen video formats 257
Windows Movie Maker software 265

Z

Zone focusing 312
Zooming
   and movie recording 253
Zoom lens
   dealing with problems 275
Zoom lens of Coolpix P510
   superzoom capability iof 271
   uses of 270
Zoom lever 33, 163
   using to call up help screens 78, 124, 164
   using to enlarge images 47, 187
Zoom Memory 157, 163
Zoom range
   35mm equivalent 269

www.ingramcontent.com/pod-product-compliance
Lightning Source LLC
Chambersburg PA
CBHW040516220526
45473CB00012B/2874